INTERIOR DESIGN VISUAL PRESENTATION

A Guide to Graphics, Models, and Presentation Techniques

SECOND EDITION

Maureen Mitton

WILEY

JOHN WILEY & SONS, INC.

This book is printed on acid-free paper. ♾

Copyright © 2004 by John Wiley & Sons, Inc. All rights reserved

Published by John Wiley & Sons, Inc., Hoboken, New Jersey
Published simultaneously in Canada

For general information on our other products and services or for technical support, please contact our
Customer Care Department within the United States at (800) 762-2974, outside the United States at
(317) 572-3993 or fax (317) 572-4002.

Wiley also publishes its books in a variety of electronic formats. Some content that appears in print may
not be available in electronic books. For more information about Wiley products, visit our web site at
www.wiley.com.

Library of Congress Cataloging-in-Publication Data:

Mitton, Maureen.
    Interior design visual presentation : a guide to graphics, models, andpresentation techniques /
Maureen Mitton.-- 2nd ed.
        p.   cm.
    ISBN 0-471-22552-5
    1. Interior decoration rendering. 2. Interior decoration--Design. 3. Graphic arts. I. Title.
    NK2113.5.M58 2003
    729'.028--dc21

                                                            2002156140

Printed in the United States of America

10 9 8 7 6 5 4 3 2 1

For
Roger, Anna, and Luc

CONTENTS

ACKNOWLEDGMENTS

This book, just like the first edition, compiles the work of many hands (and keyboards) and conversations. It has been made possible by the generous contributions of numerous people, to whom I would like to express my gratitude.

First, I must acknowledge my current and former students, who have taught me volumes and who continue give me the energy to keep going. I must thank all of the former students who contributed work to the first edition especially, including Theresa Isaacson, Leanne Larson, Ardella Pieper, Cory Sherman, and Justin Thomson. Denise Haertl, Dan Effenheim, Anne (Cleary) Olsen, and Angela Ska, now professional designers, all willingly handed over portfolios for inclusion in this edition. Current students who contributed work and help include Kristy Bokelman, Anne Harmer, and Randi Steinbrecher. And I thank former exchange students Elke Kalvelage, Jessica Tebbe, and Dirk Olbrich for allowing me to include some of their fine work.

I have been amazed and touched by the generosity of members of the design community who shared time and contributed projects: my friend Lynn Barnhouse at Meyer, Scherer & Rockcastle Architects, who contributed a great deal of work and gave hours of her time; Jane Rademacher, Lisa Miller, and Bob Albachten; and Thom Lasley, of RSP Architects.

Others who took time out of very busy schedules to contribute include Thomas Oliphant; Jim Smart, of Smart Associates; Jim Moeller, at Arthur Shuster Inc.; Craig Beddow, of Beddow Design; Deborah Kucera, of TKDA; Janet Lawson, of Janet Lawson Architectural Illustration; and Robert Lownes, of Design Visualizations; Harris Birkeland; and Aj Dumas.

I must acknowledge and thank my colleagues at the University of Wisconsin–Stout. Courtney Nystuen, a wonderful teacher and architect, contributed in many ways. Bill Wikrent, who is talented, knowledgeable, and very generous, deserves special thanks. And this edition would not have been finished in this decade without the gift of a sabbatical: thank you to the Sabbatical Committee. Jack Zellner and Kristine Recker Simpson deserve thanks for willingly contributing their fine work.

This project would not have been possible without the help of my husband, Roger Parenteau , support from our daughter, Anna, and a fair amount of terror generated by young Luc to keep things interesting.

INTRODUCTION

The practice of interior design is complex and continues to evolve. Technological and societal changes fueled by the industrial revolution and continued by more recent advancements in technology have shaped the profession in decisive ways. In a world that requires increasing professional specialization, interior design has gained recognition as an independent discipline. Work done by groundbreaking interior designers in the twentieth century has enhanced the built environment and increased the visibility of the profession. The development of educational standards, professional organizations, a qualifying exam, and legislative certification has increased the quality and credibility of practitioners and fostered design excellence.

The design of interior environments requires specialized methods of presentation, which are often omitted in standard architecture texts. This book identifies methods used in the visual presentation of interior spaces and articulates them in written and visual language. Various phases of the design process are discussed in order to reveal the connection between process and presentation. Some often overlooked basic principles of graphic design and portfolio design are also discussed.

Intended as a primer on interior design visual communication, this book presents a range of styles and techniques. The goal is to provide students and practitioners with information on visual presentation techniques and a variety of methods and materials. It is important to note that this book is not intended to impart ways of camouflaging poorly conceived design work with tricky techniques. This is not a rendering book; it is instead a portfolio of methods of communication. Good design requires, and deserves, adequate and appropriate presentation.

My desire to write the first edition of this book grew from an ongoing pedagogical need: to show students a range of examples of presentation techniques and styles. Often design students look for the "right" way to create a presentation, and this is a mistake because there are many ways of creating successful presentations. Interior design education has suffered from a lack of documentation of the many possible modes of presentation and a lack of specialized information for students. I have found that students exposed to a variety of methods and specific examples create appropriate and useful presentations, whereas students left uninformed about the possibilities often repeat the same lackluster or inappropriate type of presentation project after project.

Unlike those found in many books on rendering and presentation, many of the examples included here were executed by undergraduate design students. I've included these because I want students to see real examples of developing skills. It is important for all designers to develop drawing and sketching skills. Drawing and model building should not be reserved for the final presentation of fully developed designs. Instead, sketching, drawing, and model building must be seen as ways of seeing and exploring throughout the design process — from beginning to final presentation. I admit my desire to get interior designers to draw (and draw and draw). It is the best way to learn to visualize and develop good work.

Research for this edition made clear the significant role computer-generated imagery plays in current practice and in the academic world. Most designers use computers in creating visual presentations. Despite this, hand drawing continues to be a useful tool, particularly in producing perspective drawings. Quickly created perspective drawings offer the benefit of providing designers a visualization tool early in the design process, prior to the time finalized design drawings are complete. In addition, skills learned in drawing by hand transfer directly to computer modeling. The ability to create quick perspective sketches in client conferences and in team meetings is a highly useful tool; this is something that I have heard many times from those hiring designers. For these reasons, numerous examples of quick sketching techniques are included. Examples of computer-generated three-dimensional views are also provided because some designers create these after refining the design by hand sketching. I believe hand drawing and computer-generated imagery can sit side by side in the designer's tool kit.

I have included some examples of work done by professional illustrators, digital illustrators, and model makers to demonstrate what is being done in current practice by specialists. The work is beautiful and highly professional, and it depicts what top professionals can produce. We can learn from this work and allow it to influence our design drawings and in-process presentations.

Most chapters begin with information about specific materials and tools. Each provides written instruction in the text as well as step-by-step illustrated instructions. In teaching I've found that some students learn best by reading and others by following brief graphic guides. My goal is to provide instruction for a variety of learning styles.

For the most part this book covers conventional methods of drawing and presentation. The one exception is the material on perspective, where I have focused on estimated perspective sketching. Estimated sketching requires "eyeballing" perspectives, a method that I have found works well for students, although many educators find it horrifying. In addition to estimated sketching, information on more traditional methods of perspective drawing is included.

The examples and projects presented here range in scope from small residential student projects to huge public interior spaces designed by professionals. The projects range from purely decorative treatment of interior elements to space planning and interior architecture. It is important to note that some of the professional projects presented here are the work of architects involved in the design of interior space and exhibitions. This points to the overlap of the two professions, the breadth of current design practice, and some confusion over what the design of interior space should be called. When is it appropriate to use the term *interior architecture?* When *interior design?* Certainly that debate cannot be addressed in a book on presentation methods. For the book's title, I chose to use the term *interior design* because it describes the design of interior space, which is clearly a distinct area of specialization.

ORTHOGRAPHIC DRAWINGS

INTRODUCTION TO DRAWING

Interior design is a multifaceted and ever-changing discipline. The practice of interior design continues to evolve due to technological as well as societal changes. Computers, the Internet, and fax machines have deeply influenced and changed its practice. For example, use of computer-aided drafting and design (CADD) is standard operating procedure in current design practice, whereas 15 years ago it was just beginning to gain in popularity.

In addition to undergoing rapid technological advancement, the profession of interior design has grown in terms of scope of work, specialization, and the range of design practiced. The growth of the profession, combined with efforts toward standards and licensing, have increased its legitimacy as a serious professional discipline.

Constant change in society and in one's profession can be overwhelming and a bit frightening, and for that reason it is useful to consider the elements that remain constant in an evolving profession. In many ways, the design process itself remains constant — whether practiced with a stick in the sand, a technical pen, or a powerful computer. There are many stories about designers drawing preliminary sketches on cock-tail napkins or cheeseburger wrappers, and these stories lead us to a simple truth.

Professional designers conduct research, take piles of information, inspiration, and hard work, and wrap them all together in what is referred to as the design process, to create meaningful and useful environments. A constant and key factor in interior design is the fact that human beings — and other living creatures — occupy and move within interior spaces. To create interior environments, professional designers must engage in a process that involves research, understanding, idea generation, evaluation, and documentation. These are significant constants that exist in a changing world.

For the most part this book covers the process designers engage in and the related presentation techniques used in design communication. These processes and basic concepts are consistent, whether generated manually or by computer. Some examples included here were created manually, whereas others were computer generated. Regardless of how drawings and graphics are generated, they are part of a process of discovery, exploration, and creation.

This chapter covers what is often referred to as drafting, as well as other forms of two-dimensional graphics. The term DRAFTING refers to measured drawings done with specialized tools and equipment. The truth is that not all drawings used in the process of interior design are drawn with the aid of tools. Often those drawings created in the preliminary stages of the design process are rough sketches and involve little use of drafting tools or equipment. As designs are refined, there is clearly a need for highly accurate, measured, and detailed drawings, and these are drafted with tools.

This chapter presents the materials, equipment, and tools used for manually drafted and freehand design drawings, as well as an overview of the most common drawings used in interior design practice. The information presented in this chapter is meant as an overview, not a definitive drawing or drafting reference.

MATERIALS, TOOLS, AND EQUIPMENT

The graphics and drawings used in interior design practice vary, ranging from conceptual sketches and rough layouts to measured technical drawings. The materials, tools, and equipment used to create the variety of drawings and graphics are numerous and ever proliferating. The media and tools selected must be appropriate to the task at hand. This means that their proper selection requires careful consideration of the drawing type and use, as well as an understanding of the available products. Currently many schools and most firms create the majority of design drawings digitally, using CADD programs. However, some students begin the study of drafting by creating drawings manually; for that reason a description of manual drawing tools and equipment follows. Figure 1-1 illustrates commonly used manual drafting and drawing materials and equipment, which are discussed as follows.

DRAWING SURFACES

The type of drawing surface selected directly affects the quality of the drawn image. Some surfaces accept pencil and ink readily and allow for clear, consistent imagery. Transparent papers allow for diazo reproduction (blueprinting) and can be used as an overlay to continue a drawing by transferring details from one sheet to another. Drawings produced on

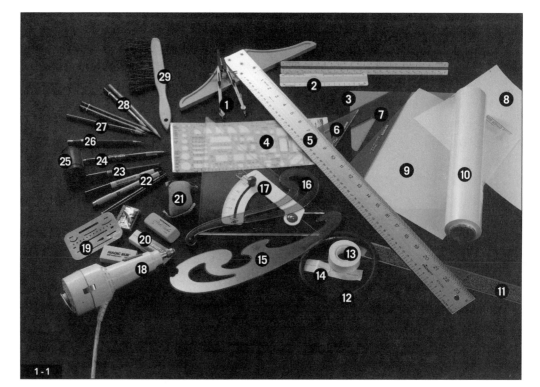

1-1

nontransparent surfaces must be reproduced by photocopying, photographic processes, or computer reproduction (scanning).

TRACING PAPER is the most common paper surface for sketching in-process design drawings and graphics. Known in various parts of the country as "trace," "flimsy," and "bumwad," this paper is highly transparent and relatively inexpensive. Tracing paper is available in cut sheets and in rolls in a variety of sizes. Rolls of tracing paper are best for interior design drawing because of the varying sizes of drawings required. Tracing paper is available in white, buff, and canary (yellow). Most designers have a personal color preference based on previous experience.

Because it is relatively inexpensive, tracing paper can be used to develop preliminary sketches and for in-process drawings. This allows for exploration through the creation of many sketches and the generation of many ideas. Tracing paper also works very well overlaid on drawings for transfer and refinement of images. Often many layers of tracing paper are overlaid as a design is refined or as a complicated perspective drawing is constructed.

Images on tracing paper can be reproduced with the use of a diazo print machine and can be easily photocopied. However, it is very delicate and subject to tearing and crumpling. For this reason, it is not the best surface for a drawing that is to be extensively reproduced.

Most final design drawings created manually are drawn on DRAFTING VELLUM, a transparent paper available in a variety of finishes and weights (thicknesses) and most often white. Drafting vellum should have a high rag or cotton content, giving it a rich finish, strength, and good stability. It is excellent for line work generated with graphite pencils. Good-quality diazo prints can be run from drafting vellum originals. Vellum is also photocopied, scanned, and photographed with excellent results.

In addition to vellum, PLASTIC DRAFTING FILMS are used for final drawings and for some design presentations. Plastic (and polyester) drafting films are expensive, tear resistant, and generally do not react to fluctuations in temperature or humidity (as do many paper surfaces). They accept ink beautifully and allow for easy ink erasure. These films require the use of special pencils. Drafting film originals produce excellent diazo prints and photocopies. For years prior to the use of CADD, plastic film and ink drawings were considered the finest for reproduction.

ADHESIVE REPRODUCTION FILM, also called appliqué film and often referred to generically as "sticky back," is used on vellum or bond drawings. Typed or printed images can be drawn or photocopied onto adhesive reproduction film. The film is then carefully measured and cut and applied to the vellum or bond paper. Matte appliqué films accept pencil well; some types are repositionable, but others are not. High-heat photocopiers may cause buckling of certain appliqué films; however, Rayven™ produces a variety of films for low-, medium-, and high-heat copiers.

Tracing paper, drafting vellum, and drafting film are commonly used in manual drawing. Nontransparent papers such as fine art drawing papers can be used with excellent results, yet they cannot be overlaid and do not reproduce well. The nature of the design process requires constant exploration and change, and transparent papers are well suited to this requirement.

Currently design drawings are reproduced on large-format photocopying machines. In many firms and studios large bond paper copies have replaced blueprints as the preferred method of reproduction.

LINE- AND MARK-MAKING IMPLEMENTS

Lines and marks record spatial information in interior design drawings and graphics. Control of line thickness and the type of stroke used are important and convey specific information. Thus, the implement used to create lines and marks is a key factor in design drawing.

GRAPHITE is mixed with clay and other elements to produce what are commonly called "lead" pencils. Graphite pencils, used in design drawing, are available in a range of hardnesses based on the mixture of clay to graphite. Graphite pencils and replaceable "leads" are coded with a standard rating system: H stands for hard, B stands for black (the softer leads). The number found next to the H or B refers to the level of hardness. For example, a 6B is softer than a 2B; an 8H is very hard. F-rated leads are at the center of the range, and HB leads are slightly harder than Bs. The softer leads are used in sketching and rendering, whereas H, 2H, and sometimes F leads are most commonly used in drafting. Polymer-based leads, which are used on plastic and polyester drafting films, are often graded differently than graphite leads.

The graphite described above is used in a variety of mark-making implements. WOODEN DRAWING PENCILS involve a graphite mixture encased in wood and are sharpened like standard wooden writing pencils. MECHANICAL PENCILS are hollow instruments that hold very fine graphite leads. These are sold in a variety of lead widths to create a range of line weights. LEAD HOLDERS are hollow implements that accept thicker leads than mechanical pencils. Although lead holders do not allow for any variety in lead widths, they do accept a range of lead types in terms of softness. Lead holders require the use of a specialized sharpener, known as a LEAD POINTER.

Specialized colored drafting pencils and leads can be used to develop drawings prior to hard-lining them. NON-PHOTO-BLUE colored pencils do not reproduce when photographed; however, they sometimes reproduce when photocopied. NONPRINT colored pencils do not reproduce in diazo prints. When appropriate, both types of pencil can be used to lay out drawings prior to completion.

One of the significant advantages of using graphite pencils is the ease of erasing. Harder leads are often the most difficult to erase, whereas soft pencil marks are easily lifted with gray kneaded erasers or pink erasers. Plastic and film erasers can be used to remove marks made with harder leads. A metal ERASER SHIELD is used to protect the drawing surface from unwanted erasing. DRY CLEANING PADS, containing art gum powder that sifts onto drawing surfaces, are available to keep drawings clean.

TECHNICAL PENS have tubular points and refillable ink reservoirs. They are available in a range of point sizes that allow for absolute control of line weight. Because they employ black ink and metal points, technical pens create the finest line work of any drawing implement. They must be used with the appropriate ink, as specified by the manufacturer.

DISPOSABLE TECHNICAL PENS combine a tubular support with a felt tip and are available in a range of point sizes. These pens require no maintenance or cleaning, making them easy to use. Although disposable pens have been known to skip, causing inconsistent line work, they have improved a great deal recently and are becoming very popular.

FELT-TIP PENS are available in a range of styles and point sizes; they are often used in sketching, exploration, and rendering. Felt-tip pens are not generally used for refined drafted drawings or working drawings.

Erasing ink marks is rather difficult and requires special erasers. Hard plastic erasers can remove ink. However, an ELECTRIC ERASER with the appropriate eraser insert is most useful in removing ink. Electric erasers are very effective but must always be used with an eraser shield. Ink marks on film are erased more easily than those on vellum. Sharp razor blades are sometimes used to scrape ink away from drawing surfaces.

A quality DRAWING BOARD is required for the creation of successful drawings. Serious students must purchase a top-quality drawing board if possible. The board should accommodate a minimum paper size of 24" by 36". Drawing boards should be covered with a specialized vinyl drawing surface, sold at drafting and art supply stores. The vinyl surface helps to improve line consistency.

T SQUARES are used in conjunction with the edge of the drawing board to provide an accurate horizontal line or right angle for drawings. PARALLEL RULERS can be attached to drawing boards using a system of screws, cables, and pulleys. This creates the sliding straightedge that is the standard in professional practice. Triangles are used with a T square to create vertical and angled lines. Adjustable and 45/45-degree and 30/60-degree triangles are readily available. Triangles should be fairly clear, easy to see through, and as substantial as possible. An inking triangle with raised edges is required when using ink. It is also useful to have a tiny triangle on hand as an aid in lettering. Triangles should never be used as a cutting edge; this will ruin them. A cork-backed metal ruler is the best edge for cutting.

DRAFTING TAPE or PRECUT DRAFTING DOTS are used to attach drawings to drawing boards. Unlike standard masking and household tape, drafting tape and dots are easy to remove from both the paper and the drawing board. A DRAFTING BRUSH is used to remove eraser debris from the drawing surface.

Measured interior design drawings require the use of a proportional scale. This allows for large areas to be reduced in size to fit on relatively small drawings. An ARCHITECTURAL SCALE is the standard scale ruler used in interior design drawing. Architectural scales are marked in a manner that makes measuring in scale fairly easy. For example, in 1/4-inch scale the ruler is marked so that each 1/4 inch measures 1 foot in scale. Architectural scales have inches marked below the zero marking; these are used to measure elements that are not exact to the foot. In transferring measurements, great care should be taken to record accurate dimensions. Scale rulers should never be used to draw against, as this would result in poorly drawn lines and damaged rulers.

TEMPLATES are most commonly constructed of plastic and are used much like stencils to draw various shapes, including circles, ellipses, furnishings, and fixtures. The more expensive templates — constructed of heavy, durable plastic — are worth the extra money. Furniture and fixture templates work well to quickly lay out and plan spaces. However, in presentation drawings furniture and fixtures drawn from templates can appear artificial and monotonous.

FRENCH CURVES are drawn against as an aid in producing curved lines. FLEXIBLE CURVES, also known as snakes, are also used as an aid in drawing curved lines. These have flexible splines that can be bent to accommodate the desired curve. These also work well for transferring curves from one drawing surface to another. A COMPASS is used for drawing accurate circles and arcs and is useful in situations where a template does not contain a circle of the required size. It is worthwhile to purchase a good compass that adjusts easily and accepts drawing leads and ink heads.

UNDERSTANDING ORTHOGRAPHIC PROJECTION DRAWINGS

The practice of interior design requires the creation and use of various types of drawing. These can be divided into three broad categories based on purpose. The first type of drawing allows the designer to explore ideas (known as ideation) and work conceptually, often in the form of sketches. The second type allows the designer to communicate to others, including members of the design team, the client, end users, consultants, and other professionals (presentation drawings). The third type of drawing conveys the technical information required for construction (construction documents or working drawings). This book focuses on the first two types of drawing, those used for exploration and presentation or graphic communication of ideas.

Unlike ideation sketches, presentation drawings and construction documents must use certain standard drawing conventions to clearly communicate and delineate the proposed design. Unlike fine art drawing, design drawing requires adherence to conventions, proportional scale, and accuracy of line. Design drawings are highly standardized so that they carry universal meaning. Or, as one early reviewer of this book put it, "Design drawing is much like a language; the drawings must convey the designer's meaning clearly."

The design drawings most commonly used in scaled delineation of interior environments are floor plans, interior elevations, sections, and reflected ceiling plans. These drawings, called ORTHOGRAPHIC PROJECTIONS, are created by projecting information about an object onto an imaginary plane known as the PICTURE PLANE. This direct projection of an object's dimensions allows orthographic projections to retain shape and proportion, making these drawings accurate and precise. Orthographic projection creates fragmentary views of an object, resulting in the need for multiple drawings. This means that because of their fragmentary nature orthographic projections become parts of a system and are mutually dependent on one another. By their nature, orthographic projections appear flat and lack the three-dimensional quality of perspective drawings. One way to visualize orthographic projection is to imagine an object enclosed in a transparent box. Each transparent plane of the enclosing box serves as the picture plane for that face of the object (Figure 1-2).

The view through the top plane of the enclosing box is called a PLAN. In a plan view only those elements seen when looking directly down at the object are drawn. Figure 1-3 depicts a roof plan.

The views through the picture planes that form the sides of the enclosing box are called ELEVATIONS. Elevations depict only what is visible when viewed directly through the picture plane (Figure 1-4).

A SECTION portrays a view of the object or building with a vertical plane sliced through it

and removed. One way of understanding section views is to imagine that a very sharp plane has been inserted into the object or building, cutting neatly into it and revealing the structure and complexity of the object's form (Figure 1-5).

A floor plan, also known as a horizontal section, portrays a view of the building with a horizontal plane sliced through it and removed, exposing the thickness of the walls and the elements below the cut line such as floor finishes and furniture (Figure 1-6).

ORTHOGRAPHIC PROJECTION DRAWINGS FOR INTERIOR ENVIRONMENTS

The special orthographic projection drawings used in delineation of interior environments are based on the concepts mentioned to this point. These drawings impart information particular to interior construction.

FLOOR PLANS

A FLOOR PLAN is a view as though looking straight down at a room or building after a horizontal cut has been made through the structure. As stated previously, a floor plan can also be called a HORIZONTAL BUILDING SECTION because the drawing is created by cutting through the building horizontally at roughly four to five feet above floor level and removing the top half. With the building cut open and viewed from above, important information such as wall, door, and window locations can be drawn to scale (Figure 1-7). Additional design elements such as fixtures and furniture can be drawn in appropriate locations to scale in a floor plan.

In the United States floor plans are most often drawn at a scale of $\frac{1}{8}$" = 1'0" or $\frac{1}{4}$" = 1'0", although this varies according to project conditions. Larger-scale floor plans are useful for presentation of complex or highly detailed spaces. Smaller-scale floor plans are

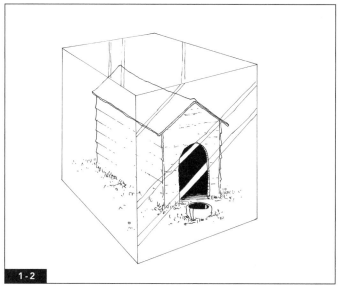

1-2

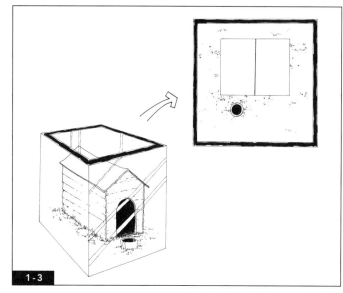

1-3

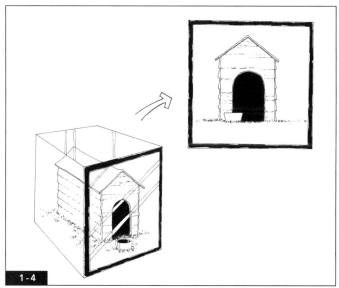

1-4

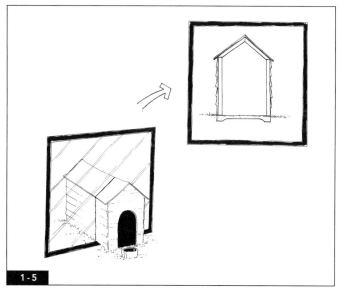

1-5

1-6

FIGURE 1-2
When an object is enclosed in a glass box, each plane of the box can serve as a picture plane.

FIGURE 1-3
The view through the top plane (picture plane) creates a plan view, in this case a roof plan.

FIGURE 1-4
The view through the picture plane enclosing the side of the box is called an *elevation.*

FIGURE 1-5
A section is a view of an object with the picture plane slicing neatly through it.

FIGURE 1-6
A floor plan is a view of the building from above with a horizontal plane sliced through it and removed to expose the thickness of the walls.

Figures 1-2–1-5 drawn by Justin Thomson.

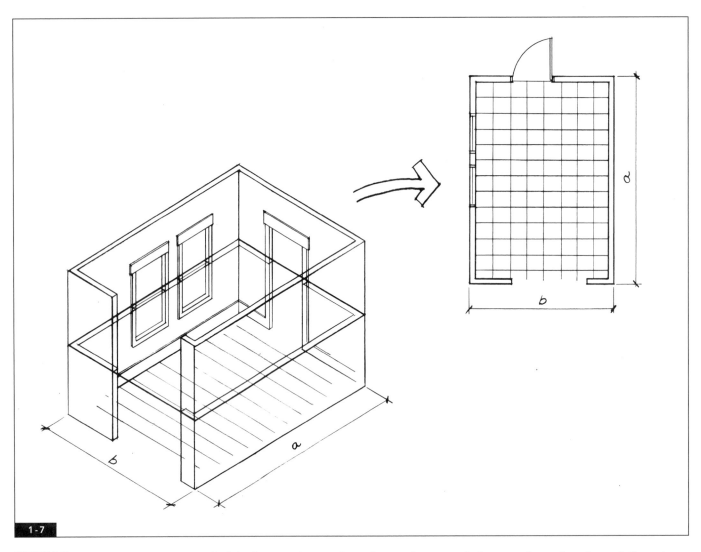

FIGURE 1-7
A floor plan is created when the picture plane cuts through the building horizontally, at 4–5' above floor level.

required for large projects and are also used as key plans in complex presentations.

In drawing floor plans it is important to convey significant spatial relationships with consistent graphic conventions. Various line weights are used to convey depths and qualities of form. In standard floor plans the boldest line weight is used to outline those elements that have been cut through and are closest to the viewer (such as full-height wall lines). An intermediate line weight is employed to outline objects that lie below the plane of the cut but above the floor plane, such as fixtures, built-ins, and furnishings. A finer line weight is used to outline surface treatment of floors and other horizontal planes, such as tile and wood grain. Objects that are hidden, such

as shelves, or above the plane of the cut are dashed or ghosted in; this must be done in a manner that is consistent throughout the presentation.

Figures 1-8a and 1-8b are examples of town-house floor plans drawn using AutoCAD software and employing standard conventions and reference symbols. Figures 1-9a and 1-9b are freehand-drawn (no tools) floor plans of the town house.

Standard doors are generally drawn open at 90 degrees to the wall and are often shown with the arc of their swing. The door frame and the space it requires must be considered in the drawing of the door system (this means the dimensions of the frame must be considered). Windowsills are typically outlined, often

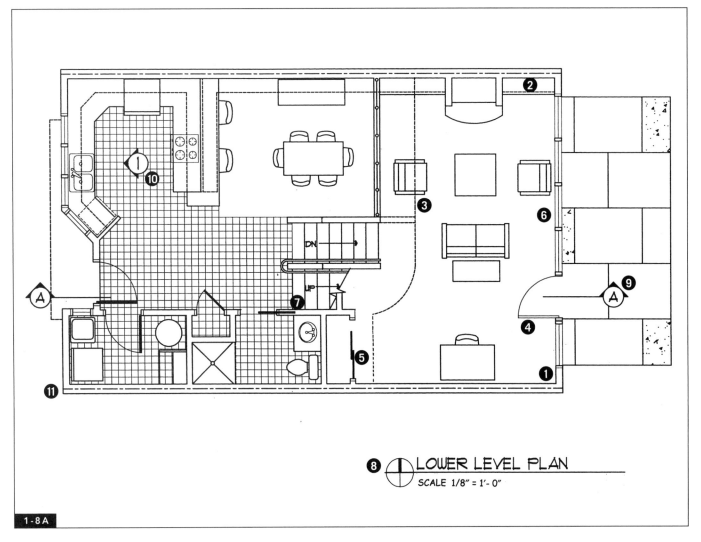

LOWER LEVEL PLAN
SCALE 1/8" = 1'- 0"

1-8A

FIGURE 1-8A
Town-house lower-level floor plan employing standard drafting conventions.

1. Boldest lines indicate the location of cut, meaning full-height walls are bold.

2. Fixtures, cabinetry, and finish materials are drawn with progressively lighter lines as they recede from the cut location.

3. Elements that are above or below the cutline (such as cabinets and soffits) are indicated with dashed lines.

4. Standard doors are drawn open at 90 degrees with the arc of swing shown.

5. Specialized doors such as bifold doors, sliding doors, and pocket doors are drawn in a way that indicates size and construction.

6. Window glass and sill lines are shown, often with a lighter-weight line than walls.

7. Stairs are drawn as broken off past the line of the cut; a special cutline is used. An arrow indicating direction from the level of the plan and the words *up* or *down* (*dn.*) are included.

8. A title, North arrow, and scale notation are required on all plans.

9. This is a section reference symbol. The arrow indicates the direction of the section view. The letter indicates the particular drawing that is referenced.

10. This is an elevation reference symbol. The arrow indicates the direction of the elevation view. The number indicates the particular drawing that is referenced.

11. This is a centerline, indicating the centerline of the shared wall in the town house.

Design by Courtney Nystuen.

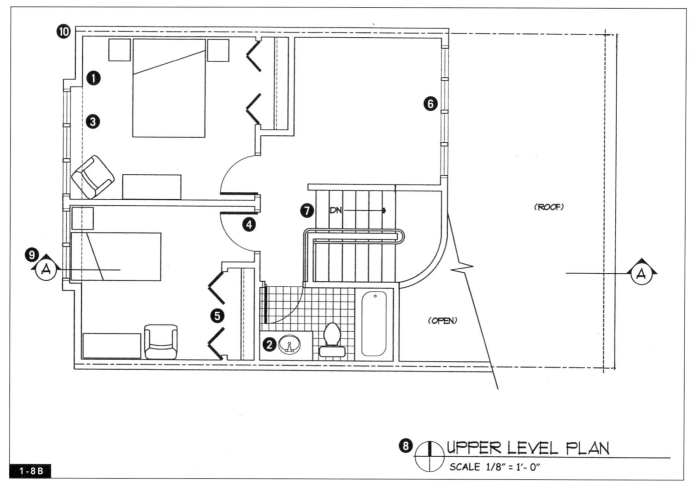

UPPER LEVEL PLAN
SCALE 1/8" = 1'-0"

1-8B

(ROOF)

(OPEN)

DN

FIGURE 1-8B
Town-house upper-level floor plan employing standard drafting conventions.

1. Boldest lines indicate the location of cut, meaning full-height walls are bold.

2. Fixtures, cabinetry, and finish materials are drawn with progressively lighter lines as they recede from the cut location.

3. Elements that are above or below the cutline (such as cabinets and soffits) are indicated with dashed lines.

4. Standard doors are drawn open at 90 degrees with the arc of swing shown.

5. Specialized doors such as bifold doors, sliding doors, and pocket doors are drawn in a way that indicates size and construction.

6. Window glass and sill lines are shown, often with a lighter-weight line than walls.

7. Stairs are drawn as broken off past the line of the cut; a special cutline is used. An arrow indicating direction from the level of the plan and the words *up* or *down* (*dn.*) are included.

8. A title, North arrow, and scale notation are required on all plans.

9. This is a section reference symbol. The arrow indicates the direction of the section view. The letter indicates the particular drawing that is referenced.

10. This is a centerline, indicating the centerline of the shared wall in the town-house.

Design by Courtney Nystuen.

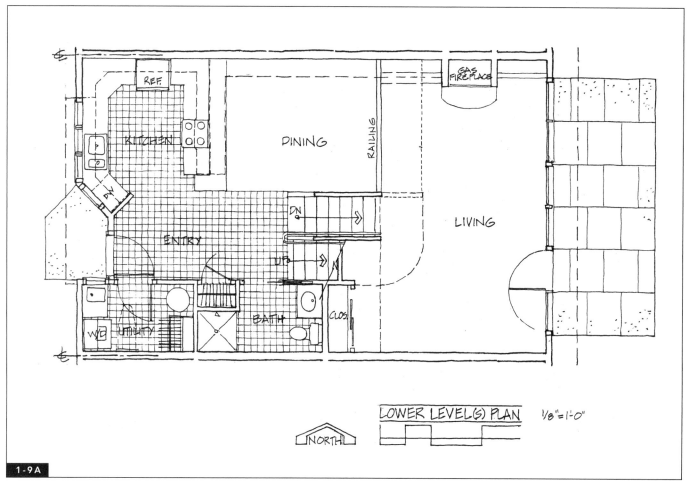

FIGURE 1-9A
Town-house lower-level floor
plan, drawn freehand employing
standard drafting conventions.
Design and drawing by Courtney
Nystuen.

with a lighter line weight at the sill only. Window frames and sheets of glass are shown in various detail as scale allows. Stairs are generally shown as broken off past the height of the plane of the cut; this is signified with a special cutline. An arrow should be included to indicate the direction of the stairs from the level of the floor plan, with the word UP or DOWN (DN.) adjacent to the directional arrow.

A title, a North arrow, and some type of scale notation should be included on all floor plans. Scale notation can be stated numerically, for example: ¼" = 1'0". Current practice often requires the use of a graphic scaling device, which allows for reduction, enlargement, and electronic transmission of the drawings.

Symbols relating the floor plan to additional orthographic views or details are often drawn on the floor plan and serve as cross-references.

Successful floor plan presentation drawings require a thorough understanding of drafting conventions. Presentation floor plans may be drawn fastidiously with tools or drawn freehand. Regardless of the style of drawing, presentation floor plans must be accurate and drawn to the appropriate scale so that they communicate the design and can be used by the designer as the project moves forward. Presentation floor plans are enhanced by the use of tone, value, color, and/or other graphic devices. The graphic enhancement of floor plans is discussed in greater detail in Chapter 5.

INTERIOR ELEVATIONS

Just as exterior elevations are created to reveal exterior elements and features, interior elevations reveal the interior features of a building. One way to understand the creation of interior elevations is to imagine ourselves inside the

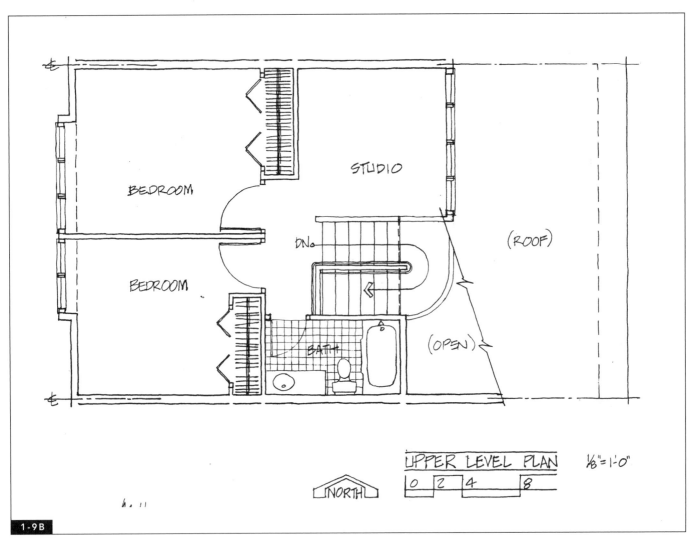

BEDROOM

BEDROOM

STUDIO

DN.

(ROOF)

(OPEN)

BATH

UPPER LEVEL PLAN   ⅛" = 1'-0"

0   2   4   8

NORTH

1-9B

FIGURE 1-9B
Town-house upper-level floor plan, drawn freehand employing standard drafting conventions. Design and drawing by Courtney Nystuen.

room we are drawing. Imagine standing inside a room facing one wall directly, with a large sheet of glass (the picture plane) inserted between the viewer and the wall. The interior elevation can then be created by outlining (projecting onto the picture plane) the significant features of the wall. Each wall of the room can be drawn in elevation by means of projecting what is visible as the viewer faces that wall directly (Figure 1-10).

Interior elevations are used extensively in professional practice. Successful elevations must clearly depict all interior architectural elements in a consistent scale. Interior elevations are typically drawn in a scale ranging from ¼" = 1'0" to 1" = 1'0". Elevations drawn to depict accessories, equipment, cabinetry, fix-

tures, and design details are often drawn at ⅜" = 1'0" or ½" = 1'0". Millwork and other highly complicated elevations are often drawn at ½" = 1'0" or larger.

All elevations require the use of differing line weights to clearly communicate spatial relationships. Typically, any portion of walls cut through and those closest to the viewer are drawn using a bold line weight. Receding elements become progressively lighter in line weight as they move farther from the picture plane. Some designers draw the line representing the ground line as the boldest, with those lines representing the top and sides of the wall drawn just slightly lighter in weight. Figure 1-11 depicts kitchen elevations for the town-house project.

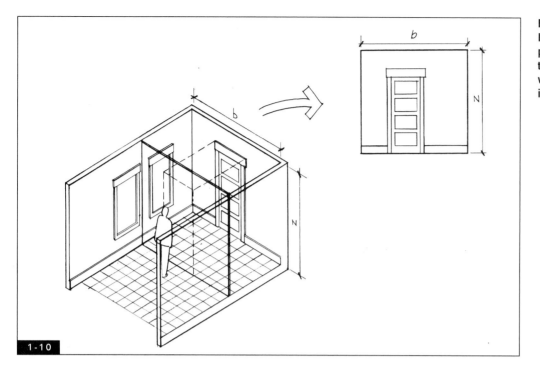

FIGURE 1-10
In drawing interior elevations, the picture plane is inserted between the viewer and wall(s). What is visible through the picture plane is drawn in elevation.

1-10

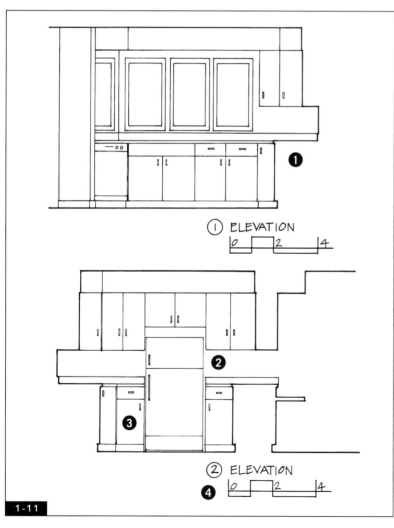

① ELEVATION
0   2   4

③ ELEVATION
0   2   4

FIGURE 1-11
Interior elevations for the town-house project.

1. Portions of walls cut into or closest to viewer are bold.

2. Receding elements are drawn with progressively lighter lines.

3. In elevations including cabinetry and or millwork, details such as countertops, door frames, and hardware should be included.

4. Interior elevations require titles, reference symbols (names or numbers), and scale notation.

Design by Courtney Nystuen.

1-11

Interior elevations can be difficult for beginning students to master. However, they deserve full attention because accurate elevations are necessary to successfully communicate key elements of a design. Figures 1-12a and 1-12b are interior elevations depicting very different design schemes for the same lobby space, indicating their importance in delineating the quality of a particular space.

Like floor plans, elevations used for design presentations vary greatly from those used for construction. Elevations used for construction drawings must necessarily contain significant dimensions as well as appropriate technical information. Those used for presentations can be drawn more freely and often contain less technical information but must be drawn accurately and in consistent scale.

For elevations to work well in visual presentations, they must be clearly keyed, noted, or referenced to the floor plan. Regardless of the referencing method used, titles must be included beneath all elevations and scale should be noted.

Drawing interior elevations by hand or digitally requires a clear understanding of the concepts involved. To this end, a case study project containing information about how elevations are constructed for an existing residence can be found in Appendix 2. Elevations used for presentations are enhanced by the use of tone, value, color, and/or other graphic devices, many of which are discussed in Chapter 5.

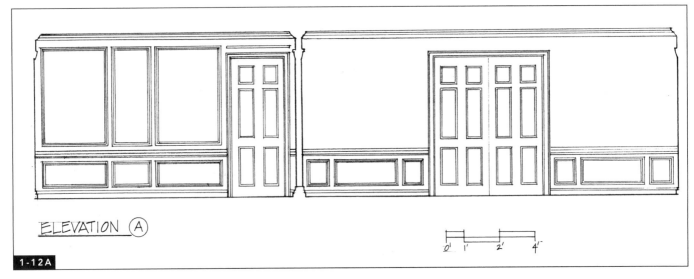

ELEVATION (A)

1-12A

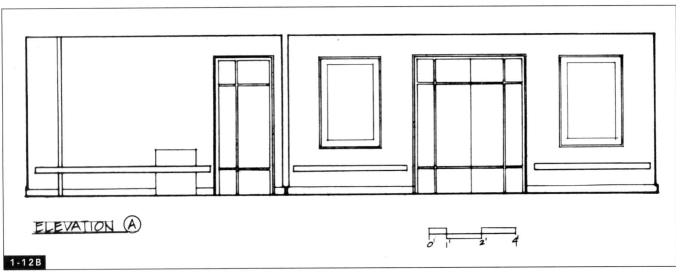

ELEVATION (A)

1-12B

SECTIONS

As described earlier, a building section is a view created as though a vertical plane has cut through the building and been removed. Unlike interior elevations, which depict only what occurs inside the interior, sections can expose the structure of the building. In drawing sections, it is important to include the outline of the structural elements as well as the internal configuration of the interior space. Sections require varied line weights as a means of describing depths and spatial relationships. It is typical to show what is cut through, and therefore closest to the viewer, in the boldest line weight; receding features and details are drawn using progressively lighter line weights.

It is important to consider carefully the most useful location (or locations) of the building to show in section. The section should be cut through the building as a single continuous plane. Sections should expose and convey important interior relationships and details such as doors, windows, changes in floor level, ceiling heights, and, in some cases, finish material locations.

Design and presentation sections differ greatly from construction sections. Construction sections require technical information to communicate information about building systems. In contrast, design sections and presentation sections focus on form, finish materials, and definition of interior space. For sections to work well in visual presentations, they must be clearly keyed, noted, or referenced to the appropriate floor plan. Generally, sections are referenced to the floor plan with use of a symbol that denotes the locations of the vertical cut. Figure 1-13 is an example of a hand-drawn (with tools) design section for the town-house project.

FIGURE 1-13
Building section for the town-house project.

1. **Boldest lines indicate location of cut.**

2. **Receding elements are drawn with progressively lighter lines.**

3. **Sections require titles, reference symbols (names or numbers), and scale notation.**

Design by Courtney Nystuen.

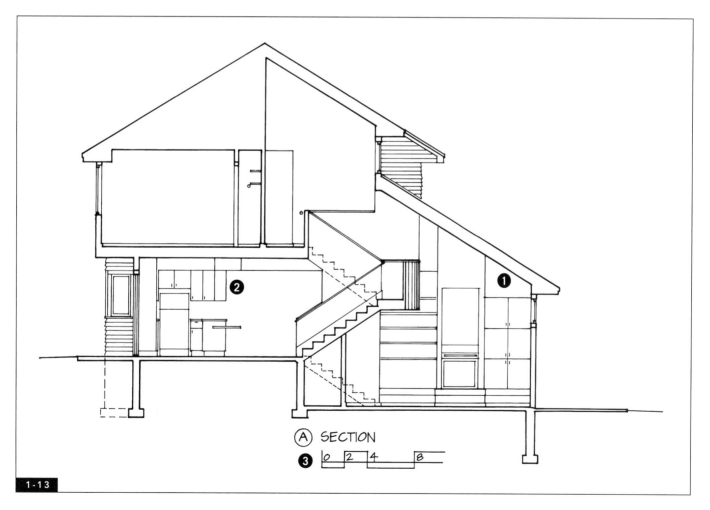

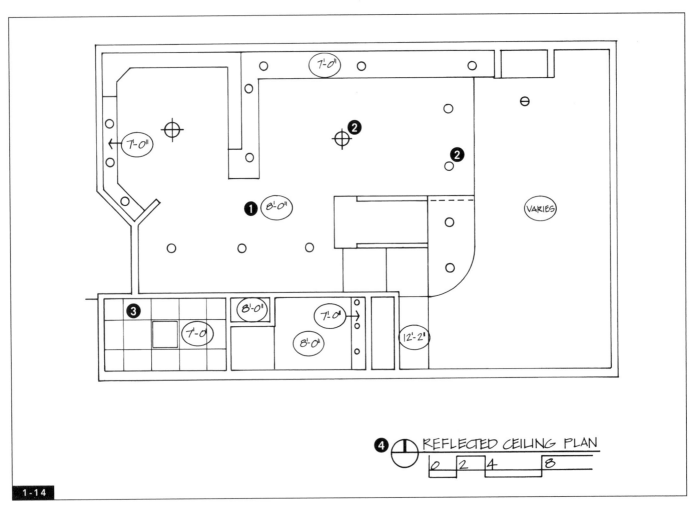

FIGURE 1-14
Simple reflected ceiling plan for town-house project.

1. Ceiling heights are noted and enclosed in a symbol.

2. Light fixture locations are noted with various symbols and are keyed to a legend.

3. Finish materials such as gypsum board, wood, and ceiling tiles are indicated in scale.

4. Reflected ceiling plans require titles, North arrows, and scale notation.

Design by Courtney Nystuen.

REFLECTED CEILING PLANS

REFLECTED CEILING PLANS are often used in conjunction with floor plans, elevations, and sections to communicate interior design. Reflected ceiling plans communicate important information about the design of the ceiling, such as materials, layout and locations of fixtures, and ceiling heights. A reflected ceiling plan is drawn as though a giant mirror were on the floor reflecting the elements located on the ceiling. The use of reflective imagery allows for the ceiling plan to have exactly the same orientation as the floor plan.

There is often a distinction between ceiling plans used for presentation and those used for construction. Typically, ceilings plans created for construction are highly technical and include a great deal of information. Reflected ceiling plans used in design presentations can

be simplified. Most often reflected ceiling plans used in presentations include simplified lighting information, ceiling heights, and finish materials, whereas precisely measured, complex technical lighting plans are required for construction. Figure 1-14 is a simple reflected ceiling plan for the town-house project appropriate for use in a design presentation. More complex ceiling plans used for different projects can be found in Figures C-71a, C-71b, and C-72.

Together, floor plans, elevations, sections, and ceiling plans communicate information about the quality of an interior environment. Because these drawings are abstracted, fragmented versions of three-dimensional form, they depend on one another to communicate effectively.

The orthographic projections covered in this chapter relate directly to the communication and design of interior space. Differing versions of orthographic projections are used for construction and presentation, but they are used in one form or another on virtually all projects.

Additional types of orthographic drawing are used to communicate the features of buildings and building sites. Site plans, foundation plans, demolition plans, roof plans, framing plans, exterior elevations, wall sections, and design details are also used in the design of buildings. Designers of interior space must be knowledgeable about the nature of these drawings, how they are created, and how they relate to the interior architecture of a building.

LETTERING

Traditionally, floor plans, elevations, and sections contained notes and dimensions written in a standardized style of hand lettering. However, recent changes in technology allow for creation of type that can be applied to hand-drawn orthographic projections. Lettering and type can be computer generated, printed on adhesive reproduction film ("sticky back"), and applied to drawings. Lettering is also created by specialized machines (lettering machines) that print on adhesive-backed tape that can be applied to drawings. Lettering machines can be used to produce type in a range of sizes, styles, and colors. In addition, all of the com-

FIGURE 1-15
Hand-lettering reference.

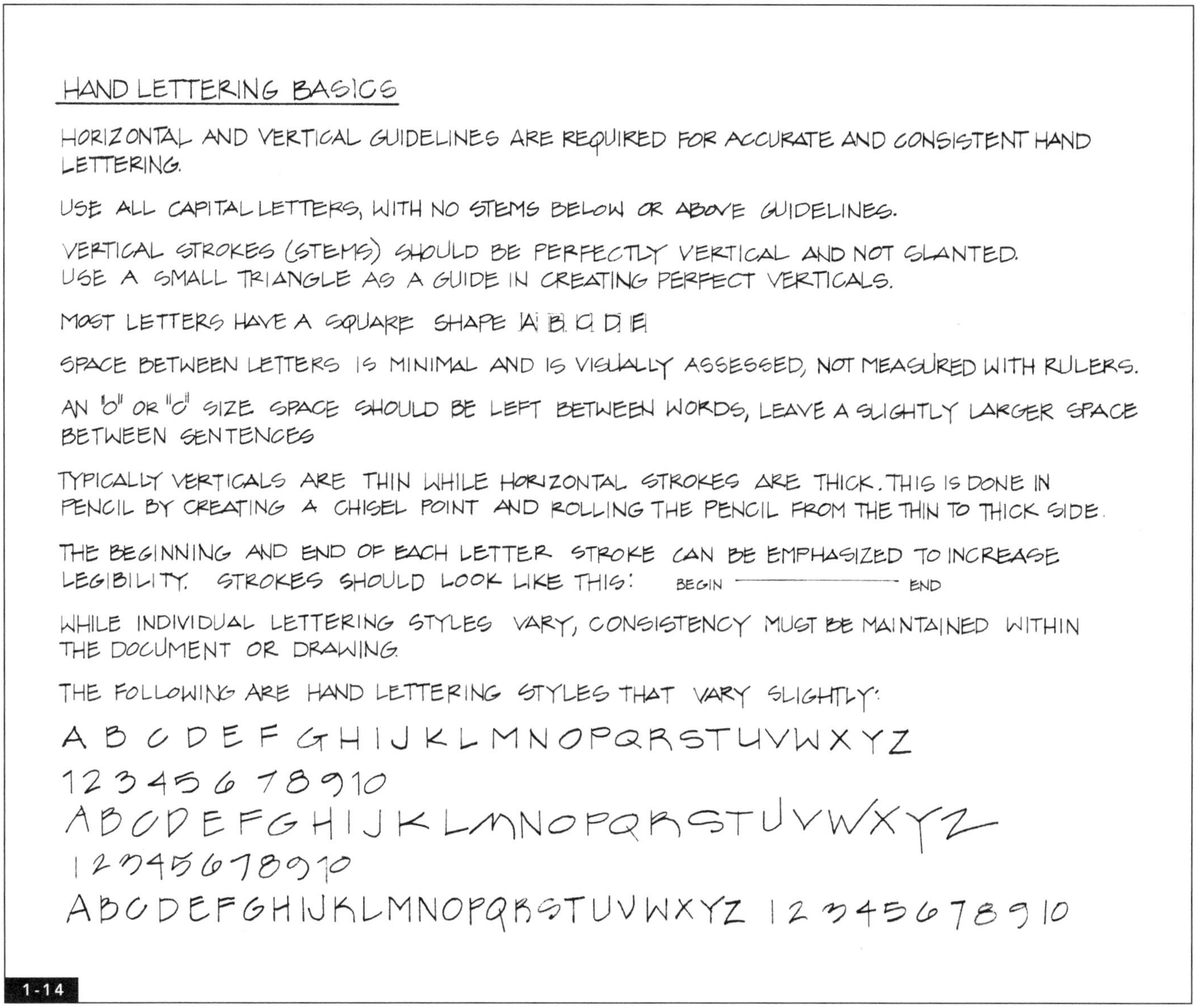

HAND LETTERING BASICS

HORIZONTAL AND VERTICAL GUIDELINES ARE REQUIRED FOR ACCURATE AND CONSISTENT HAND LETTERING.

USE ALL CAPITAL LETTERS, WITH NO STEMS BELOW OR ABOVE GUIDELINES.

VERTICAL STROKES (STEMS) SHOULD BE PERFECTLY VERTICAL AND NOT SLANTED. USE A SMALL TRIANGLE AS A GUIDE IN CREATING PERFECT VERTICALS.

MOST LETTERS HAVE A SQUARE SHAPE A B C D E

SPACE BETWEEN LETTERS IS MINIMAL AND IS VISUALLY ASSESSED, NOT MEASURED WITH RULERS.

AN "O" OR "C" SIZE SPACE SHOULD BE LEFT BETWEEN WORDS, LEAVE A SLIGHTLY LARGER SPACE BETWEEN SENTENCES

TYPICALLY VERTICALS ARE THIN WHILE HORIZONTAL STROKES ARE THICK. THIS IS DONE IN PENCIL BY CREATING A CHISEL POINT AND ROLLING THE PENCIL FROM THE THIN TO THICK SIDE.

THE BEGINNING AND END OF EACH LETTER STROKE CAN BE EMPHASIZED TO INCREASE LEGIBILITY. STROKES SHOULD LOOK LIKE THIS: BEGIN —————————— END

WHILE INDIVIDUAL LETTERING STYLES VARY, CONSISTENCY MUST BE MAINTAINED WITHIN THE DOCUMENT OR DRAWING.

THE FOLLOWING ARE HAND LETTERING STYLES THAT VARY SLIGHTLY:

A B C D E F G H I J K L M N O P Q R S T U V W X Y Z
1 2 3 4 5 6 7 8 9 10
A B C D E F G H I J K L M N O P Q R S T U V W X Y Z
1 2 3 4 5 6 7 8 9 10
A B C D E F G H I J K L M N O P Q R S T U V W X Y Z 1 2 3 4 5 6 7 8 9 10

1-14

monly used CADD programs allow for consistent, standardized type to be readily applied to the appropriate location on a drawing.

Even with these changes in technology, it is useful to develop the ability to hand-letter in a consistent standardized style. Many designers still create presentation drawings by hand, and for the sake of visual consistency, hand lettering is crucial. Hand lettering is also often used on quick sketches and design details, and for dimensions and revisions of drawings.

There are some basic rules for lettering design drawings, as well as some stylistic elements that influence letter form. Guidelines are required for all lettering locations. Horizontal guidelines create the lines on which the lettering rests. Consistent spacing between the lines of lettering is required. Vertical guidelines must be drawn so that the lines of type are aligned consistently. Lettering for design drawings is typically all capitals, allowing all letters to fit within a single pair of guidelines, with no tips or tails above or below the guidelines. Letters should have perfectly vertical strokes; the vertical strokes should not slant to the left or to the right. A tiny lettering triangle is used as a straightedge in making vertical strokes. Figure 1-15 is a hand-lettering reference.

DIMENSIONS

Dimensions, required on all construction drawings, are sometimes necessary on drawings used for presentation purposes. Their inclusion is based on the project and the presentation audience. Dimensions must be accurate, complete, and readable. Horizontal dimensions should read across the sheet from left to right. Vertical dimensions must read from the left-hand edge so as not to require rotating the drawing in a variety of directions.

Dimension lines should be of a thin, crisp line weight that sets them apart from wall and other construction lines. The lines leading from the area dimensioned to the dimension lines (known as leader lines) should be spaced slightly apart from construction lines.

Dimensions should be written above the dimension lines, so that they are underlined by them. Dimensions are best written in feet and inches. For example, 2'-4" is written, not 28". The single exception is made for items measuring less than one foot; these are listed in inches only. Figure 1-16 is a town-house upper-level floor plan using standard dimensioning conventions for interior. Figure 1-17 is a town-house lower-level floor plan employing standard conventions for locating interior and exterior dimensions outside of the plan boundaries.

COMPUTER-AIDED DRAFTING AND DESIGN (CADD)

It is important to note that the conceptual basis for orthographic drawings and drafting conventions is the same whether created by hand or through the use of electronic tools. The meaning communicated in a floor plan is the same whether the drawing is created by hand or with the use of a CADD program.

While the debate rages on as to the "best" CADD program, most of the commercial design firms that I have interviewed use Auto-CAD® software and expect entry-level designers to have a working knowledge of it. I have noted more variation in terms of CADD software used by residential design firms. My many interviews with those who hire professional interior designers have consistently shown that all employers expect recent graduates to come equipped with high-level CADD skills. Clearly this book is not the guide to any software program; instead the focus is on the concepts and conventions that convey information in design drawings. Some recently published AutoCAD guides have proven highly useful, and those are listed in the references.

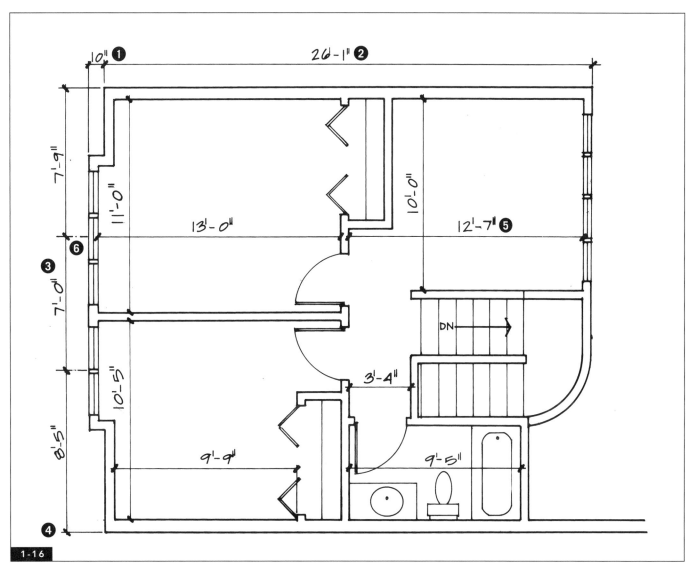

FIGURE 1-16
Dimensioned upper-level floor plan for town-house project, delineating conventions for interior dimensions.

1. Dimension lines should be light and crisp.

2. Horizontal written dimensions sit above the dimension lines and read left to right.

3. Vertical written dimensions sit above the dimension lines and read from left.

4. Leader lines run from the building location being dimensioned to the dimension lines. Leader lines should not touch the building; instead they should be drawn slightly away.

5. Dimensions are written in feet and inches unless less than one foot.

6. Dimensions measured from centerlines must be clearly indicated. Windows and doors are commonly measured to centerlines.

Design by Courtney Nystuen.

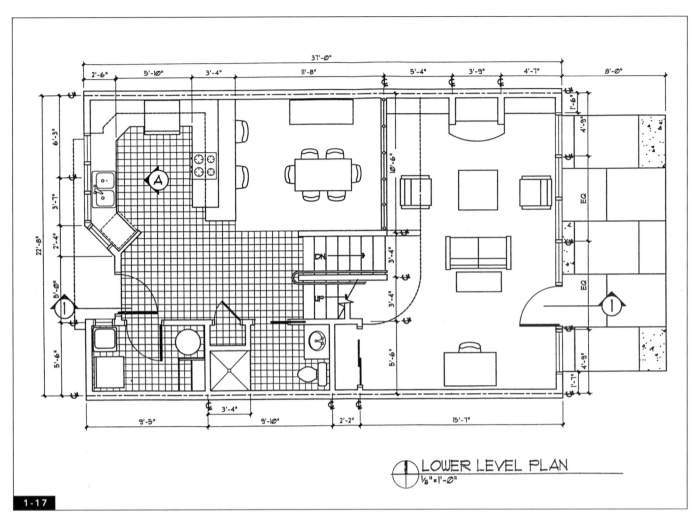

LOWER LEVEL PLAN
1/8" = 1'-0"

1-17

FIGURE 1-17
Dimensioned lower-level floor plan for town-house project, employing standard conventions for locating interior and exterior dimensions outside of the plan boundaries.

REFERENCES

Ching, Frank. *Architectural Graphics*. New York: John Wiley & Sons, 1996.

———. *A Visual Dictionary of Architecture*. New York: John Wiley & Sons, 1995.

Forseth, Kevin, and David Vaughn. *Graphics for Architecture*. New York: John Wiley & Sons, 1998.

Kirkpatrick, Beverly, and James Kirkpatrick. *AutoCAD® for Interior Design and Space Planning*. Upper Saddle River, N.J.: Prentice Hall, 2000.

Liebling, Ralph. *Architectural Working Drawings*. New York: John Wiley & Sons, 1990.

Porter, Tom. *Architectural Drawing*. New York: Van Nostrand Reinhold, 1990.

Smith, C. Ray. *Interior Design in 20th Century America: A History*. New York: Harper & Row, 1987.

Trachte, Judith. *A Quick Start Guide to AutoCAD® for Interior Design*. Upper Saddle River, N.J.: Prentice Hall, 2000.

THE DESIGN PROCESS AND RELATED GRAPHICS

INTRODUCTION TO THE DESIGN PROCESS

The complexity of the design process requires that at various points along the way designers communicate aspects and outcomes of the process to clients and consultants. Like professionals, students must present in-process projects to team members, instructors, and guest critics. Visual presentations must vary to accommodate the process of design and to communicate both process and outcome.

In *Interior Design Illustrated,* Francis Ching identifies three basic stages of design process: analysis, synthesis, and evaluation. According to Ching, analysis involves defining and understanding the problem; synthesis involves the formulation of possible solutions; and evaluation involves a critical review of the strengths and weaknesses of the proposed solutions.

Interestingly, these three basic stages of design process are used by design practitioners in a variety of disciplines. Industrial designers, graphic designers, exhibition designers, and others often engage in a similar process. Of course, the design disciplines vary a great deal in terms of professional practice and final outcome. For this reason, actual interior design process and project phases are quite distinct and are more elaborate than the three basic stages may indicate.

For purposes of contractual organization, the process of design engaged in by architects and interior designers in the United States has been divided into five basic project phases: (1) PROGRAMMING, (2) SCHEMATIC DESIGN, (3) DESIGN DEVELOPMENT, (4) CONSTRUCTION DOCUMENTATION, and (5) CONTRACT ADMINISTRATION. These phases are derived from the American Institute of Architects (AIA) Owner-Architect Agreement for Interior Design Services and the American Society of Interior Designers (ASID) Interior Design Services Agreement. Both of these documents serve as contracts for design services and reflect the current design process and project management in the United States. Figure 2-1 is a description of design phases and related visual presentation methods.

Peña, Parshall, and Kelly, writing in *Problem Seeking,* identify the actual design process as taking place in the first three project phases. They state that "programming is part of the total design process but is separate from schematic design." The authors go on to link schematic design and design development as the second and third phases of the total design process. This chapter is intended as an exploration of the three phases of the design process identified by Peña, Parshall, Kelly, and others and as a study of the draw-

PROJECT PHASE	TYPICAL TASKS AND ACTIVITIES	TYPICAL MEANS OF VISUAL PRESENTATION
Programming also known as pre-design	**In depth analysis and documentation of needs, requirements goals and objectives.** Can include: identification of space and adjacency requirements analysis; asset assessment; specialized needs assessments; codes and accessibility research and identification of conceptual and thematic issues. As well as; analysis of architectural or site parameters; and analysis of scheduling and budget.	Most often written information compiled in a programming report. Often includes problem identification, diagrams, charts, matrixes, and may include some orthographic drawings and early fit studies. May include preliminary scheduling graphics.
Schematic Design also known as the preliminary design phase	**Preliminary conceptual, spatial, conceptual, and technical design of project.** Includes preliminary space planning often using; relationship diagrams; matrices; bubble diagrams; blocking diagrams; stacking plans; and fit plans. As well as initial furnishings, fixtures and equipment design/layout. Development of projects conceptual and thematic issues. Color, material and finish studies. Preliminary code review. Preliminary budgetary information.	Graphic presentation of preliminary design; can include relationship diagrams; blocking and fit plans; preliminary space plan(s); preliminary furnishing and equipment layouts; preliminary elevations and sections; preliminary 3-D drawings; preliminary color and materials studies; and study models. Presentation may also include graphic presentation of conceptual and thematic issues using sketches, diagrams, and mixed media.
Design Development	**Refinement of finalized design.** Includes space plan and design of interior construction elements and details. Often involves incorporation of lighting, electrical, plumbing, and mechanical systems design; as well as data and telecommunication systems integration. Often includes millwork design and detailing. Also includes color, materials, and finish selection. Design and specification of furnishings, fixtures, and equipment, as well as refinement of budgetary and scheduling information.	Finalized, refined design presentation incorporating all necessary components of design. Graphic presentation of finalized design can include conceptual diagrams; space plan(s); and plan(s) for furnishings, fixtures and equipment, as well as elevations; sections; ceiling plans; 3-D drawings; colors, materials, and finish samples; scale models and mockups. Multimedia presentations can incorporate all of the above elements plus sound and animation.
Construction Documents	**Preparation of drafted, working drawings and/or contract documents.** Includes preparation of drawings, schedules, details, and specifications, as well as coordination and integration of consultants documents. Can include preparation of specialized equipment and/or furnishings documents for bidding by purchasing agents. May include purchasing documents.	Preparation of contract documents. Often includes submission to general contractor(s) and purchasing agents for bid and to appropriate agencies for plan check.
Construction Administration	**Guide and review construction and installation.** Can include periodic site visits and creation of progress reports. Coordination and review of shop drawings and sample submittals. May include clarification and interpretation of drawings, as well as possible review of billing and payment. Preparation of punch list. May include move coordination and supervision of furnishings, fixtures and equipment installation.	Communication with contractors, agencies and clients is primarily written and verbal. May include scheduling, budgetary, and administrative graphics.

Adapted from: AIA Owner-Architect Agreement for Interior Design Services' and the ASID Interior Design Services Agreement'.

2-1

FIGURE 2-1
Project phases and related visual presentation methods.

ings and graphics used to communicate, document, inform, and clarify the work done during these phases.

PROGRAMMING

The experienced, creative designer withholds judgment, resists preconceived solutions and the pressure to synthesize until all the information is in. He refuses to make sketches until he knows the client's problem. . . . Programming is the prelude to good design. (Peña, Parshall, and Kelly, 1987)

Programming, also known as predesign or strategic planning, involves detailed analysis of the client's (or end user's) needs, requirements, goals, budgetary factors, and assets, as well as analysis of architectural or site parameters and constraints. Information gathered about the user's needs and requirements is often documented in written form, whereas architectural or site parameters are often communicated graphically through orthographic projection. These two distinct forms of communication, verbal and graphic, must be brought together in the early stages of design.

Some firms employ professionals to work as programmers and then hand the project over to designers. It is also common for project managers and/or designers to work on project programming and then continue to work on the design or management of the project. It could be said that programmers and designers are separate specialists, given the distinctions between programming (analysis) and design (synthesis). However, many firms and designers choose not to separate these specialties or do so only on very large or programming-intensive projects.

In practice, programming varies greatly from project to project. This is due to variation in project type and size and to the quantity and quality of information supplied by the client (or end user). In some cases clients provide designers with highly detailed written programs. In other situations clients begin with little more than general information or simply exclaim, "We need more space, we are growing very fast" or "Help, we are out of control." In situations such as the latter, research and detective work must be done to create programming information that will allow for the creation of successful design solutions.

It is difficult to distill the programming process used in a variety of projects into a brief summary. Clearly the programming required for a major metropolitan public library is very different from that required in a small-scale residential renovation. It is important, therefore, to consider what all projects relating to interior environments share in terms of programming.

All projects require careful analysis of space requirements for current and future needs, as well as analysis of work processes, adjacency requirements, and organizational structure (or life-style and needs-assessment factors in residential design). Physical inventories and asset assessments are required to evaluate existing furniture and equipment as well as to plan for future needs. Building code, accessibility, and health/safety factors must also be researched as part of the programming process.

In addition to this primarily quantitative information, there are aesthetic requirements. Cultural and sociological aspects of the project must also be identified by the designers. All of these should be researched and can be documented in a programming report that is reviewed by the client and used by the project design team. When possible, it is important to include a problem statement with the programming report. The problem statement is a concise identification of key issues, limitations, objectives, and goals that provide a clearer understanding of the project. With the programming report complete, the designers can begin the job of synthesis and continue the design process.

ECO
TOYS Programming Information

Company History:
Eco Toys is a young, dynamic company. Larry Leader, the company president started the company in 1985. The company designs and produces toys for preschoolers, using recycled plastic products. Eco Toys has enjoyed tremendous success and growth in the last five years. Owing to recent growth, the company must move to larger, better organized design and marketing offices.

Company Structure and Organization:
The president is at the center of all company operations and constantly interacts with all members of his staff. Mr. Leader depends a great deal on his assistant Steve Stable. Although Mr. Leader is in touch with all levels of operation, he has set up the company in a horizontal organizational structure. This means that all members of the Eco Toys staff have equal status and power and are seen as important contributors to the organization. The design of the space should reflect the organizational structure of the company.

General Requirements:
Because of the non hierarchical organizational structure, all workstations must be exactly the same size. As a means of encouraging team meetings and sharing within departments small (8' x 8') individual workstations have been requested. As a result of complicated egress conditions, the existing door locations must be retained.

Department Information and Requirements:

Entry/Reception: Very public, must visually represent company's mission. Requires reception desk with work surface and transaction counter, task seating. Guest seating for 6. Must allow space for movement of children into toy test center. Must be near conference room, toy test center and close to marketing dept.
Conference Room: Very public and attractive, seating for 10 at tables with additional seating available. Requires multimedia center. View if possible. Immediately adjacent to toy test center (with visual connection), close to reception, and near marketing dept.
Toy Testing Center: Open and flexible space for use by 4 - 6 preschool age children. Must be visually connected to conference room and adjacent to entry and conference room.
Design Dept.: 2 designers and 2 assistants. All individual work spaces must accommodate CADD station, plus layout space, 2 file drawers, and handy reference storage. Adjacent to model shop; a messy, noisy, enclosed space -120 sq. ft. min. Adjacent to engineering dept. Nearby team meeting space with casual seating for 4, and room for plotter, display area, and filing.
Marketing Dept.: 2 marketing managers and 1 assistant. All individual work spaces must accommodate a P.C., 2 file drawers, and handy reference storage. Must have adjacent team space with table and seating for 5. Must be near conference room, toy test and reception area.
Engineering Dept.: 2 engineers. All individual work spaces must accommodate CADD station, and lay-out space, two file drawers, and handy reference storage. Must be adjacent to design dept. and near design team space.
Accounting Dept.: 2 accountants. Individual work spaces must accommodate a P.C. and printer, 2 file drawers, and handy reference storage. Requires some privacy and no major interaction with other departments, with the exception of the President.
President: Pres. plus assistant (2 total); must accommodate P.C. and printer, 2 file drawers, and handy reference storage. President to have small conference table (to seat 4). Near all depts. and break room.
Break Room: Generous counter space, base and wall cabinets, sink, refrig., microwave, and commercial coffee makers. Seating for 8 minimum.
Copy/Mail: Room for copy machine and adjacent 5 lineal ft. of collating space, room for 16 mailboxes, paper, and supply storage. Convenient to corridor.
Storage: Generous heavy-duty shelving. Must be enclosed and private, requires shelving and ventilation for Local Area Computer Network.

2-2A

FIGURE 2-2A
Programming information for the sample project.

FIGURE 2-2B
Floor plan for the sample project.
By Leanne Larson.

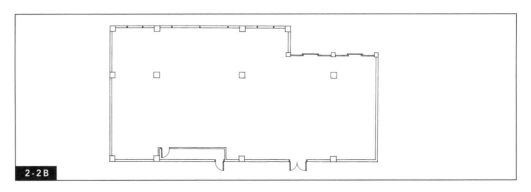

2-2B

Residential projects generally require less intensive programming graphics. Programming is a significant element of the residential design process; however, the relationships, adjacencies, and organization of the space are often simplified in relation to large commercial and public spaces. For this reason the following discussion focuses primarily on commercial design, where a significant amount of visual communication of programming information is often required.

Clients, consultants, and designers require graphic analysis as a way of understanding programming data and information. Diagrams, charts, matrices, and visual imagery are comprehended with greater ease than pages of written documentation. It is useful to develop ways of sorting and simplifying programming information so that it can be easily assimilated.

Successful graphic communication of both the programming process and the programming report can help to create useful information from overwhelming mounds of raw data. A sample project created to illustrate the drawings and graphics used in the various phases of the design project is referenced throughout this chapter. Figure 2-2a contains written programming information regarding the sample project. Figure 2-2b is a floor plan indicating the given architectural parameters of the project.

PROGRAMMING ANALYSIS GRAPHICS

Many designers find it useful to obtain early programming data and incorporate it into graphic worksheets. Using a flip-chart pad, brown kraft paper, or other heavy paper, the programmers can create large, easy-to-read graphic documents. These sheets are created so that they may be understood easily by the client and can therefore be approved or commented on. Often the eventual project designers find these sheets useful as a means of project documentation.

The book *Problem Seeking* (Peña, Parshall, and Kelly, 1987) provides an additional tech-

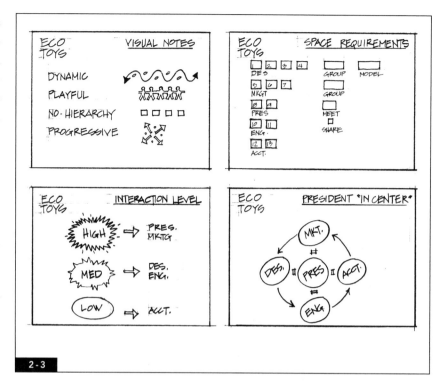

FIGURE 2-3
Examples of programming analysis graphics for the sample project.

nique for the graphic recording of information generated in the early stages of programming, using a device known as analysis cards. Analysis cards allow for easy comprehension, discussion, clarification, and feedback. The cards are drawn from interview notes and early programming data. Based on the notion that visual information is more easily comprehended than verbal, the cards contain simple graphic imagery with few words and concise messages. The cards are most successful if they are large enough for use in a wall display or presentation and if they are reduced to very simple but specific information. Figure 2-3 illustrates program analysis graphics for the sample project. See Figure C-6 for a color version of a programming analysis graphic.

PROGRAMMING MATRICES

Matrices are extremely useful tools in programming, incorporating a wealth of information into an easily comprehended visual tool. An adjacency matrix is commonly used as a means of visually documenting spatial proximity, identifying related activities and services, and establishing priorities. Adjacency ma-

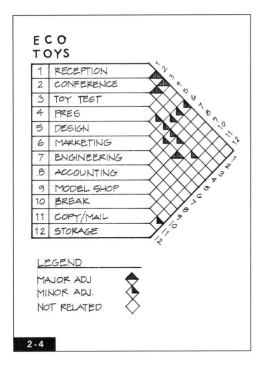

FIGURE 2-4
Simple adjacency matrix for the sample project.

FIGURE 2-5
Another type of adjacency matrix for the sample project.

ECO TOYS

	RECEPTION	CONFERENCE	TOY TEST	PRES.	DESIGN	MARKETING	ENGINEERING	ACCOUNTING	MODEL SHOP	BREAK	COPY/MAIL	STORAGE
RECEPTION	·	●	●	O	O	◐	O	O	X	O	O	O
CONFERENCE	●	·	●	O	O	◐	O	O	X	O	O	O
TOY TEST	●	●	·	O	O	◐	O	O	X	O	O	O
PRES.	O	O	O	·	◐	◐	◐	◐	O	◐	O	O
DESIGN	O	O	O	◐	·	O	◐	O	●	O	O	O
MARKETING	◐	◐	◐	◐	O	·	O	O	O	O	O	O
ENGINEERING	O	O	O	◐	◐	O	·	O	O	O	O	O
ACCOUNTING	O	O	O	◐	O	O	O	·	O	O	O	O
MODEL SHOP	X	X	X	O	●	O	O	O	·	O	O	O
BREAK	O	O	O	◐	O	O	O	O	O	·	O	O
COPY/MAIL	O	O	O	O	O	O	O	O	O	O	·	◉
STORAGE	O	O	O	O	O	O	O	O	O	O	◉	·

LEGEND
● MAJOR ADJACENCY
◐ MINOR ADJACENCY
O NOT CLOSELY RELATED
X UNDESIRABLE

2-5

trices vary in complexity in relation to project requirements. Large-scale, complex projects often require highly detailed adjacency matrices. Figures 2-4 and 2-5 illustrate two types of adjacency matrix.

A criteria matrix can distill project issues such as needs for privacy, natural light, and security into a concise, consistent format. Large-scale, complex design projects may require numerous detailed, complex matrices, whereas smaller, less complex projects require more simplified matrices. Criteria matrices are used in residential design projects and in the programming of public spaces. Smaller projects allow for criteria matrices to be combined with adjacency matrices. Figure 2-6 illustrates a criteria matrix that includes adjacency information. Special types of matrix are used by designers on particular projects.

Programming graphics, such as project worksheets, analysis cards, and a variety of matrices, are widely used in interior design practice. These are presented to the client or end user for comment, clarification, and approval. Many of these graphics are refined, corrected, and improved upon during the programming process and are eventually included in the final programming report.

SCHEMATIC DESIGN

With the programming phase completed, designers may begin the work of synthesis. Another way of stating this is that with the problem clearly stated, problem solving can begin. The creation of relationship diagrams is often a first step in the schematic design of a project. Relationship diagrams serve a variety of func-

FIGURE 2-6
A combination criteria and adjacency matrix, computer generated. By Leanne Larson.

ECO TOYS

		Adjacencies	# of Dept Members	Seating Req's	Public Access	Privacy	Plumbing	Data/Phone	Special Req's	Comments
1	Reception	②③<u>6</u>	1	6 min	●			●	Y	Visually rep mission; used by adults & children; "dynamic & playful"
2	Conference	①③<u>6</u>		10+	●			●	Y	"Dynamic & playful"; multimedia center; multiple lap-top /computers
3	Toy Test	①②		4-6	●			○	Y	Used by preschoolers; open, flexible, playful
4	President	<u>5 6 7 8</u> <u>10</u>	2	4				●	Y	PC, printer, 2 file drawers, ref storage for each 8' x 8' work space
5	Design	⑨⑦	4	4 min				●	Y	CADD, lay-out, 2 file drawers, ref storage for each 8' x 8' work space
6	Marketing	①②<u>3</u>	3	5 min				●	Y	PC, printer, 2 file drawers, ref storage for each 8' x 8' work space
7	Engineering	⑤	2					●	Y	CADD, lay-out, 2 file drawers, ref storage for each 8' x 8' work space
8	Accounting	<u>4</u>	2			●		●	Y	PC, printer, 2 file drawers, ref storage for each 8' x 8' work space
9	Model Shop	⑤				○	●	○	Y	Messy & noisy; enclosed
10	Break Room	<u>4</u>		8 min			●	○	Y	Relaxing & inviting; gen counters; refrig, microwave, sink, coffee makers req
11	Copy/Mail							○	Y	5 lineal feet collating space; 16 mailboxes; storage
12	Storage					●			Y	Generous heavy-duty shelving; ventilation

Legend

①	Major Adjacency	○	Secondary Requirement
<u>1</u>	Minor Adjacency	Y	Yes, See Comments
●	Mandatory Requirement	X	Undesirable

2-6

tions that allow the designers to digest and internalize the programming information. Relationship diagrams also allow the designer to begin to use graphics to come to terms with the physical qualities of the project.

One type of relationship diagram explores the relationship of functional areas to one another and uses information completed on the criteria and adjacency matrices. This type of one-step diagram can be adequate for smaller commercial and residential projects. Larger-scale, complex projects often require a series of relationship diagrams. Diagrams of this type do not generally relate to architectural or site parameters and are not drawn to scale. Most specialized or complex projects require additional diagrams that explore issues such as personal interaction, flexibility, and privacy requirements.

BUBBLE DIAGRAMS

As relationship diagrams begin to incorporate and account for necessary requirements and

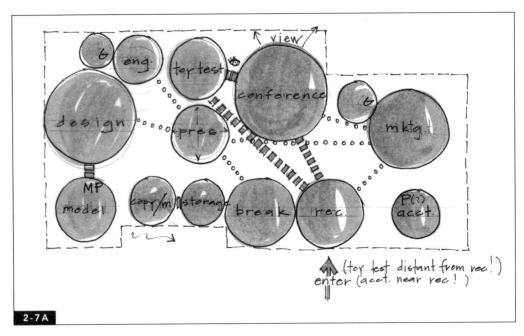

2-7A

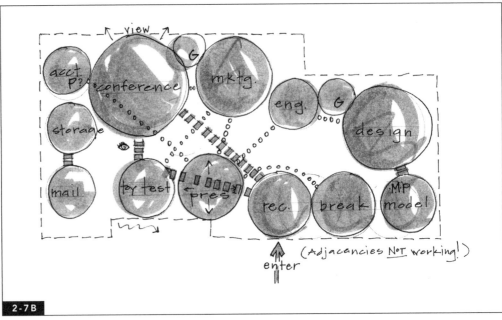

2-7B

adjacencies, they can become refined into what are generally referred to as BUBBLE DIAGRAMS. Bubble diagrams take the project one step further in the schematic design process. Often bubble diagrams relate approximately to the actual architectural parameters (the building space) in rough scale. In addition, they often incorporate elements identified in criteria and adjacency matrices through the use of graphic devices keyed to a legend. Figures 2-7a–2-7e are a sequence of bubble diagrams for the sample project. See Figure C-7 for a color version of a bubble diagram. It is important to note that a primary purpose of these early schematic diagrams is to generate a number of options. Brainstorming many ideas is highly advisable. Designers with years of experience use brainstorming techniques, as should students of design. Successful design requires sparks of creativity in every phase, and these sparks are fostered by nurturing idea generation. Rarely does the first try (or even the first

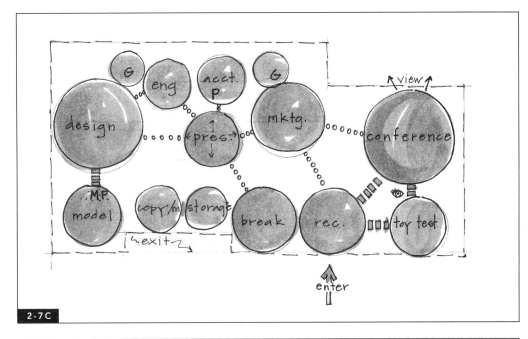

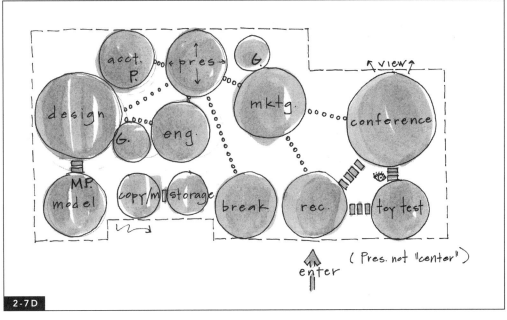

FIGURES 2-7A, 2-7B, 2-7C, 2-7D
Bubble diagrams for the sample project.

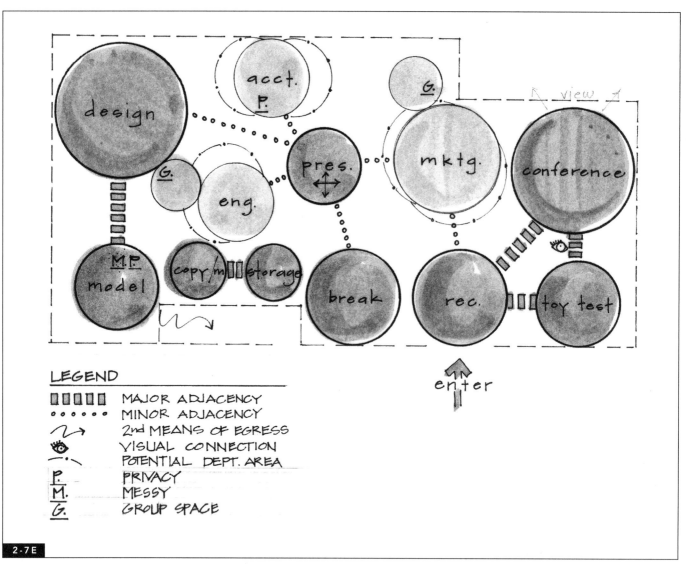

LEGEND

▯▯▯▯▯	MAJOR ADJACENCY
○○○○○○	MINOR ADJACENCY
↝	2nd MEANS OF EGRESS
👁	VISUAL CONNECTION
—·—·—	POTENTIAL DEPT. AREA
P̲.	PRIVACY
M̲.	MESSY
G̲.	GROUP SPACE

2-7E

FIGURE 2-7E
Final successful bubble diagram for the sample project.

several) create a masterpiece or a workable solution. It is often the combination of several diverse schemes that eventually generates a good solution.

BLOCKING DIAGRAMS

Bubble diagrams are part of a continuous process of refinement. One diagram may have useful components that can be combined with elements of another. As this process of refinement continues, designers often proceed to BLOCKING DIAGRAMS.

Before moving to blocking diagrams, design students benefit from the creation of space studies, also known as area prototype sketches. Each area or function is sketched in scale with furniture and equipment included, and these sketches can be used for purposes of approximation in the blocking diagram. Space study sketches are also helpful in the design of systems furniture, allowing students to explore possibilities and gain insight into the use of these products. See Figures 2-8a, b, c for examples of space studies.

Blocking diagrams can be generated on tracing paper taped over a scaled, drafted floor plan of the existing or proposed building. In rare cases projects do not involve the use of existing architectural parameters because the interior space will dictate the final building form. In these cases, bubble diagrams and blocking plans are sometimes the genesis for the even-

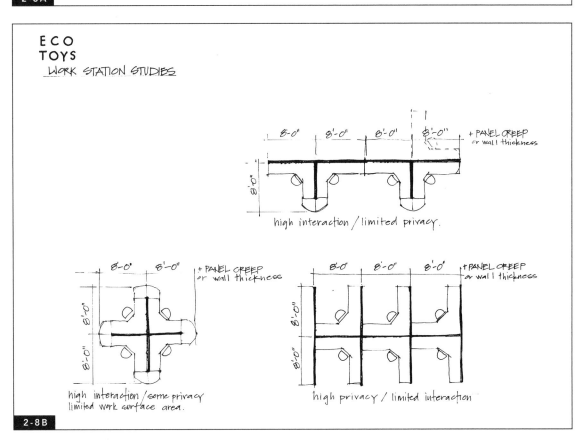

E C O
T O Y S
SPACE STUDIES

8'-6"   8'-6"   16'-0"

9'-0"   9'-0"   9'-0"

COPY/MAIL   STORAGE   MODEL SHOP

16'-0"

14'-0"

TOY TEST

14'-0"

14'-0"

KITCHEN/BREAK

18'-0"

18'-6"

RECEPTION

16'-0"

20'-0"

A.V. (VIEW?)

CONFERENCE

2-8A

E C O
T O Y S
WORK STATION STUDIES

8'-0"   8'-0"   8'-0"   8'-0"   + PANEL CREEP
or wall thickness

8'-0"

high interaction / limited privacy.

8'-0"   8'-0"   + PANEL CREEP
or wall thickness

8'-0"

8'-0"

high interaction / some privacy
limited work surface area.

8'-0"   8'-0"   8'-0"   + PANEL CREEP
or wall thickness

8'-0"

8'-0"

high privacy / limited interaction

2-8B

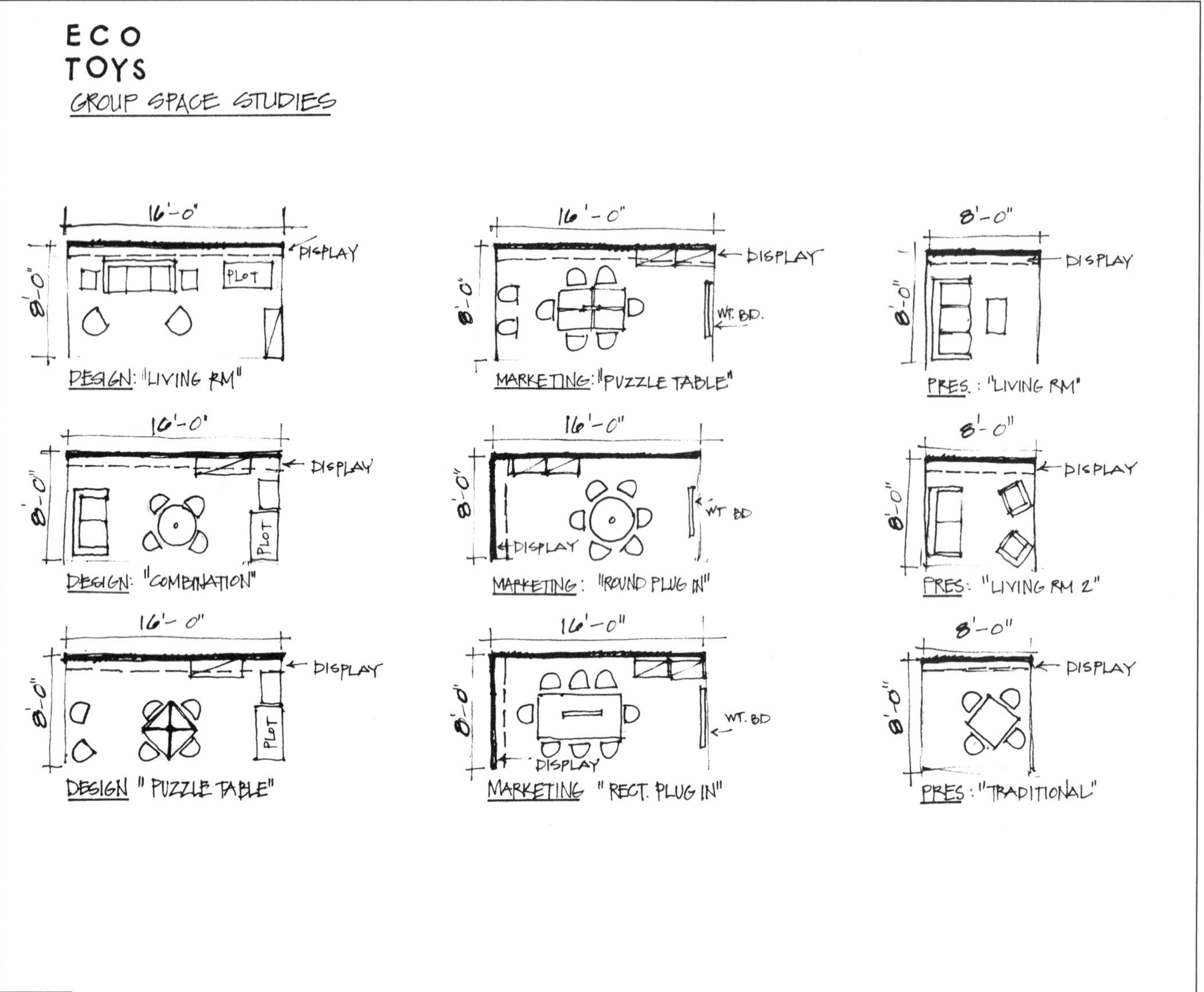

ECO
TOYS
GROUP SPACE STUDIES

DESIGN: "LIVING RM"

MARKETING: "PUZZLE TABLE"

PRES.: "LIVING RM"

DESIGN: "COMBINATION"

MARKETING: "ROUND PLUG IN"

PRES.: "LIVING RM 2"

DESIGN "PUZZLE TABLE"

MARKETING "RECT. PLUG IN"

PRES.: "TRADITIONAL"

2-8C

tual building plan. It is increasingly common for designers to begin the blocking plan process on CADD and take the project through the rest of the design process using CADD. Some designers find that space planning on CADD is frustrating and therefore plot out a CADD drawing and work over it with tracing paper.

As stated, blocking diagrams are generally drawn to scale and relate directly to the architectural parameters or the existing building plan. Blocking plans are generally drawn with each area or function represented by a block of the appropriate square footage; circulation areas are often blocked in as rectilinear corridors. Figures 2-9a, b, c are blocking diagrams.

Some experienced designers move quickly to blocking diagrams, forgoing the use of bubble diagrams, whereas others dislike the blocky, confining nature of blocking diagrams. Many designers develop a personal system of schematic diagrams that is a combination of bubble and blocking diagrams. The approach and graphic quality of schematic diagrams used by individual designers vary greatly, yet the underlying purpose is consistent. Designers use these diagrams to move from verbal and simplified graphic notation toward true scale and the eventual realization of architectural form.

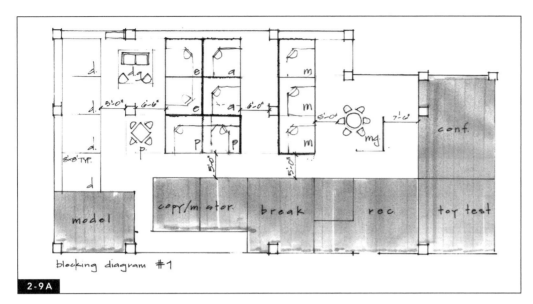

blocking diagram #1

2-9A

FIGURES 2-9A, 2-9B, 2-9C
Blocking diagrams for the sample
project. Note that these blocking
diagrams focus on the layout of
individual work spaces.

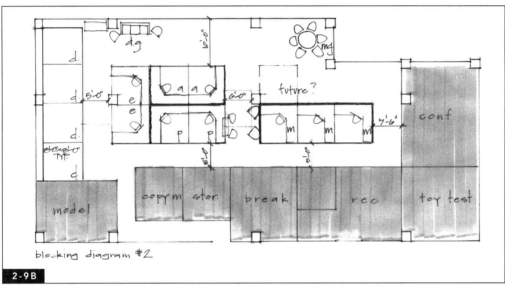

blocking diagram #2

2-9B

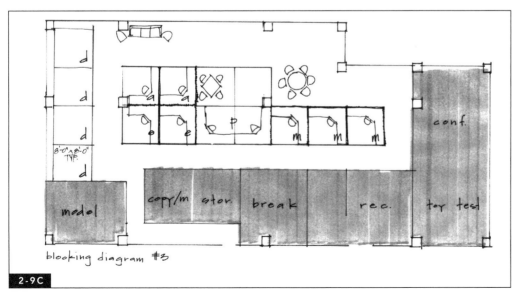

blocking diagram #3

2-9C

FIT PLANS AND STACKING PLANS

A FIT PLAN can be considered a further refinement of the blocking diagram. Basically the fit plan is a test determining whether the requirements and needs clarified in programming fit into a given space. In some cases, fit plans are drawn up when a client reviews a piece of real estate or a potential site. In other cases, fit plans are drawn up to indicate the way a proposed office tower may eventually be laid out. These types of fit plan are generated for both real estate professionals and end users.

In still other situations the fit plan is part of the final stage of the space-planning process. For this reason, fit plans often contain furniture and equipment accurately drawn to scale as a means of testing the space plan for fit and for client review.

A STACKING PLAN is used when a project occupies more than one floor of a building. Often the interrelationships of departments or workgroup locations are examined in a stacking diagram. Generally stacking diagrams are created early in the design process as a means of evaluating the use of each floor before refined space planning is done.

CONCEPTUAL DESIGN

The schematic design phase is often a time when designers explore symbolic representation for the conceptual foundation of a project. Although relationship, bubble, and blocking diagrams represent functional and spatial requirements, they sometimes do little to illuminate the conceptual nature of a project. It is often useful to employ an abstract diagram or graphic device to represent the conceptual qualities of a project.

One means of illustrating conceptual project themes is the use of a design PARTI. Frank Ching, in *A Visual Dictionary of Architecture* (1995), defines a parti as "the basic scheme or concept for an architectural design represented by a diagram." A design parti can take a wide range of forms, from a highly simplified graphic symbol to a more complex plan diagram. Some designers use a conceptual diagram such as a parti as an aid in bringing together the functional and conceptual components of a design. The parti, or another conceptual diagram, can be used throughout the design process as a conceptual anchor for the project. Designers sometimes employ the parti extensively, and it may be the foundation for the design and appear as a logo or project icon on all presentation graphics.

A formal design parti is not sought for all design projects. Most projects do, however, include a considerable number of thematic issues. Views, geography, climate, building context and site, functional requirements, and cultural issues may contribute to the project on a conceptual level. Often the existing building form provides project constraints in the design of interior environments. Most designers find it useful to articulate and explore conceptual and thematic issues early in the schematic phase of a project. Some designers find it useful to create three-dimensional conceptual studies in the form of models (see Chapter 6). In professional practice the methods of presentation of conceptual components of a project are varied and highly personal, and involve both verbal and graphic notations.

For purposes of organization, space planning and conceptual development are discussed separately here. However, in design practice these elements are brought together in the early stages of project design. Bubble diagrams often incorporate conceptual elements, and a design parti can serve as an organizational anchor in the space-planning process. It is important to see the schematic/conceptual design phases as a continuous process of refinement whereby all elements are brought together. Figures 2-10a, b, c are conceptual sketches that might be generated during the drawing of blocking diagrams.

As the project evolves and blocking diagrams make way for a schematic space plan, it is often helpful to consider the totality of the design through the use of preliminary eleva-

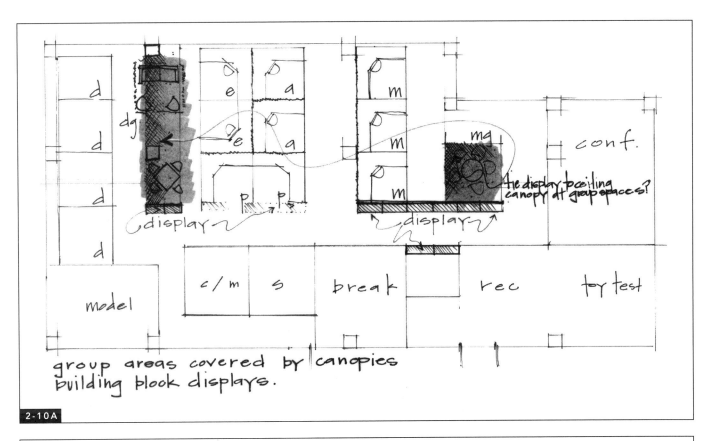

group areas covered by canopies
building block displays.

2-10A

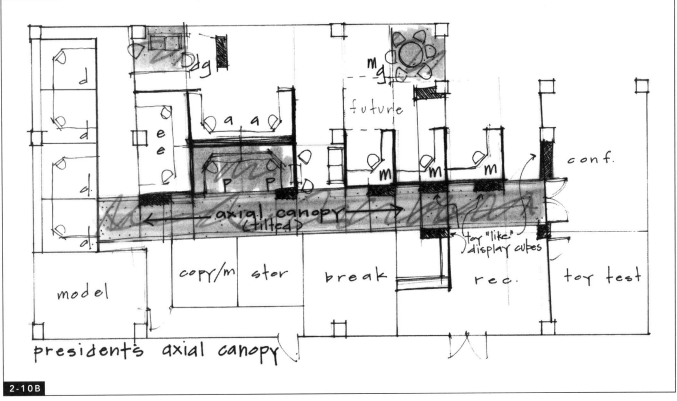

presidents axial canopy

2-10B

FIGURES 2-10A, 2-10B, 2-10C
Conceptual blocking diagrams for the sample project.

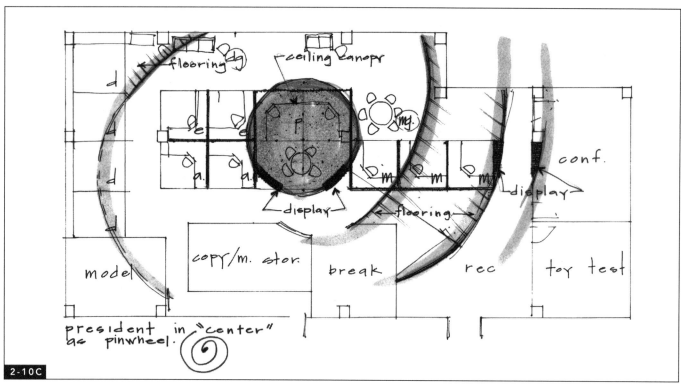

2-10C

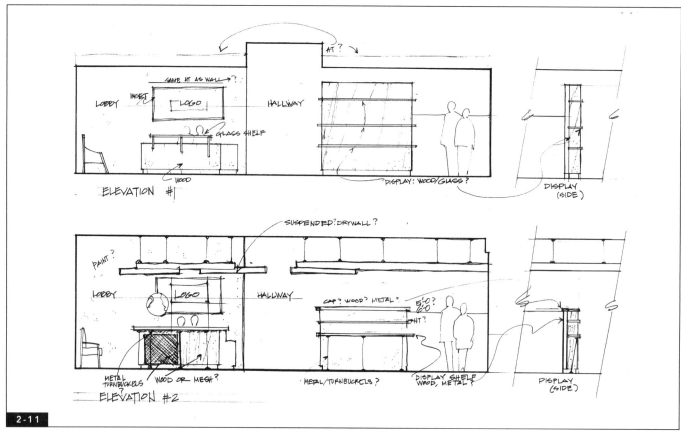

2-11

FIGURE 2-11
Two preliminary elevations of varying approaches for the design shown in the blocking diagram in Figure 2-10c.

tions. Preliminary elevations, much like early perspective studies, allow for more complete understanding of the total volume of a space. Preliminary elevations can be used as a means of ideation or idea generation, and therefore it is useful to attempt more than one approach as the elevations are undertaken. Two such preliminary elevations of varying approaches for the design shown in the blocking diagram in Figure 2-10c can be found in Figure 2-11.

SCHEMATIC DESIGN PRESENTATION GRAPHICS

The preliminary design(s) created in this process of continual refinement must be evaluated by the designer or design team, as well the client, for the project to continue successfully. Presentation of the preliminary design may be highly informal or formal, depending on the nature of the project. In all cases it is useful to consider the purpose of the presentation as well as its audience. The audience for a preliminary presentation may include the client, consultants, real estate professionals, and those with financial interests in the project. Prior to the creation of any presentation, it is worthwhile to take time to assess the audience for the presentation; identifying and understanding this audience is imperative to the quality of the communication.

In addressing members of the design team or design consultants, a presentation may consist of rough sketches and multiple layers of paper. Designers and most consultants are familiar with orthographic drawings and can wade through some confusing and messy drawings and notes. Many clients, however, require easy-to-understand graphic images as a means to understanding the schematic presentation. The client must understand the preliminary design to evaluate and approve it, which is necessary for the project to continue successfully.

The preliminary client presentation must communicate the underlying project research and the constraints that have led to the preliminary design. These include preliminary budg-

etary information, preliminary scheduling information, research of appropriate building codes, and programming information. Generally at a minimum the preliminary schematic design presentation requires a floor plan as a means of communicating the space plan. When the project involves more than one floor, each floor plan and stacking plan is typically included in the preliminary presentation.

The preliminary presentation floor plan(s) may be drawn freely, drafted with tools, or generated on CADD. Regardless of the means of drawing or drafting, the floor plan should be drawn to scale and include a North arrow and titles. If the designers wish to communicate several design schemes, the various floor plans must be labeled clearly with some sort of notation system, such as "Scheme 1" or "Concept 1."

Some preliminary presentations include programming information, floor plans, and minimal additional graphics, whereas other projects require preliminary presentations that include additional drawings such as elevations, sections, and preliminary perspective drawings, as well as models and materials samples. The following chapters cover some of these additional forms of preliminary presentation. A successful presentation of the preliminary schematic design communicates information to the client and other interested parties and allows for input, comments, criticism, and approval. Figures 2-12a and 2-12b are examples of a schematic design presentation for the sample project and are based on issues covered to this point. Figures 2-13a and 2-13b are examples of a professional schematic design presentation.

Most often designers come away from a preliminary presentation with lists of suggestions from the client. These range from minor corrections or clarifications to major changes in functional, conceptual, or aesthetic aspects of the design.

The information generated by feedback to the first schematic presentation allows the designers to move forward in the refinement of

FIGURES 2-12A, 2-12B
Schematic presentation for the sample project,
graphite on drafting film.

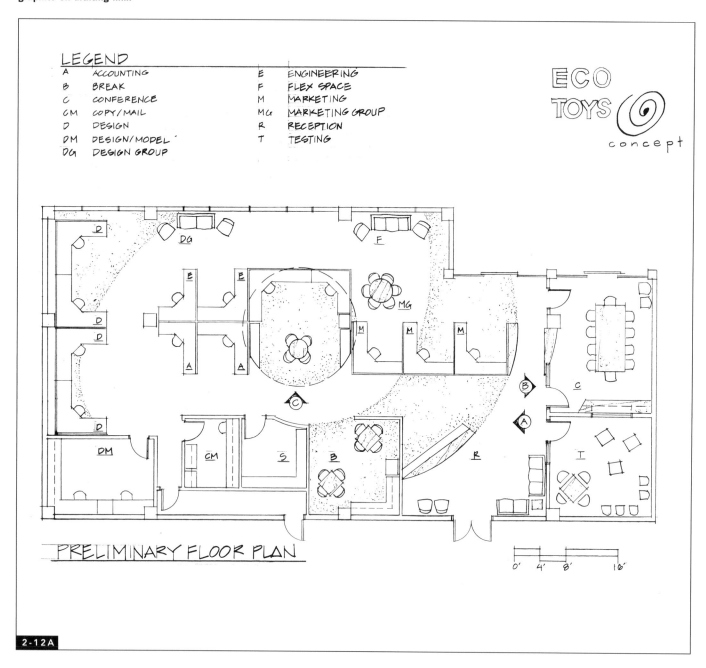

LEGEND

A	ACCOUNTING	E	ENGINEERING
B	BREAK	F	FLEX SPACE
C	CONFERENCE	M	MARKETING
CM	COPY/MAIL	MG	MARKETING GROUP
D	DESIGN	R	RECEPTION
DM	DESIGN/MODEL	T	TESTING
DG	DESIGN GROUP		

ECO TOYS concept

PRELIMINARY FLOOR PLAN

0' 4' 8' 16'

2-12A

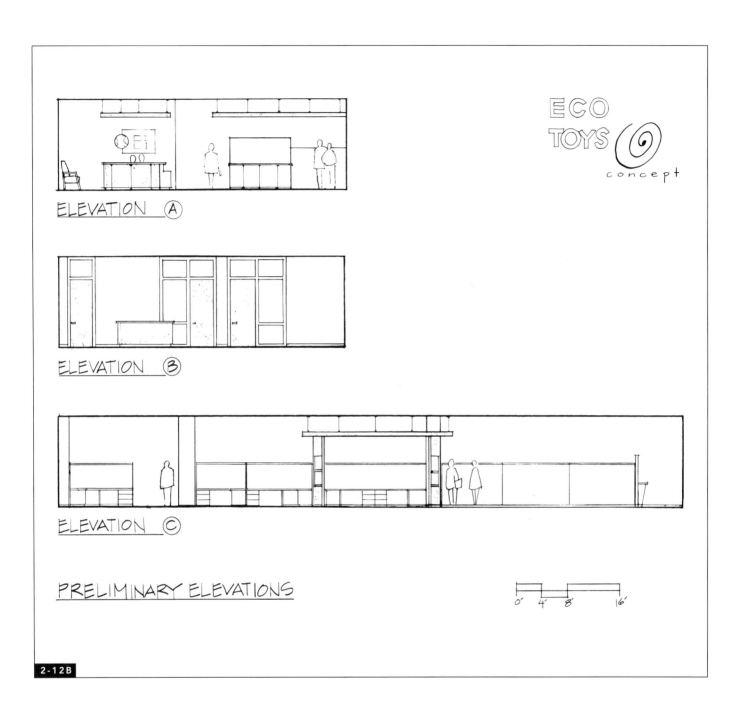

ELEVATION (A)

ELEVATION (B)

ELEVATION (C)

PRELIMINARY ELEVATIONS

ECO TOYS
concept

0'   4'   8'   16'

2-12B

FIGURES 2-13A, 2-13B
Professional schematic design presentation, ink and graphite on vellum and bond paper. By Bruck Allen Architects Inc. Project team: Christopher Allen, Mark Bausback, Brian Church, and Randall Rhoads.

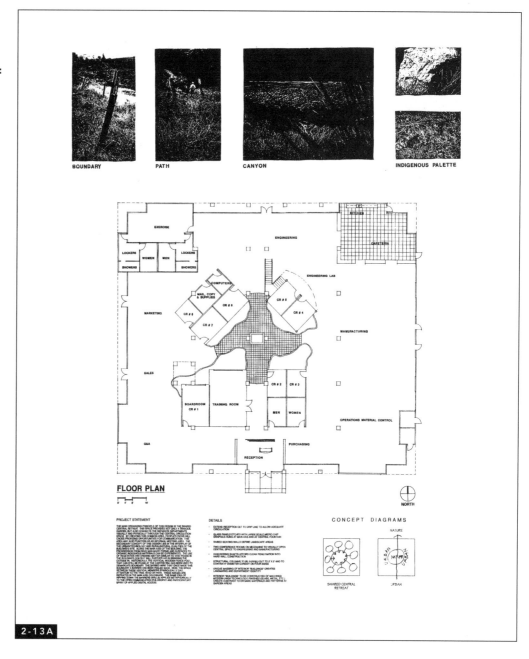

the design. Depending on project requirements and constraints, and the number of changes requested by the client, more schematic presentations may be required. It is common for smaller, less complicated projects to receive quick general approval, allowing the designers to move forward in the design process. Larger projects can require many additional meetings and presentations before the client grants approval of the schematic design.

In interviewing designers, I have found great variety in the formality, visual quality, and quantity of information included in preliminary design presentations. Clearly there is a range of styles of presentation, and firms have varying standards. Even with this great variety, there seem to be elements of consistency. Most designers describe a need to communicate very clearly in early presentations and to make sure that the client understands

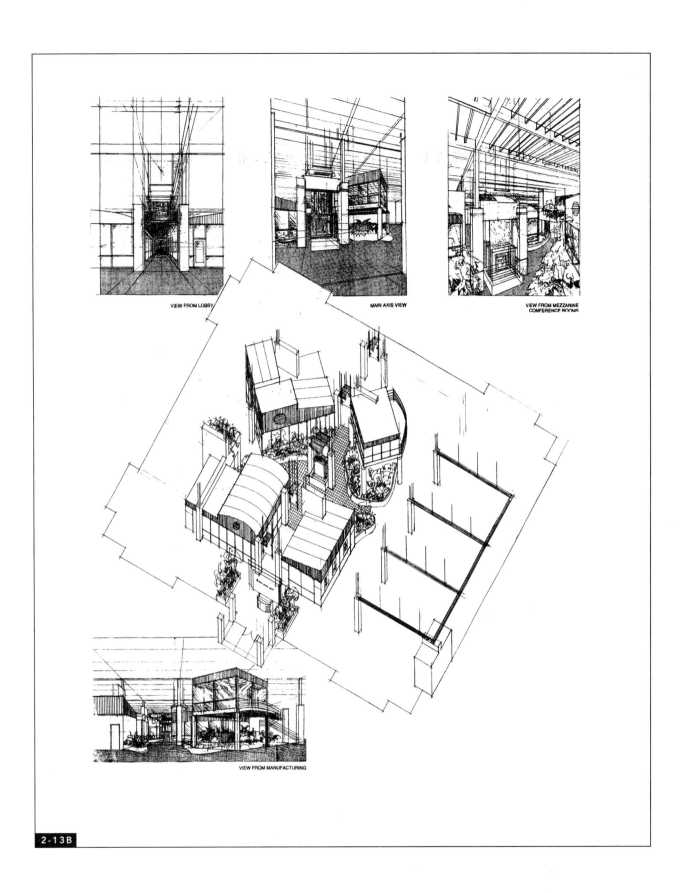

VIEW FROM LOBBY

MAIN AXIS VIEW

VIEW FROM MEZZANINE
CONFERENCE ROOMS

VIEW FROM MANUFACTURING

2-13B

the elements of the design presented. Most also describe the importance of making clear the very preliminary nature of the design. Many designers find that clients need time to settle into ideas; thus, pinning things down too early can be frightening and frustrating for them.

DESIGN DEVELOPMENT

The design development of a project involves finalizing the space plan and fully developing all of the components of the design. All aspects of the design must come together and be resolved in this phase of the project. It is useful for students to know that the goal is to have the design of a project completed in the design development phase. It is important to keep in mind that the phase following design development is construction documentation, which involves preparation of the project for construction. In large firms the project is often handed from the design team to the production team upon completion of design development.

In a perfect world, every detail would be considered and resolved in the design development phase of a project. For the most part, design development drawings are drafted accurately and to scale. Some designers create design development drawings that are somewhat sketchy, and others create extremely precise, highly detailed drawings. In either case, the entire volume of a space must be explored and refined to ensure a successful design project and to allow for a smooth transition into the construction documentation phase of the project.

The presentation made upon the completion of the design development phase is often seen as the comprehensive final design presentation of a project. This presentation must include every possible element of the design to ensure clear communication of the final design. Orthographic drawings — including detailed floor plans, ceiling plans, detailed elevations, sections, and design details — are generally part of the presentation. In addition, technical drawings, millwork drawings and samples, materials samples, and furnishings and fixtures samples and images are often included in the final design development presentation.

Smaller projects often move quickly from schematic to design development and involve minimal presentations. More complex projects require many interim presentations and meetings. Weekly or biweekly design meetings are not uncommon on large or complex projects. Final design presentations vary enormously because of the variety of projects and working styles of designers. Clearly there is no existing industry standard for the preparation of design development presentations. It is with pride and sometimes secrecy that firms and designers create successful presentations.

Although design presentations reflect the concerns, aesthetics, and tastes of designer(s) and client, communication is the one constant in their preparation. The final design presentation must clearly communicate all elements of the design. For the project to move forward, the design must be understood and approved by the client. In addition to the client or end user, a wide range of individuals may have to review and approve the design.

Projects dependent on public funding, such as libraries and municipal buildings, often require public review of the design. Many require design approval of municipal agencies or local community groups. Investors and consultants must often review design presentations before a project can move forward. All of these individuals form the eventual audience for the design presentation, and understanding this audience is key to the successful communication of the design.

The following chapters offer information on additional visual devices employed in the design and presentation of projects. These are discussed separately for purposes of clarity, but all are used throughout the design process as a means of exploring and communicating the design.

REFERENCES

Ballast, David. *Interior Design Reference Manual.* Belmont, Calif.: Professional Publications, 1995.

Ching, Frank. *A Visual Dictionary of Architecture.* New York: John Wiley & Sons, 1995.

Guthrie, Pat. *Interior Designers' Portable Handbook.* New York: McGraw-Hill, 1999.

Harwood, Bouie. "An Interior Design Experience Program, Part II: Developing the Experiences." *Journal of Interior Design* 22(1), 15–31.

Henley, Pamela. *Interior Design Practicum Exam Workbook.* Belmont, Calif.: Professional Publications, 1995.

Karlen, Mark. *Space Planning Basics.* New York: Van Nostrand Reinhold, 1993.

Koberg, Don, and Jim Bagnall. *The Universal Traveler.* Menlo Park, Calif.: Crisp Publications, 1991.

Peña, William, Steven Parshall, and Kevin Kelly. *Problem Seeking.* Washington, D.C.: AIA Press, 1987.

3

PARALINE AND PERSPECTIVE DRAWINGS

INTRODUCTION TO THREE-DIMENSIONAL VIEWS

Drawings depicting three-dimensional views differ greatly from orthographic drawings in that they offer a more natural view of space. It is important to note that these three-dimensional views (also known as pictorial drawings) are useful at every phase of the design process. Pictorial drawings work well in the various phases of the design process as a method of examining and refining ideas, and should not be reserved merely as a means of final project presentation.

The purpose of this chapter is to present a wide range of three-dimensional drawing methods and procedures. These methods range from freehand sketches to measured, hard-lined perspective illustrations. Students of design should seek a method or methods that work well for them as individuals. The goal, then, is to find drawing methods that are useful as tools throughout the design process and to realize that pictorial drawing is a way of seeing that is useful for all designers.

Unlike orthographic projections, three-dimensional views allow for a single depiction of a large portion of an interior space. This type of drawing can also help clients to clearly understand the design of a project. In addition,

three-dimensional views of a space allow the designer to see and explore the entire volume of space and make design decisions accordingly.

Many designers create these drawings by hand, but computers are increasingly used for the generation of perspective drawings. Some designers state that they can explore the total volume of a space in the preliminary design phases only when drawing it in perspective by hand. Many designers have mentioned that they use a combination of hand sketching and computer-generated perspective imagery.

Increasingly design graduates are expected to have the ability to create three-dimensional views both by hand and with the use of computers. This is because understanding the basics of creating hand-drawn three-dimensional views allows a designer to work more effectively by computer and also grants the ability to create quick sketches in client meetings (and elsewhere).

Some designers use computer-generated three-dimensional imagery from the inception of a project and create no hand drawings at any point in the design process. Software used by those working this way includes AshlarVellum® and Form•Z® from Auto*des*sys*. Others generate two-dimensional design drawings on AutoCAD (various releases) and then use these to generate three-dimensional views on AutoCAD.

This chapter provides step-by-step instructions on a range of hand-drawn perspective methods. However, given the range of software available, there are no explicit directions on creating computer-generated perspective drawings because each software product has very distinct properties. It is also worth noting that hand-drawing works effectively early in the schematic design phase as a means of generating many varied ideas about a given space. Using the quick sketching techniques covered in this chapter will help a designer generate a wide range of ideas rapidly without first creating plans and elevations.

Pictorial drawings are created as line drawings (or wire frames) and used as such in presentations or are rendered upon completion. Some perspective and paraline line drawings work very well in communicating a design to an audience without the addition of value or color rendering. This is especially true if additional descriptive items such as materials and finishes samples are also used in the presentation. Therefore, it is worthwhile to attempt to generate descriptive line drawings that communicate a design successfully and to see rendering as a secondary step in the drawing process.

The tools and materials used in pictorial drawings are similar to those used in orthographic projection drawings and the other forms of graphic communication mentioned previously. An abundance of tracing paper is probably the most important material in the production of perspective drawings. The transparency and low cost of tracing paper make it highly useful as a visualization tool. As soon as a drawing becomes confusing to sort out, a new sheet of tracing paper can be overlaid. When tracing paper is used as an overlay, a variety of colored pencils can be used as a visual aid in the construction of three-dimensional drawings.

Both pencils and pens can work well in the construction of three-dimensional views when working by hand. Although the choice of implements is highly personal, quick-sketching methods are best accomplished with marking pens that provide quick visual impact. Marking pens also eliminate the use of erasers, which actually helps with visualization. This approach is tough at first but worth the effort.

Hand-drawn refined measured paraline and perspective drawings are most often constructed in pencil on tracing paper, with many layers of paper and a variety of colored pencils used. These drawings often require the use of drafting tools but are also drawn freehand by some individuals. The final hard-lined measured paraline or perspective line drawing is often done on high-quality vellum or drafting film with drafting pencils or ink pens. This allows for the line drawing to be reproduced by a variety of reprographic methods on a variety of papers. Once reproduced, the drawing may be incorporated into a presentation with or without rendering. Information on rendering and reprographics is available in Chapter 5.

PARALINE DRAWINGS

PARALINE DRAWINGS are quick, accurate, and useful in the communication of interior form. The method of construction of these drawings is based on the relationship of three principal axes (x, y, and z). Although there are several types of paraline drawing, all share common characteristics: (1) paraline drawings have parallel lines drawn as parallel, and lines do not converge to vanishing points; (2) vertical lines are drawn as true verticals in paraline drawings; and (3) paraline drawings are drawn using some method of proportional scale.

PLAN OBLIQUE DRAWINGS

One type of paraline drawing commonly used in the communication of interior environments is known as a PLAN OBLIQUE. Figure 3-1 provides a quick reference of plan oblique construction. Plan obliques can be constructed quickly because they are drawn by projecting directly off the floor plan. Drawing a plan oblique requires the rotation of the floor plan to appropriate angles as measured against a horizontal baseline. The most common angles of plan rotation or orientation are 30 degrees–60 degrees and 45 degrees–45 degrees, although plan obliques may be drawn at any two angles that together equal 90 degrees. Vertical elements are drawn by projecting loca-

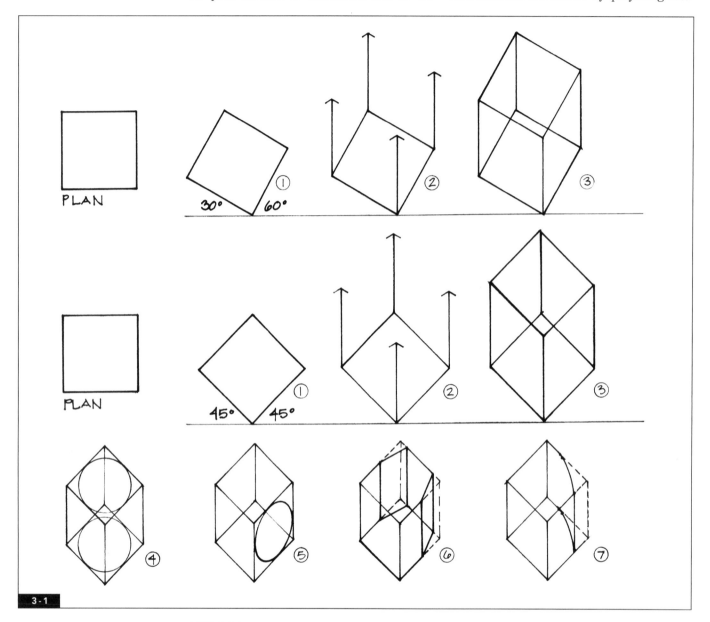

FIGURE 3-1
Quick reference: plan oblique construction.

1. Rotate scaled plan to appropriate angles (shown here, 30 degrees–60 degrees and 45 degrees–45degrees).

2. Draw vertical lines upward to appropriate height in scale.

3. Lines parallel to the base plane (the floor plan) are drawn at the same angles as plan.

4. Circles found on the plan and its parallel planes are drawn as circles.

5. Circles found on vertical planes are drawn as ellipses.

6. Create an enclosing box to measure and locate nonaxonometric lines.

7. Create an enclosing box to measure and plot irregular and curvilinear lines and planes.

tions vertically from the plan to the appropriate height. Horizontal elements are drawn using the same angles as those used in the orientation of the plan.

Because they are generally projected from existing plans, these drawings are created quickly and can be used throughout the design process as an aid in seeing and understanding the environment. The angle of rotation changes the orientation of the drawing and must be considered in the construction of these drawings. The angle of rotation used allows for varying views and emphasis on particular portions of the space. Often plan obliques employ some method of visual elimination of portions of walls to depict the space successfully. This is often done by cutaway views or by ghosting in portions of walls.

Circles and curvilinear forms can be drawn in plan obliques using a number of methods. Circles found in the true-size planes on plan oblique drawings retain their true size and form. This means that a true circle found in a plan (and on surfaces parallel to the plan) remains a true circle in a plan oblique. Circles or curvilinear lines found on the vertical non-frontal planes (those drawn at angles extending from the plan) appear as ellipses. (For additional information on ellipse construction see Figures 3-14 and 3-15.)

The location of free-form curvilinear lines can be approximated by plotting locations on the plan and extending them vertically to the appropriate height. Curvilinear forms found on nonfrontal planes can be approximated using a grid to plot locations and transferring them to the appropriate location of a gridded area on the oblique drawing.

Objects or lines that are not parallel to any of the three primary axes are not measurable in scale and can be tricky to draw. To draw nonaxonometric lines and objects, an enclosing box can be created within the axonometric framework. The enclosing box can provide measuring lines with which to locate the end points of the object lines. Nonaxonometric

lines that are parallel to one another remain parallel in plan oblique drawings.

Plan oblique drawings are quick to create and are useful as an aid in the design process. However, although they are a simple and effective means of visualization for the designer, they can be confusing for clients who are not accustomed to viewing this type of drawing. Figures 3-2, 3-3, and 3-4 are examples of plan oblique drawings.

ISOMETRIC DRAWINGS

An ISOMETRIC is a paraline drawing based on the use of 30-degree angles. Unlike plan obliques, isometrics cannot be constructed by simple rotation and projection of the plan. Instead, the drawing of an isometric requires the reconstruction of the plan in scale with the two ground-plane axes (x and y axes) at 30 degrees. All elements that are parallel to the ground plane are drawn at 30 degrees. As in other types of paraline drawings, vertical elements remain vertical in isometric drawings. Scale measurements can be made along any of the three principal axes (x, y, and z). Figure 3-5 provides a quick reference of isometric construction.

All circles and circular lines in isometric drawings are drawn as ellipses. Readily available isometric ellipse templates can be used in isometric drawing. For additional information on ellipse construction, see Figures 3-14 and 3-15. Lines not parallel to the three principal axes are created by using an enclosing box method to locate the object(s). Isometric drawings offer a balanced view and the least distortion of any paraline drawing. They are also rather easy to create in most CADD programs.

Isometric drawings can be used at any phase of the design process as a means of communicating form and spatial relationships. Isometrics are also used in technical and construction documents. Although isometrics offer some advantages, they are somewhat inflexible and do not emphasize any particular portion of the space.

FIGURE 3-2
A plan oblique drawing of a residential storage area.

FIGURE 3-3
A plan oblique drawing of a residential basement remodeling project.

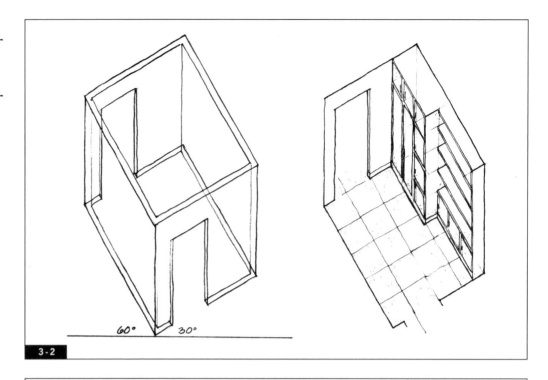

60°   30°

3-2

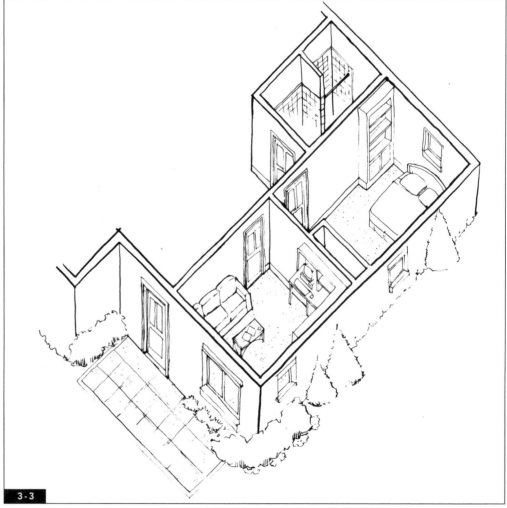

3-3

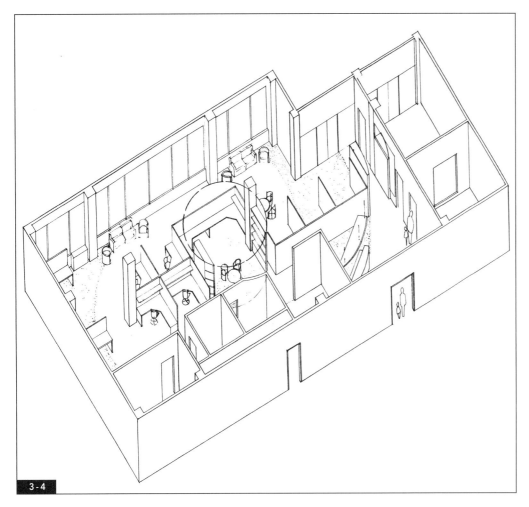

FIGURE 3-5
Quick reference: isometric construction.

1. Redraw plan, in scale, with x and y axes at 30 degrees.

2. Draw vertical lines upward to appropriate height in scale.

3. Lines parallel to the x and y axes are drawn at the same angles as plan.

4. All circles are drawn as ellipses in an isometric drawing.

5. Create an enclosing box to measure and locate nonaxonometric lines.

6. Create an enclosing box to measure and plot irregular and curvilinear lines and planes.

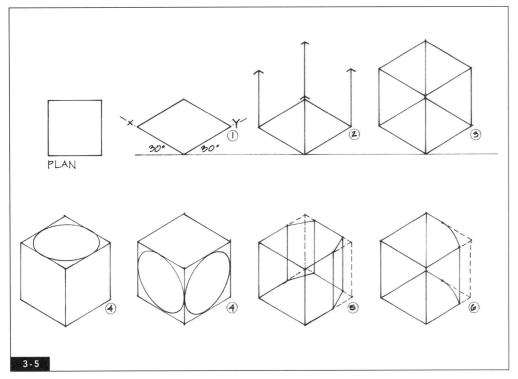

PLAN

PERSPECTIVE DRAWINGS

PERSPECTIVE DRAWING offers a natural view of interior space and for this reason is commonly used in design presentations. Many design students (and some design professionals) have difficulty creating clear, natural-looking perspective drawings. This is unfortunate because perspective sketching and drawing is an excellent design tool that can — and should — be used throughout the design process to generate and refine ideas. Using perspective drawing only in finalized design presentations can result in weak design projects and lost opportunities for discovery.

An understanding of basic perspective principles allows designers to draw quickly and fairly accurately. Quick perspective drawings are helpful as visualization tools for designers. In addition, an understanding of basic principles and estimated sketching techniques allows for the creation of fresh, attractive drawings that can be used in design presentations.

The ability to draw simply measured or estimated freehand perspectives allows for the rapid expression of ideas, which helps in the generation of ideas and solutions. Certainly the capacity to produce laboriously created mechanical perspective drawings is important in design practice, but equally important is the ability to express ideas rapidly. It is worth stating that some CADD programs require that the design be complete and fully expressed in plan and/or elevation drawings prior to the generation of a three-dimensional view, which also points to the need for skills with quickly hand-drawn perspectives.

PERSPECTIVE BASICS

Creating successful pictorial drawings requires a working knowledge of basic principles of perspective. Many of these principles remain constant regardless of the method of drawing employed. Therefore, it is worthwhile for students to become well acquainted with the fundamental terms and principles of perspective drawing.

Understanding the concept of the picture plane is fundamental to understanding perspective drawing. The PICTURE PLANE is an imaginary transparent plane through which the area to be drawn is viewed. It can be visualized as a giant sheet of glass standing between the viewer and the area to be drawn. Once the drawing is begun, the surface of the drawing paper represents this picture plane. We cannot create successful perspective drawings without first visualizing the picture plane and its relationship to the items to be drawn on the surface of the paper. Understanding that the paper surface can be seen as a reproduction of the picture plane is fundamental to good perspective drawing (Figure 3-6).

It is the relationship of an object to the picture plane (and to the location of the viewer) that creates a given perspective view of the object. For example, a box that has its front face (plane) parallel to the picture plane is in a position that creates a one-point perspective drawing (Figure 3-7).

Turning the box so that the entire front corner is on edge in relation to the picture plane creates a two-point perspective view of the box (Figure 3-8).

Tweaking the box so that only the top (or bottom) corner touches the picture plane creates a three-point perspective view of the box (Figure 3-9).

All three types of perspective employ a HORIZON LINE representing the viewer's eye level. A box held high above the viewer's eye level (horizon line) allows a view of the bottom of the box. As the box is moved below the eye level of the viewer (the horizon line), a view of the top of the box is possible. In all types of perspective drawing, perspective lines converge to a VANISHING POINT (or points, in two- and three-point perspectives).

The general location of the viewer is often called the STATION POINT. It is from this point in space that the item is seen by the viewer. Another important perspective principle, shared by all three types of perspective, is the CONE OF VI-

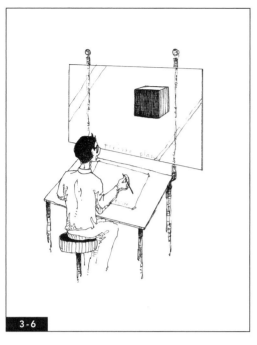

3-6

3-7

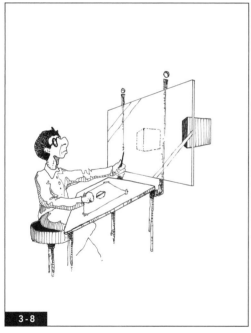

3-8

3-9

FIGURE 3-6
In perspective drawing the picture plane is an imaginary viewing plane that can be represented by the drawing surface.

FIGURE 3-7
A box drawn in one-point perspective has its front plane parallel to the picture plane.

FIGURE 3-8
A box drawn in two-point perspective has its front corner viewed on edge in relation to the picture plane.

FIGURE 3-9
All planes of the box are oblique to the picture plane when viewed in three-point perspective.

Drawings by Justin Thomson.

SION. The cone of vision represents the angle of view, or sight range of the viewer. This concept is based on the reality that humans cannot view all of a space at a given time. As we approach a given space, we focus on one area at a time, owing to the natural limitations of our vision.

The cone of vision, or angle of view, can be seen as representing the natural limits of human sight. Elements that exist within the cone of vi-

sion of the viewer can generally be drawn without excessive distortion. Those elements that exist outside of the cone of vision become distorted and cannot be drawn successfully.

Perspective drawings show objects becoming smaller as they recede toward the vanishing point(s); that is, items decrease in size as they move away from the viewer. This perspective principle is referred to as DIMINUTION OF SIZE. As

FIGURE 3-10
Quick reference: one-point perspective principles. Perspective lines converge to a single vanishing point (V.P.), located on the horizon line (H.L.). The front faces of the cubes and the back wall of a room are viewed parallel to the picture plane. Those elements with faces touching the picture plane can be drawn in scale. One-point perspective drawings have true vertical, horizontal, and perspective (depth) lines. Items located outside of the cone of vision (C.V.) tend to appear distorted.

a result, a box drawn correctly will appear larger when closest to the viewer and smaller as it moves farther from the viewer. Because items diminish in size, they cannot be measured consistently in scale; therefore, a variety of methods of measurement have been devised.

Although there are a number of nuances that create more complicated relationships of object to picture plane and horizon line, those mentioned here are fundamental perspective relationships. An effective way to become skilled at drawing in perspective is to practice drawing simple boxes in various relationships to the picture plane and to the horizon line. The ability to sketch a box in perspective in such various relationships allows for the eventual capability to draw more complex objects constructed from boxlike forms. To sketch boxes in perspective successfully, additional information about perspective drawing is required.

ONE-POINT PERSPECTIVE

One-point perspective views portray an object or environment with one plane parallel to the picture plane. In addition to this parallel orientation to the picture plane, one-point perspective views make use of one vanishing point, located along the horizon line, to which all perspective lines converge. The horizon line is a horizontal line that represents the viewer's eye level, usually between five and six feet from the floor. One-point perspective is considered the easiest type of perspective to draw because the entire plane that is parallel to the picture plane can be measured in scale. Figure 3-10 illustrates one-point perspective principles.

Ease of construction of one-point perspective is also based on the fact that lines that are vertical in reality remain vertical, horizontal lines remain horizontal, and only lines indicating perspective depth are drawn converging to

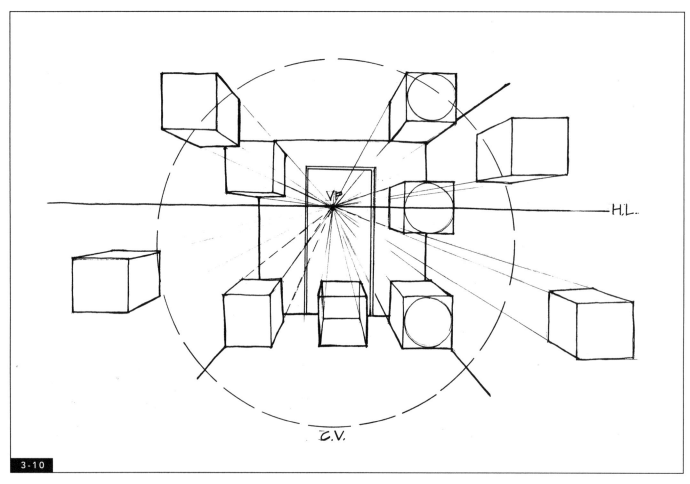

3-10

the vanishing point. Although they are easy to draw, one-point perspective views can be unnatural-looking and can become distorted. Despite their drawbacks, one-point perspective drawings are highly useful during the early stages of design and are often used by designers for ideation (idea generation).

TWO-POINT PERSPECTIVE

Two-point perspective drawings portray objects and volumes on edge in relationship to the picture plane. Another way of stating this is that two-point perspective depicts the primary faces of a volume oblique to the picture plane. This means that two-point perspectives offer a view of the front corner of objects or the rear corners of rooms and environments. In two-point perspective, an object's edge (or the corner of a room) is drawn first and can be used as a vertical measuring line from which perspective lines recede toward two vanishing points. The two vanishing points lie on the horizon line, one to the left and one to the right. As with one-point perspective drawings, the horizon line is always horizontal and represents the viewer's eye level. Figure 3-11 illustrates the principles of two-point perspective.

Apart from the horizon line and elements that lie along the horizon line, there are no horizontal lines found in accurate two-point perspective drawings. Instead, lines that are not true verticals converge to one of the two vanishing points. Only one vertical measuring line can be drawn in scale owing to the fact that perspective lines converge to two vanishing points, causing objects to look smaller as they recede away from the viewer toward the vanishing points. Two-point perspective drawings can be tricky to measure and confusing to create. However, two-point perspective drawings appear more natural and suffer from less distortion than other types of perspective.

FIGURE 3-11
Quick reference: two-point perspective principles. Perspective lines converge to two vanishing points (V.P.s), located on the horizon line (H.L.). Boxes are viewed from the front corner, and rooms generally from the back corner in relation to the picture plane. Two-point perspective drawings have true vertical lines as well as perspective (depth) lines. In two-point perspective, the front edge (or back edge) touching the picture plane can be measured in scale. Items located outside of the cone of vision (C.V.) tend to appear distorted. As with all forms of perspective, items appear to diminish in size as they recede from viewer.

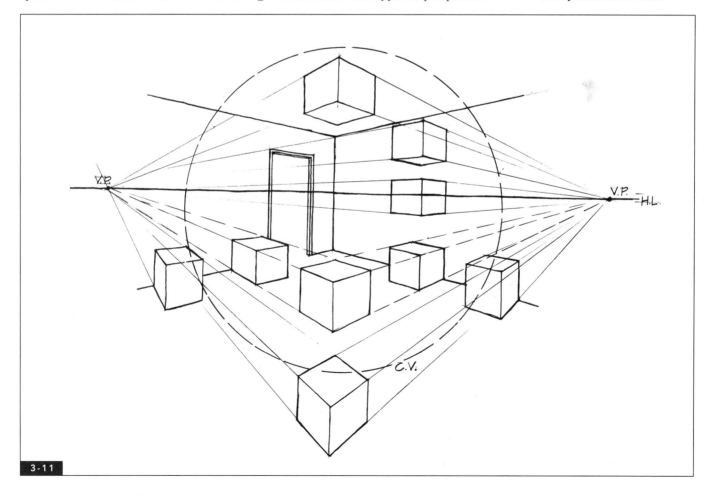

3-11

THREE-POINT PERSPECTIVE

Three-point perspective is not commonly used in traditional illustration of interior space. Three-point perspective portrays an object or volume with all principal faces oblique to the picture plane. All lines in this type of perspective converge to vanishing points. Generally three-point perspectives are constructed with two vanishing points on the horizon line, one to the left and one to the right, with an additional vanishing point above or below the horizon line. It is best to center the third vanishing point above or below the left and right vanishing points. Figure 3-12 is a quick reference to three-point perspective principles.

The use of three vanishing points creates highly dynamic drawings that may easily become distorted. Because all lines converge to vanishing points, no true-scale measuring line can be employed. This means that drawing three-point perspectives requires good visualization skills. Three-point perspective is most useful for portraying single objects, such as furniture or products, that by design should be dynamic, unusual, or attention-grabbing. Three-point perspective creates an "ant's-eye view" or "bird's-eye view" and is also used in some types of animation.

FIGURE 3-12
Quick reference: three-point perspective principles. Perspective lines converge to three vanishing points (V.P.s), two located on the horizon line (H.L.) and one usually above or below the horizon line. All planes of a box are oblique to the picture plane. All lines drawn in three-point perspective drawings converge to a vanishing point. No portion of a three-point perspective drawing can be measured in scale. Items located outside the cone of vision (C.V.) tend to appear distorted. As with all forms of perspective, items appear to diminish in size as they recede from viewer.

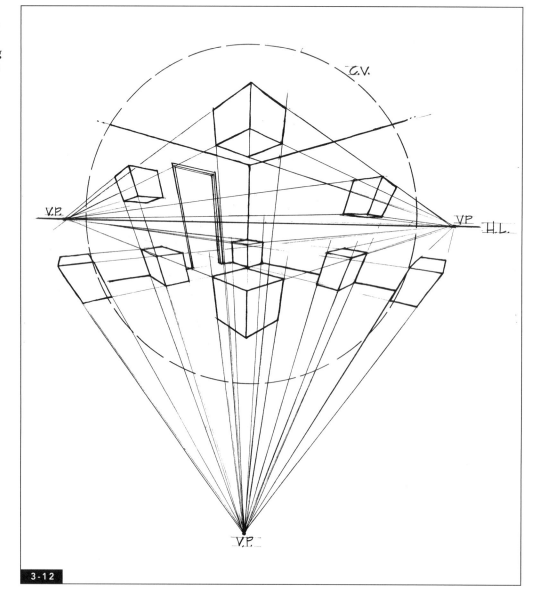

3-12

DEVELOPING VISUAL SKILLS

To develop visual skills and learn to "see" in perspective, students should practice drawing simple square-looking boxes in one-, two-, and three-point perspectives. I believe that the ability to draw accurate-looking boxes lies at the heart of successful perspective drawing. Figure 3-13 illustrates important principles of perspective sketching.

Boxes drawn in two-point perspective will appear distorted when the two vanishing points are located too close to each other on the horizon line. The vanishing points should be kept far enough apart to create an angle of 90 degrees or greater at the front edge of the cube. At the same time, the front edge of the cube should be less than 140 degrees (see Figure 3-13).

In two-point perspective the front corner (also known as the vertical leading edge) of an object is often used as a VERTICAL MEASURING LINE. This line can be scaled and then used to measure portions of the object that recede toward the vanishing points. Vertical measuring lines allow for fairly accurate measurement of vertical elements of drawings. In principle, this line is the only element of a drawing that can be accurately scaled because the front corner that serves as a measuring line is touching the picture plane — or is very close to it (see Figure 3-13).

For dimensions that cannot be measured on vertical surfaces, a number of very simple proportional devices can be employed. One such method of proportional perspective measurement involves the use of diagonal lines as a means of subdividing squares and rectangular planes in perspective. Each face of a square can be subdivided into visually equal portions at the intersection of two diagonals. The intersection of diagonals drawn from corner to corner of a square locates the midpoint of that square. Rectangular planes are also divided in this manner. Diagonal subdivision of rectangular planes is a significant perspective principle

and is useful in all methods of perspective drawing (see Figure 3-13).

The use of diagonals can also aid in adding, extending, and duplicating boxes drawn in perspective. One method of doing this requires locating the midpoint of a single box or cube, then drawing a diagonal from the bottom corner of the cube through the midpoint of the far side of the cube. The diagonal is then extended from the midpoint to the top perspective line (that which recedes to the vanishing point). Where the diagonal meets the perspective line of the original cube, a new vertical is drawn, creating a second square that is visually equal in perspective (see Figure 3-13).

It is useful to learn to draw boxes with elements that have slanted surfaces, such as gabled roofs. These slanted surfaces do not fall on the primary horizon line. Instead the lines that form the slanting surfaces converge at a point directly above or below the vanishing point for the box. This point, known as a VANISHING TRACE (after Ching, 1975), is a line to which all parallel lines in the same plane will converge. A vanishing trace is employed because lines that are parallel always converge at a common point (see Figure 3-13).

A vanishing trace is also useful in relation to drawing stairs. Stairs can be drawn by first plotting the base of the stair (the width and depth as found on the floor plane). The height of the stair must then be located on a height plane. The height plane must be divided equally (use the forward vertical as a measuring line) in increments that equal the required number of risers. The first riser can be found by drawing a line from the appropriate vanishing point forward through the noted riser height and onward to the riser location as noted on the floor plan.

The next step involves drawing the vanishing trace. A vanishing trace is found by drawing a diagonal line from the forward location of the height of the riser to the top of the stair run (as measured on the height plane) and onward to a location directly above the vanishing point.

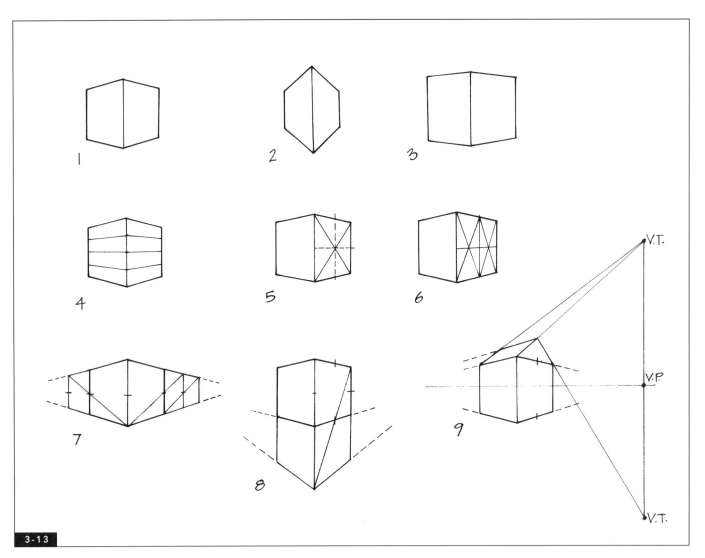

3-13

FIGURE 3-13
Quick reference: sketching in two-point perspective.

1. Practice drawing boxes that look square.

2. Boxes look distorted when the front corner equals less than 90 degrees — this means V.P.'s are too close.

3. Boxes look distorted when the front corner equals greater than 140 degrees — this means V.P.'s are too far apart.

4. The front corner can be divided equally to serve as a measuring line.

5. Bisecting diagonals divide a square drawn in perspective.

6. Diagonals also divide rectangles.

7. Boxes can be extended using diagonals. Extend a diagonal from bottom corner through midpoint of a square. Where the diagonal meets the perspective line (line to V.P.), a new box is formed.

8. Diagonals can also extend a box vertically.

9. Slanting parallel lines converge at a common point. This point is called a vanishing trace (after Ching, 1975), or V.T., and is directly below or above the V.P.

With this vanishing trace located, a second diagonal is drawn to the opposite side of the stair. Risers and treads are then located where measuring increments brought forward from vanishing points intersect with diagonals. Figure 3-14 gives instructions for stair construction.

Circles and curves are drawn as ELLIPSES in perspective. An understanding of ellipses and how they are drawn can help create natural-looking perspective drawings (Figures 3-15 and 3-16). Understanding the relationship of the major and minor axes of an ellipse is essential to successful perspective drawing. The MAJOR AXIS is an imaginary line that is found at the widest part of an ellipse, and the MINOR AXIS is found at the narrow diameter of the ellipse. An ellipse's major axis is greater than its minor axis. The major and minor axes always appear at right angles (90 degrees) to each other regardless of the position of the object. When found on horizontal planes, such as floors and ceilings, an ellipse's major axis is horizontal.

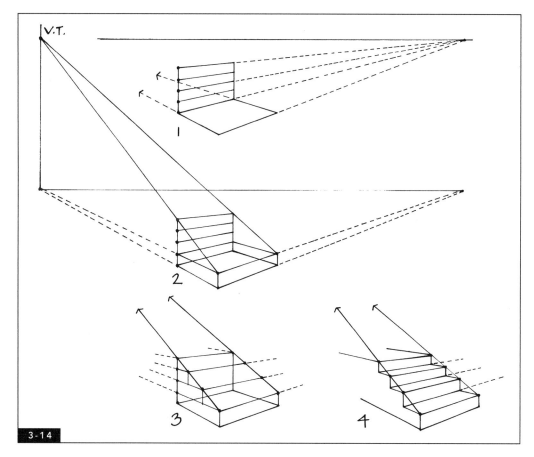

FIGURE 3-14
Sketching stairs in two-point perspective.

1. By measurement or estimation, plot the width and depth of the stairs on the floor plan. Locate a height plane by extending vertical lines to the appropriate height (the top of the stair run). Divide the height plane to create the appropriate number of risers.

2. Draw a line from the vanishing point through the height plane at the first riser measurement; this creates the first riser. Draw a diagonal line from the forward height of the first riser through the top of the height plane and continue this diagonal until it is directly above the V.P.; this is the vanishing trace (V.T.). Draw a second diagonal from the vanishing trace to the location opposite the forward riser.

3. Draw lines from the V.P. through each riser measurement on the height plane. Continue these lines until they intersect with diagonals; these are the forward riser locations.

4. Tread locations are found by extending vertical lines down to the next riser measurement; lines indicating treads converge to the appropriate vanishing point.

The centerline of a cylinder or cylindrical object is drawn as an extension of the minor axis. Because it is an extension of the minor axis, this centerline always appears at a right angle to the major axis. This means that the centerline of a complicated object, such as the axle of a wheel or the cylindrical base of a piece of furniture, can be drawn as an extension of the minor axis.

Understanding the relationship of the minor and major axes and the location of the centerline can eliminate distortion in the drawing of circular forms in perspective, and allows for freehand sketching of ellipses as well as construction of complex linear perspectives.

One method of ellipse construction involves using planes as an approximation guide for the ellipse (Figure 3-16). This is done by first drawing a plane, which resembles a square in perspective, then dividing the square using a diagonal. On each diagonal, approximately two-thirds of the distance from the center point of the square, a dot (or mark) is drawn. The ellipse is then approximated by drawing curved lines from the dots on the diagonals to the midpoints of each side of the plane. With the rough approximation complete, the major and minor axes can be approximated to aid in refinement. The minor and major axes should not be confused with the diagonal divisions of the plane, as these are separate items.

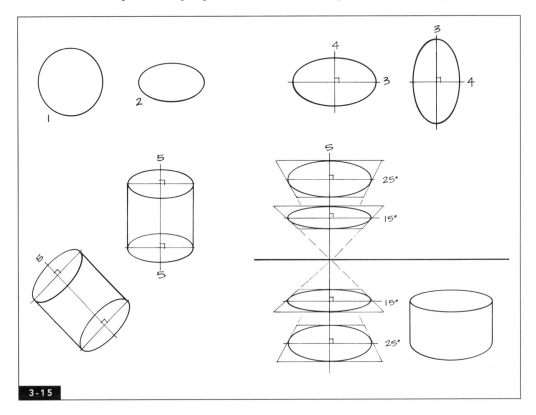

3-15

FIGURE 3-15
Ellipses.

1. Circle.

2. Ellipse. In perspective drawings, circles are drawn as ellipses.

3. The major axis is found at the widest diameter of an ellipse.

4. The minor axis is found at the narrow diameter and is always at 90 degrees to the major axis.

5. The centerline of a cylinder is drawn as an extension of the minor axis (also at 90 degrees to major axis).

6. When found on a horizontal plane such as a floor, the major axis is horizontal. Our view of the ellipse varies according to the location of our eye level (horizon line); elliptical templates are used to easily approximate the various views.

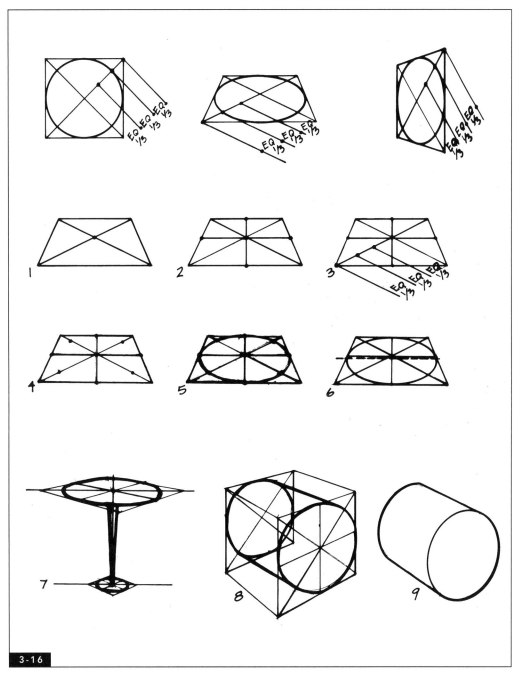

FIGURE 3-16

Quick reference: estimated ellipse construction. Based on their geometry, as shown at the top of the figure, ellipses can be estimated by creating an enclosing plane and plotting locations on diagonals:

1. Create an enclosing plane that appears square in perspectve; divide the plane with diagonals (as in diagonal division). Mark the center as located by the diagonals.

2. From the center mark, extend lines vertically and horizontally; these lines will define midpoints of the enclosing plane. Mark the locations where these lines are tangent to (touching) the enclosing plane.

3. Divide each half of the diagonal into thirds and make marks at these locations.

4 and 5. Sketch the ellipse by locating the mark two-thirds from center and drawing connecting curvilinear lines from the two-thirds mark to the adjacent midpoint mark. Refine the ellipse by visual assessment.

6. Note: quarter divisions of the square are not the major and minor axes. These divisions are for estimation purposes only. The major axis is actually slightly forward of center (dashed line).

7. The central leg of this table is formed by a center line extending from the top minor axis to the lower minor axis.

8. A full cylinder can be sketched using an enclosing cube to create the forward and rear planes; these are then used to form the required ellipses.

9. Refine the final drawing by visual assessment.

Many designers use elliptical templates to create accurate ellipses and curvilinear forms. The use of elliptical templates is based on the locations of the major axis, the minor axis, and the centerline of the form. When templates are used, the two-thirds estimating method is not employed.

Clearly, methods mentioned for drawing ellipses underscore the need to be able to draw a square-looking box accurately. This skill is perhaps the single most effective tool in freehand perspective drawing. It is worthwhile for students to practice by filling pages with boxes drawn to look square in two-point perspective. Once this skill has been developed, the box is drawn as an enclosing form, like a packing crate, then portions of the box are subtracted to reveal the object within (Figure 3-17). Starting with a simple box, and adding boxes using diagonal division, allows us to sketch items in boxes that are not square but may be elongated in a number of directions. Figures 3-18 and 3-19 depict the steps involved in creating drawings in which an enclosing cube is employed to construct items that are quite different in form from the original enclosing cube.

The ability to visually assess freehand perspective drawings that have been constructed from simple boxes lets us understand and see form and spatial relationships. Employing the principles of perspective mentioned thus far allows for better drawing and for the use of perspective drawing as a design tool.

FIGURE 3-17
Quick reference: two-point sketching using estimated boxes.

1. Sketch a box that approximates the dimensions of the object. Make sure the vanishing points are generously spaced. Create a measuring line at the front corner of the box. Mark equal divisions of the measuring line (these can be eyeballed or estimated with diagonal division).

2. Use the measuring line and diagonal division to rough out details and proportions.

3. Overlay with clean tracing paper and refine details.

4. Use a clean overlay for a final drawing; a combination of freehand and drafted lines often look best. Drawing by Leanne Larson.

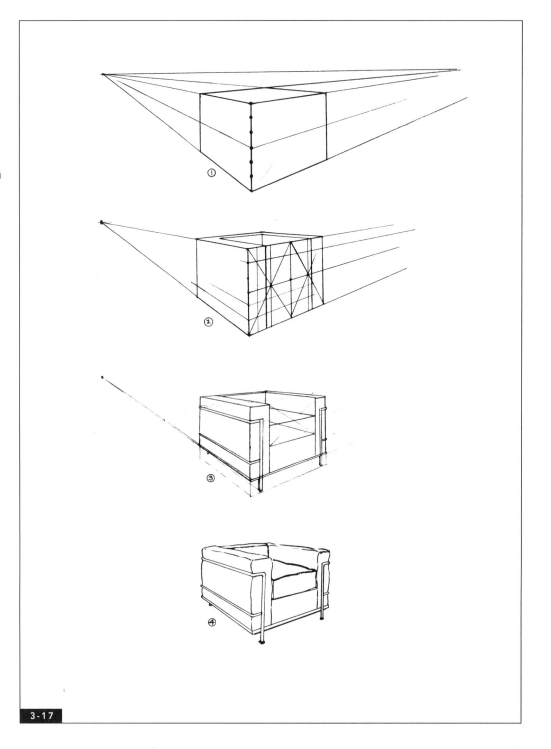

3-17

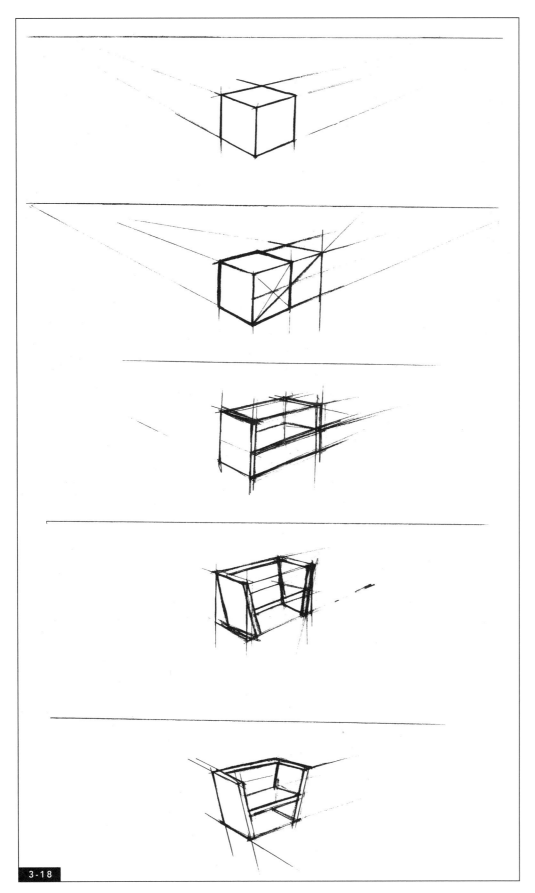

3-18

FIGURE 3-19
This series of sketches indicates
the steps involved in using an
enclosing cube to rough out proportions for a preliminary sketch
of an information desk.

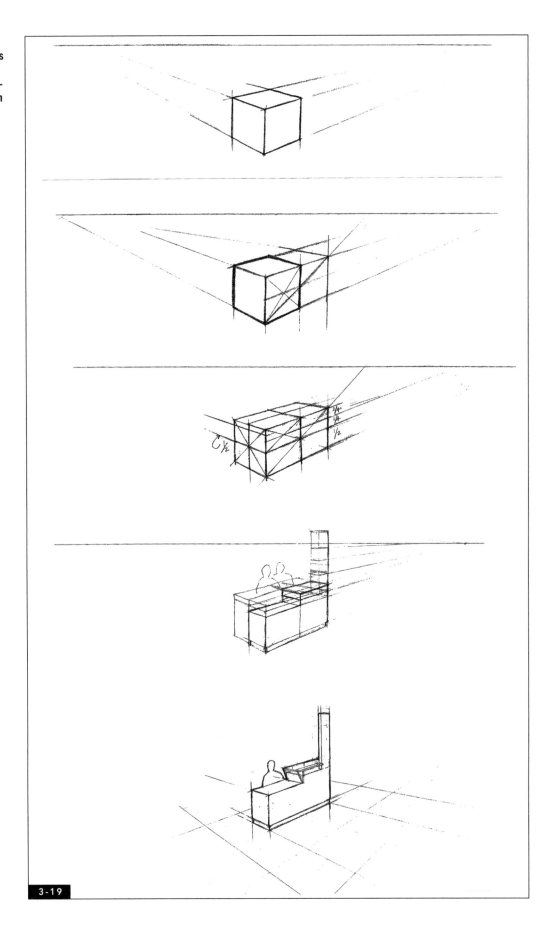

3-19

REFERENCES

Ching, Frank. *Architectural Graphics.* New York: John Wiley & Sons, 1996.

———. *A Visual Dictionary of Architecture.* New York: John Wiley & Sons, 1995.

Drpic, Ivo. *Sketching and Rendering Interior Space.* New York: Whitney Library of Design, 1988.

Forseth, Kevin, and David Vaughn. *Graphics for Architecture.* New York: John Wiley & Sons, 1980.

Hanks, Kurt, and Larry Belliston. *Rapid Viz.* Los Altos, Calif.: William Kaufman, 1980.

McGarry, Richard, and Greg Madsen. *Marker Magic: The Rendering Problem Solver for Designers.* New York: Van Nostrand Reinhold, 1993.

Pile, John. *Perspective for Interior Designers.* New York: Whitney Library of Design, 1985.

Porter, Tom. *Architectural Drawing.* New York: Van Nostrand Reinhold, 1990.

4 DRAWING AND SKETCHING INTERIOR ENVIRONMENTS

ESTIMATED ONE-POINT INTERIOR PERSPECTIVE DRAWINGS

The same concepts that allow us to sketch objects using enclosing boxes can be employed in sketching interior environments. There are many methods of measured linear perspective drawing that work well in the creation of accurate, beautiful drawings. However, it is important to note that all of the most accurate and refined methods of perspective drawing require a great deal of time, ranging from one hour to eight hours or more. These may be appropriate for final design development presentations, but time constraints require designers to develop quick sketching techniques in order to use drawings throughout the design process. Quick sketching is beneficial as a design tool, a presentation tool, and a way of seeing the world and recording details successfully.

The easiest method of quick sketching interior environments has as its foundation the box-sketching techniques discussed previously. This estimated method allows us to create a perspective of a ten-foot-square room by drawing a giant ten-foot-square box in one-point perspective. Figure 4-1 is a quick reference to this estimated one-point perspective

method. It is important to note that this method is unusual in that it requires that a square-looking room is estimated, necessitating visual accuracy developed by practice.

The estimated sketch method is started by drawing a horizontal line to serve as the horizon line; this is the viewer's eye level. A square (that serves as the back wall of the room) can then be drawn that is 10' by 10' (in any appropriate scale or eyeballed). The horizon line should bisect the square at its vertical midpoint. Next, a single vanishing point is located on the horizon line slightly left or right of center. Perspective lines indicating depth are created by drawing lines from the vanishing point through all four corners of the square. The overall depth of the room is simply estimated.

The key to this method is the ability to estimate the forward depth of the square room. The depth must be estimated in a way that makes the room look square. This is the tricky part — which takes some practice. Once this is accomplished, architectural elements can be drawn by using measurements found on the back wall (the original square) and estimating depth. Diagonal bisection of planes can be used to find depths of walls and corresponding objects.

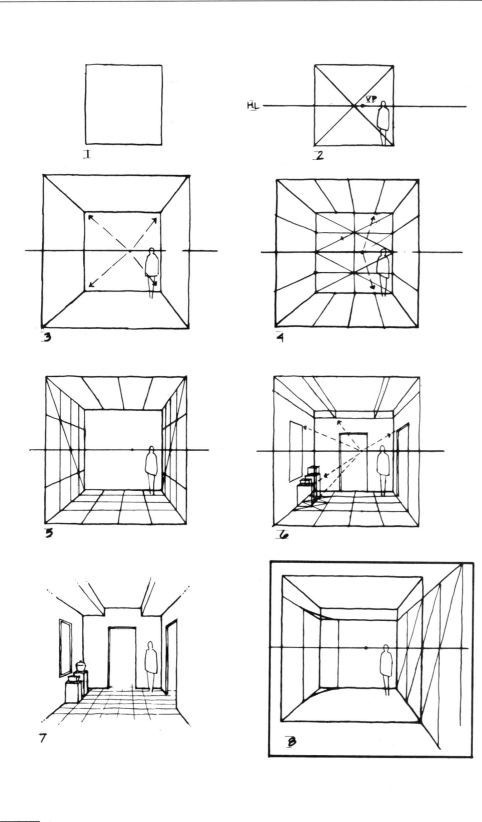

FIGURE 4-1
Quick reference: estimated one-point interior sketching.

1. Draw a 10' x 10' square in a workable scale (½" or 1").

2. Divide the square using diagonals. Draw a horizontal line through the center. This is the horizon line (H.L.); it is at roughly 5' high. Place a vanishing point on the horizon line slightly left or right of center.

3. Draw perspective lines from the V.P. through the corners of the original square, creating wall and ceiling lines. Now estimate the depth of the room — make it look square.

4. Use diagonals to divide the original square (see Figure 3-13), which is now the back wall. By dividing the back equally in four, you will create 30' height increments.

5. If necessary, a grid can be estimated through diagonal division. On side walls, verticals are located where height lines intersect diagonals.

6. Use measuring increments (created in step 4) or a grid to locate objects and architectural elements.

7. Use a clean overlay to create a line drawing.

8. To raise or lower the ceiling, simply draw lines from the V.P. to the appropriate height on the back wall and extend these lines forward. Diagonal extensions can be used to enlarge the room (see Figure 3-13). Curves are found by plotting and sketching in appropriate locations.

Because many rooms do not have ten-foot ceilings, it is often necessary to "lower" the ceiling by redrawing it at eight to nine feet. This is accomplished by locating the desired height on the back wall (the original measured square) and cutting the wall off at the desired height. Similarly, ceilings can be raised by adding the appropriate dimension to the back wall (the original square) and extending the walls to the desired height.

Most rooms are not perfectly square, and this method allows for the original 10' by 10' square to serve as the starting point for a room of another shape. Dividing and adding to the room using diagonal bisection allows for the creation of a variety of room sizes. Once again, the ability to see and create the original square

room and use it as a guide for drawing a more complicated environment is the key to the success of this method.

In drawing estimated one-point interior perspectives, complicated items or architectural elements are easiest to draw when placed on the wall(s) parallel to the picture plane. The location of the single vanishing point is important because walls and objects located very close to their vanishing points can become quite distorted. It is useful to draw a few quick thumbnail sketches of the space, using the estimation method, to locate the vanishing point and visualize the space being drawn. Thumbnail sketches aid in the location of an appropriate view of the space and the location of the vanishing point.

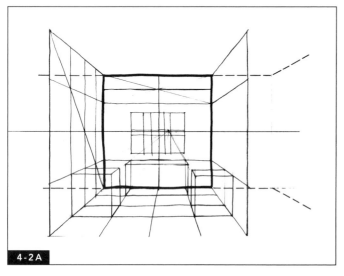

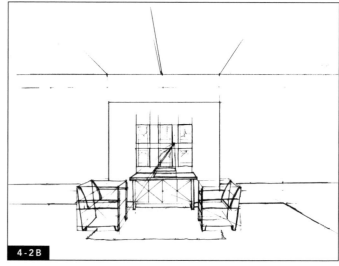

FIGURE 4-2A
This first step in constructing this drawing requires drawing the square-looking room shown in Figure 4-1 and modifying it. The bold lines in this drawing indicate the back wall of the orignal 10' x 10' room; dashed lines indicate the areas in which the room was elongated to set up the structure of the larger environment (in this case a hotel lobby and hallway). With the basic proportions of the environment complete, furnishings and additional elements can be roughed in.

FIGURE 4-2B
The drawing can be continued by adding necessary details and refining design elements.

FIGURE 4-2C
A final clean copy of the drawing can be traced and readied for rendering if necessary. Figures C-24a, b, c show the process of color-rendering this drawing.

The estimated method is an approximation method. Measurements are based on rough approximations. For example, the horizon line is placed at roughly five feet in height, providing a view of the space from a five-foot eye level. We can imagine that most pieces of furniture fit into a 30-inch-high packing crate. Therefore, much of the furniture is roughed in as 30-inch-high boxes. Human figures drawn to scale should be included in interior perspectives and are best placed with eye levels at (or near) the horizon line. More information regarding scale figures can be found in Appendix 4.

This method of quick sketching, using rough approximations, allows designers to draw space as they design it. It also allows perspective drawing to be integrated into the design process during the schematic design and design development phases of a project prior to the completion of a full set of orthographic drawings. (Figures 4-2a, b, c, 4-3a, b, c, and 4-4a, b, c). Practice generating these types of drawing can provide the skills necessary for drawing quickly and directly in client meetings with simple pens and no tools (Figures 4-5a and 4-5b). Most of the more refined methods of linear perspective require complete scaled plans and elevations, thus necessitating that the design be complete prior to the creation of the perspective drawings. The more refined perspectives are useful as a means of presentation but are not as helpful as a quick means of exploring design options or brainstorming.

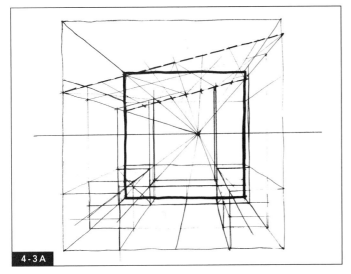

4-3 A

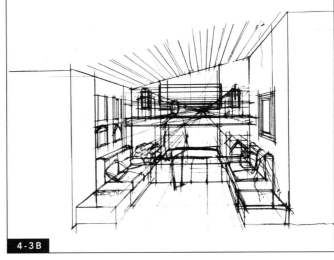

4-3 B

4-3 C

FIGURE 4-3A
This first step in constructing this drawing requires drawing the square-looking room shown in Figure 4-1 and modifying it. The bold lines in this drawing indicate the back wall of the orignal 10' x 10' room; dashed lines indicate the areas in which the ceiling was altered, in this case to indicate a shed roof in a small New Mexico cabin. With the basic proportions of the environment complete, furnishings and additional elements can be roughed in.

FIGURE 4-3B
The drawing can be continued by adding necessary details and refining design elements.

FIGURE 4-3C
A final clean copy of the drawing can be traced and readied for rendering if necessary. Figure C-39 is a color rendering of this drawing.

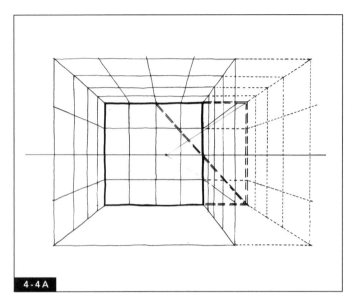

4-4A

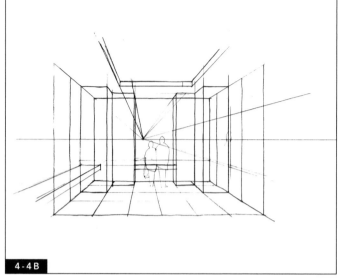

4-4B

FIGURE 4-4A
The first step in constructing this drawing requires drawing the square-looking room shown in Figure 4-1 and modifying it. The bold lines in this drawing indicate the back wall of the orignal 10' x 10' room; dashed lines indicate the areas in which the room was altered, in this case to create a much larger exhibition space.

FIGURE 4-4B
With the basic proportions of the environment complete, the basic design elements can be roughed in.

FIGURE 4-4C
Given the complexity of this environment, some extra steps are required to refine the design. Signage can be generated, photocopied, and pasted onto the drawing.

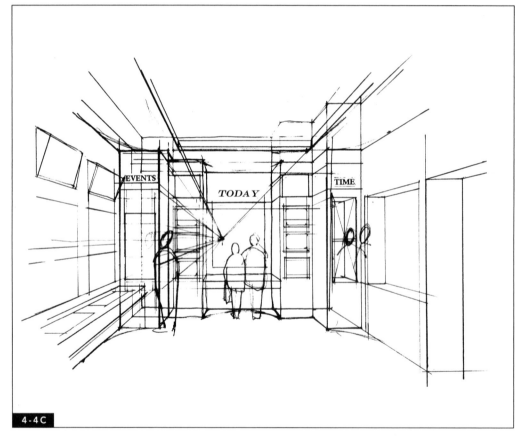

4-4C

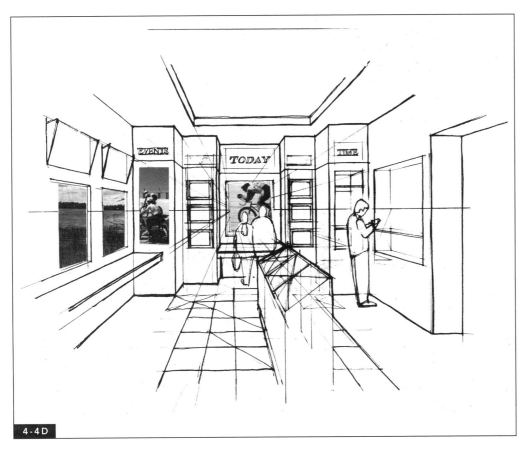

4-4D

FIGURE 4-4D
Additional elements can be
copied onto the drawing surface
as the drawing is completed. Figure 4-16 illustrates this drawing
as manipulated digitally.

4-5A

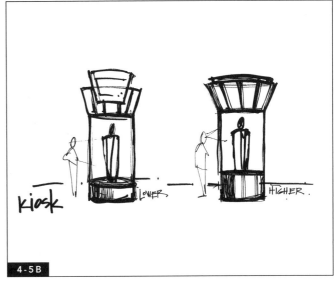

4-5B

FIGURES 4-5A, 4-5B
Practicing estimated one-point
sketching leads to the ability to do
quick sketches in client and team
meetings. This group of drawings
was sketched in less than ten
minutes using ink pens.

ESTIMATED TWO-POINT INTERIOR PERSPECTIVE DRAWINGS

One-point interiors are helpful and easy to create but are limited in use because of problems with distortion, particularly in drawing furniture and freestanding objects. Because of the limitations of one-point perspective, it is important to learn to draw two-point interior perspectives quickly using the estimation method.

The same concepts used in drawing boxes and estimated one-point interiors are employed in estimated two-point perspective sketching. In the two-point method a 10' by 10' square room is drawn first as a guideline for further development. Figure 4-6 is a quick reference for the estimated two-point perspective method.

The 10' by 10' room is created by first drawing a single vertical measuring line with four equal segments noted (in any appropriate scale

FIGURE 4-6

Quick reference: estimated two-point interior sketching.

1. Draw a single vertical line to serve as a measuring line. Divide the line into four equal segments. At the midpoint, draw a horizontal line; this is the horizon line (H.L.).

2. Place two vanishing points on the H.L., one near to (N.V.P.) and one far from (F.V.P.) the measuring line. Draw lines from each V.P. through the top and bottom of the measuring line. This creates floor and ceiling lines. Now estimate the depth of room — make it look square.

3. Draw lines from each V.P. through all increments on the measuring line; these will serve as height measurement lines.

4. To create a grid, draw diagonals on each wall. Then, at the intersection of the diagonal and each height line, draw a vertical.

5. Use the grid to estimate architectural elements and objects. Note: grids are not always necessary; for simple spaces it is best to simply estimate measurements.

6. Use a clean overlay for tracing and refining the drawing.

7. Raise or lower the ceiling by estimating the desired height. Extend the room using diagonal division (see Figure 3-13).

8. Curved surfaces are estimated by using a grid.

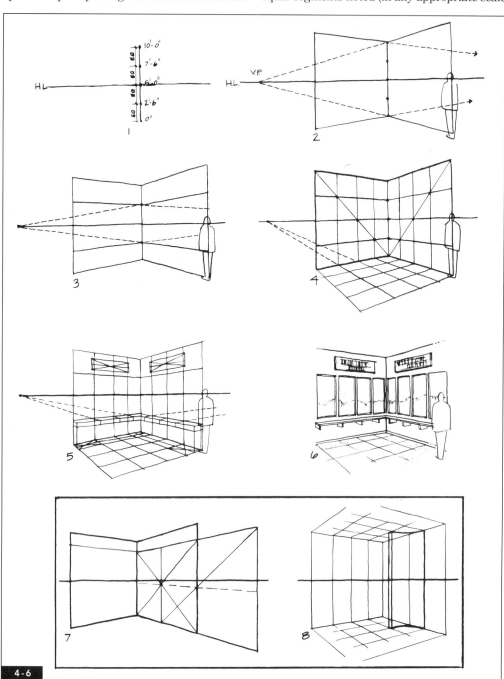

4-6

or eyeballed). This vertical measuring line serves two important functions: first, it is the only true measuring device in the drawing; second, it can become the back corner of the room(s) being drawn. A horizontal line is then drawn through the middle of the vertical line (bisecting it at the five-foot mark). This is the horizon line or viewer's eye level.

Two vanishing points must be placed on the horizon line. One should be located fairly close to the vertical measuring line; this is referred to as the near vanishing point. The second should be located far from the vertical measuring line; this is referred to as the far vanishing point.

Next, draw a line from the near vanishing point to the very bottom of the vertical measuring line and extend it forward, creating the floor line. Repeat the process with the far vanishing point. Lines are then drawn from each vanishing point to the top (the tenth increment) of the vertical measuring line and extended forward, creating the ceiling line.

At this point in the drawing we have created the floor, two walls, and the ceiling location of the room. The depth of the room must now be estimated. The overall room depth is approximated by visually assessing the room and creating a square-looking box of a room. As with one-point estimation, this is the tricky part. The key is the ability to *estimate* the depth of a 10' by 10' square room, which takes some practice.

With the use of this method, architectural elements and freestanding objects are located by measurement and estimation. The vertical measuring line can be used to find vertical measurements; these are taken from the vanishing point through the vertical measuring line and plotted on the appropriate wall. In cases where objects are freestanding, heights can be determined by extending a line from the vanishing point through the appropriate height on the wall to the location of the object. Depths are estimated using diagonal division and extension — dividing the walls with diagonals and finding the midpoint of the room at the intersection of the two diagonals.

The originally estimated square room can be modified to create a lower or higher ceiling by simply extending or reducing the dimensions of the original vertical measuring line and extending lines to the vanishing points. The walls of the room can be reconfigured easily by diagonal subdivision and extension. The ability to see and create the original square-looking room and use it as a guide for drawing a more complicated environment is the key to the success of this method.

In drawing two-point interior perspectives, complicated items and architectural elements are easiest to draw when placed on the wall created by the far vanishing point. This is because the wall generated by the near vanishing point tends to become distorted. A common distortion problem in two-point perspective drawing is caused by locating the two vanishing points too close to each other. This creates a distorted, unnatural-looking view of the space. If in the process of using this method your drawing becomes distorted, it is best to start over with the vanishing points located farther from each other.

As with one-point sketches, it is useful to do a few thumbnail sketches of the space to locate the vanishing points and visualize the space being drawn. Thumbnail sketches allow for the location of an appropriate view of the space and the proper positioning of the vanishing points.

The estimated two-point perspective method is an approximation method. Measurements are based on rough approximations. For example, the horizon line is placed at roughly five feet in height. This gives the drawing the overall view at eye level of the viewer. We can imagine that most pieces of furniture fit into a 30-inch-high packing crate. Therefore, much of the furniture can be sketched into the space as 30-inch-high boxes. Human figures drawn to scale should be included in interior perspectives and are best placed with eye levels located at or near the horizon line. This method of estimating two-point perspective drawings perspective allows drawing to be integrated into the design process during the schematic design and design development phases of a project (Figures

4-7a, b, c, d, 4-8a, b, c and 4-9a, b, c show the various steps in constructing "estimated" two-point perspective drawings for a range of projects).

Methods of estimated sketching, using rough approximation as described here (also known as "eyeballing" drawings), permit de-signers to draw a space as they design it. This type of sketching allows perspective drawing to be integrated into the design process. Sketching in perspective lets us visualize spaces three-dimensionally rather than merely view space in plan, where a sense of volume is

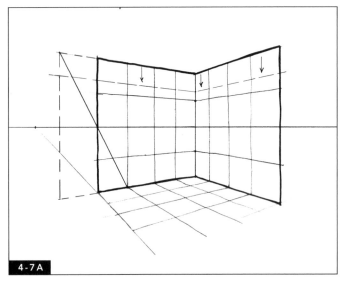

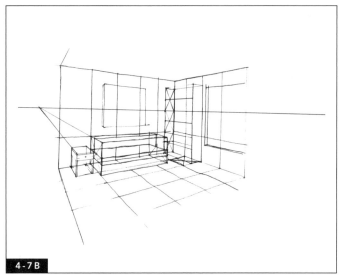

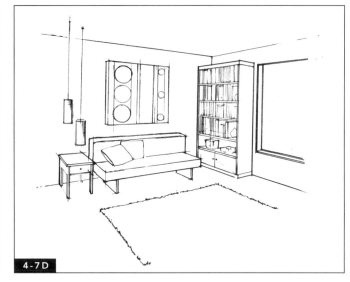

FIGURE 4-7A
This first step in constructing this drawing requires drawing the square-looking room shown in Figure 4-6 and modifying it. The bold lines in this drawing indicate the back wall of the orignal 10' x 10' room; dashed lines indicate the areas in which the room was elongated (to the left) and the ceiling was lowered to roughly eight feet above the floor.

FIGURE 4-7B
With the basic proportions of the environment complete, furnishings and additional elements can be "roughed in."

FIGURE 4-7C
The drawing is then continued by adding necessary details and refining design elements.

FIGURE 4-7D
A final clean copy of the drawing can be traced and readied for rendering if necessary. In preparing this more refined drawing, templates were used for hanging lamps and tools were used for edges of furniture. Figures C-24a, b, c show the process of color-rendering this drawing.

often missing. Visualization skills are fundamental to the design of interior environments.

Most of the more refined methods of linear perspective require complete scaled plans and elevations, thus necessitating the design to be complete prior to the creation of the perspective drawings. The more refined perspectives often appear highly realistic in contrast to the estimated methods. Refined, measured linear perspectives are most useful as a means of presentation for clients, end users, real estate professionals, investors, and the general public.

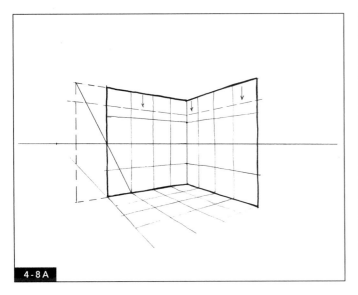

4-8A

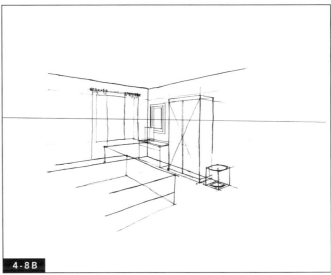

4-8B

4-8C

FIGURE 4-8A
This first step in constructing this drawing requires drawing the square-looking room shown in Figure 4-6 and modifying it. The bold lines in this drawing indicate the back wall of the orignal 10' x 10' room; dashed lines indicate the areas in which the room was elongated (to the left) and the ceiling was lowered to roughly eight feet above the floor.

FIGURE 4-8B
With the basic proportions of the environment complete, furnishings and additional elements can be roughed in. The drawing is then continued by adding necessary details and refining design elements

FIGURE 4-8C
A final clean copy of the drawing can be traced and readied for rendering if necessary. In preparing this more refined drawing, templates and tools were used.

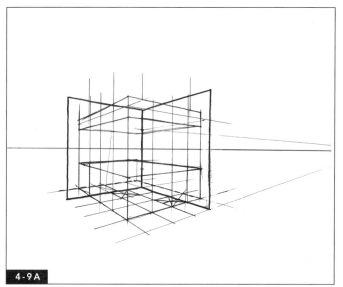

4-9A

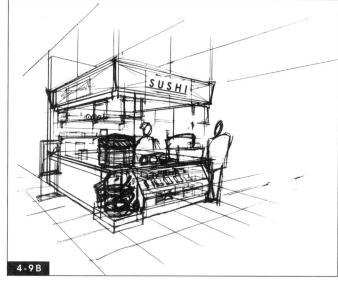

4-9B

FIGURE 4-9A
This first step in constructing this drawing requires drawing the square-looking room shown in Figure 4-6 and modifying it. The bold lines in this drawing indicate the back wall of the orignal 10' x 10' room; dashed lines indicate the areas in which the room was elongated (to the rear of the original square).

FIGURE 4-9B
With the basic proportions of the environment complete, the basic design elements can be roughed in. This particluar drawing was done very early in the design process and was used to consider the entire volume of the retail design. Type was printed and pasted into the signage area as a means of understanding scale isues.

FIGURE 4-9C
A final clean copy of the drawing can be traced and readied for rendering if necessary. In preparing this more refined drawing, some elements were drawn freehand while tools were used for others. The type shown in the previous figure was modified (by hand) to relate directly to the right vanishing point.

4-9C

REFINED LINEAR PERSPECTIVE METHODS

The perspective drawing concepts and skills covered thus far can help us gain valuable visualization skills. These skills are easily transferred to the refined, measured methods of linear perspective. Therefore, the ability to draw well in estimated perspective allows us to draw well in refined, precisely measured perspectives.

The ability to create refined perspective presentation drawings is useful for all environmental designers. Most firms have at least one employee (and often several) who is considered to be a perspective drawing or rendering specialist. Such individuals are often called upon to do much of the detailed perspective drawing and rendering for the firm. These drawings are generally created well into the design process and are not used as preliminary ideation sketches. It is also quite common for firms to hire professional design illustrators and renderers to create highly detailed drawings as required for particular project presentations. Firms often select a particular professional illustrator's style to enhance a project. This points to the fact that there is never a single way to illustrate space; there is a range of stylistic approaches.

A wide variety of methods of measured perspective drawing are used in practice. I have found that certain methods work best for certain people. People who draw well in measured perspective employ the particular method that works best for them. For this reason a variety of methods are discussed briefly and illustrated in the following sections. Students should experiment with the described methods to discover a personal method of measured perspective drawing.

TWO-POINT PLAN PROJECTION METHOD

Two-point plan projection, also known as the "common method" or the "office method," is used by students and professionals alike. A comparable method is used commonly for ex-terior perspectives, and a similar one-point method is used as well. The plan projection method requires a completed scaled floor plan and scaled elevations, which means the project must be well resolved for this method of drawing to take place. Figures 4-10a and 4-10b illustrate step-by-step plan projection instructions.

This method is completely different from any perspective methods discussed previously. Although it is useful and highly accurate, it can be confusing at first because it requires going back and forth from plan view to perspective view. To minimize confusion, one must understand that the floor plan is used to set up the final perspective elements and measurements. In this method the floor plan is manipulated to provide information that is projected onto the perspective drawing.

To begin this method, decisions must be made as to what view of the space is desired, the location of the viewer, and the cone of vision. Key elements of the space must be included within a 60-degree cone of vision. With decisions made regarding the areas to be shown and the orientation of the viewer, the plan is set up against the picture plane (also drawn in plan).

The plan setup must also include the location of the viewer in plan; this is known as the station point, but I like my students to think of it as the head of the viewer in plan. The station point, or location of the viewer, is extremely important to the success of this method. The location of the station point dictates the view of the space, as well as the cone of vision and other key elements, such as the location of the vanishing points.

With the plan set up against the picture plane and the station point located, the vanishing points can be located on the picture plane in plan. This is done by drawing lines from the station point parallel to the walls of the room (or building) that terminate at the picture plane. This method requires that lines be drawn from the station point to the location on the plan, to the picture plane, and then projected onto the perspective drawing.

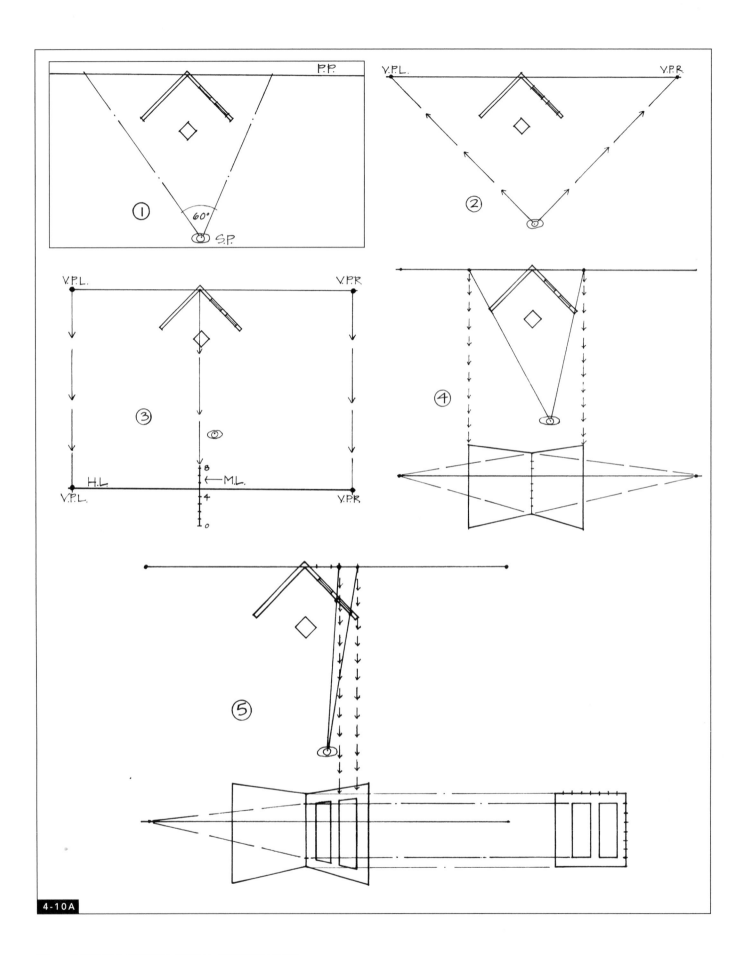

FIGURE 4-10A
Quick reference: two-point plan projection.

1. Draw a horizontal line; this is the picture plane (P.P.). Select the desired angle of view and orient the plan so that the rear corner touches the picture plane. Locate the station point (S.P.); make sure all desired elements fit within a 60-degree cone of vision projecting from the S.P. to the desired areas in plan. Locate the station point one to three times the height of the interior space from the focal point of the drawing.

2. Draw lines from the S.P. to the P.P. that are parallel to the walls of the floor plan; the locations of the intersections of these lines and the P.P. are the setup vanishing points, vanishing point right (V.P.R.) and vanishing point left (V.P.L.).

3. Draw a horizontal line below the plan setup; this is the horizon line (H.L.). Project the location of V.P.L. and V.P.R. vertically to the H.L.; this relocates the vanishing points. Project a line from the rear corner of plan vertically to the H.L.; this will be the measuring line (M.L.). It can be measured in scale (to match plan); it will also be the back corner of the room. The horizon line must be located at 5' to 6' in scale on the M.L. (normal eye level).

4. Draw lines from the V.P.L. through the top and bottom of the M.L. These are the wall and floor lines. Repeat this step with V.P.R. Next, draw lines from the S.P. through the ends of walls (in plan) to the P.P. Project these locations vertically onto the drawing.

5. Draw lines from the S.P. through window locations, or any other elements (in plan), to the P.P. Project these locations vertically onto the drawing. Heights are determined by measuring from M.L. or from an available elevation.

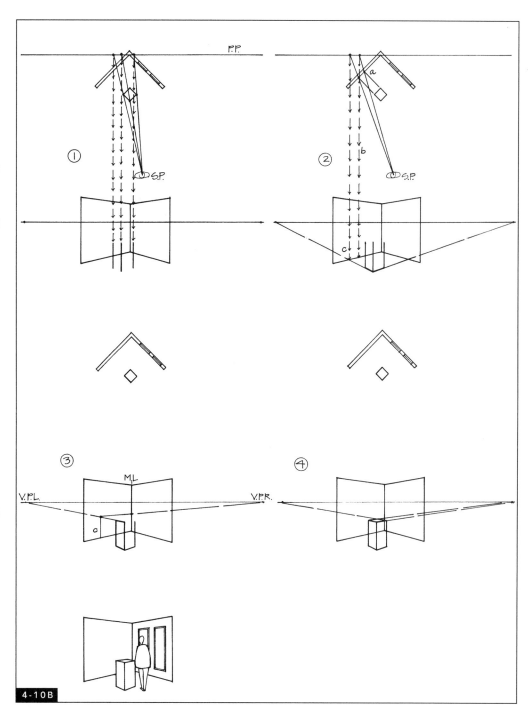

FIGURE 4-10B
Quick reference: locating freestanding objects using plan projection.

1. Draw lines from the S.P. through the edges of the object and extend them to the P.P. Project these locations vertically onto the drawing.

2. To find a floor location, first transfer the furniture location onto walls in plan setup (a). Then draw lines from the S.P. to locations on walls; extend the lines to P.P. Next project locations on the P.P. vertically to the appropriate wall in the drawing (b).

Draw a line from the V.P. to the location where the wall projection meets the floor (c); extend these lines forward onto the object to find the floor location.

3. Find the height of objects by drawing a line from V.P. (in this case, V.P.R.) through the appropriate height on the M.L. to the wall location (c).

4. The object is completed with lines drawn to the appropriate vanishing points.

Hint: Often when a drawing looks wrong or "off," it is because a location was not projected from the P.P.

Most students find it helpful to recognize two separate types of activity within this method: (1) those set up in plan and related to the picture plane and (2) those then projected from the picture plane to the perspective drawing. Measurements of width and depth are projected from the picture plane onto the perspective drawings. Heights are taken from the measuring line or elevation(s) and tranferred to the appropriate location.

The plan projection method is generally accurate and provides an excellent perspective framework. But it can be time-consuming and sometimes leads to unexpected distortion, requiring the entire process to be completed a second time. I find that the method works best for environments based on simple geometric forms rather than those based on complex or organic forms. Figures 4-11a – 4-11j delineate the various steps in a plan projection method drawing for a residential project.

FIGURE 4-11A

1. In beginning the drawing, the desired view must be selected. In this case the plan is oriented to provide a view of the rear corner of the kitchen to include the kitchen cabinets.

2. The picture plane should pass through the rear corner of the plan with the walls you wish to include in the drawing on the left and right.

3. Create a station point directly below the rear corner of the plan (there are other ways to do this, but this is the easiest). The station point indicates the location of the viewer. This point should be located roughly 2–3 times the height of the room (in the same scale as the plan).

4. Draw a line (dashed here) from the station point to the picture plane; this line must be parallel to the back walls of the room in plan.

5. The actual perspective drawing is begun by projecting the location of the back corner down vertically through the station point and well below (or above) the plan.

6. The line projected in 5 now becomes the measuring line. This line is drawn to the desired height of the room (in this case nine feet), in the same scale as the original plan

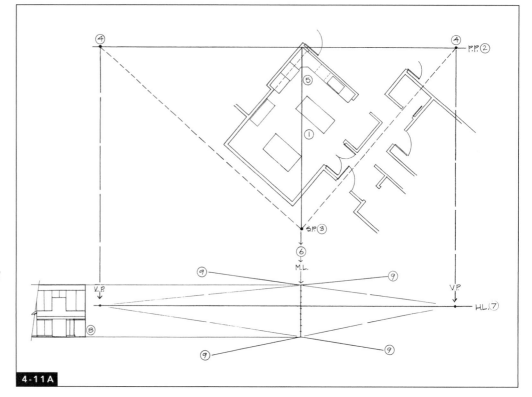

was created. It is helpful to draw "tic marks" that indicate one-foot increments on the measuring line.

7. A horizontal line is now drawn to serve as the horizon line for the perspective drawing. In most drawings it should be located at eyeball height, in this case 5'5". The vanishing points should be projected vertically directly from the picture plane onto this new horizon line.

8. If desired, an elevation can be placed alongside the perspective drawing to aid in establishing height measurements.

9. Wall and ceiling lines can now be drawn from opposite vanishing point to the appropriate heights on the measuring line.

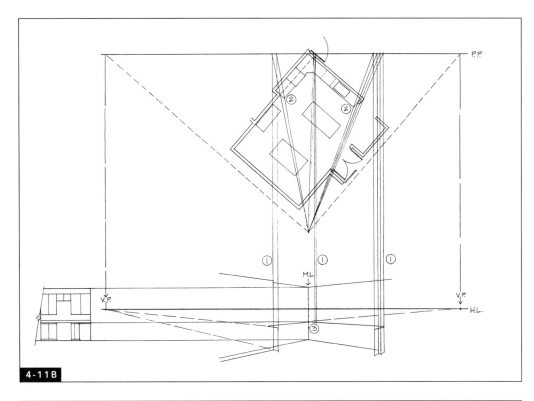

4-11B

FIGURE 4-11B

1. Wall and object locations are found by locating the item on the plan and projecting a line from the station point to the location on the plan, onward to the picture plane, and down onto the drawing.

2. In this case a line is drawn from the station point to the cabinet, onward to the picture plane, and then projected vertically from the picture plane to the drawing. Note: If your drawing looks weird, you are not projecting consistently down from the picture plane.

3. The height of the lower cabinets is found by counting off the measuring line, in this case 3'. Some people prefer to obtain the height dimensions by transferring them from the adjacent elevations.

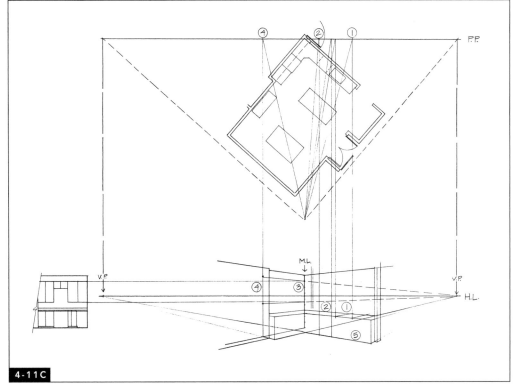

4-11C

FIGURE 4-11C

1. The sink location is found by drawing a line from the station point to the front corners of the sink, onward to the picture plane, and then onto the drawing.

2. The dishwasher is found by drawing a line from the station point to the front corners of the dishwasher, onward to the picture plane, and then onto the drawing.

3. To find the heights of the wall cabinets it is necessary to first locate the height on the original measuring line (in this case the height information is transferred from the adjacent elevation).

4. Because the cabinets are recessed into the wall (see plan), it is necessary to draw a line from the station point to the rear edge of the cabinet, onto the picture plane, and project this location onto the drawing.

5. The lower cabinets are completed when lines are drawn from the edges of the cabinets to the appropriate vanishing points.

FIGURE 4-11D

1. The angled portion of the lower cabinets is created by drawing a line from the station point to the edges of the angled portion onward to the picture plane, and then the lines are projected onto cabinets in the drawing.

2. The location of the stove is found by drawing a line from the station point to the front corners of the stove, onward to the picture plane, and then down onto the drawing.

3. This piece of furniture is located by drawing lines from the station point to the three visible edges of the object, onward to the picture plane, and then onto the drawing. The height of the object is determined by locating it on the measuring line and then transferring, by use of the vanishing point (dashed lines).

4. The upper cabinets can be completed by working from the measuring line and the vanishing points, similarly to step 3 above.

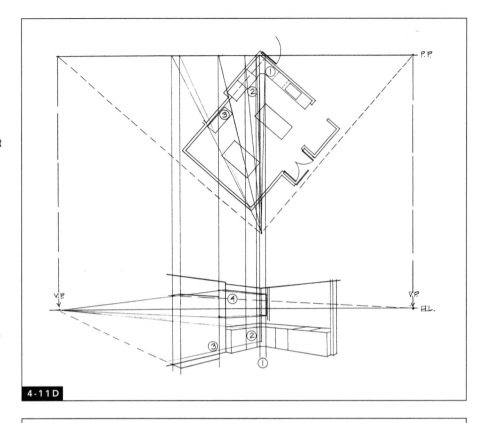

FIGURE 4-11E

1. The island, which is freestanding, is drawn using a combination of projected lines. Lines are drawn from the station point to the three visible edges of the island, onward to the picture plane, and then down to the drawing, creating the island's corner locations.

2. Because the item is freestanding, its height and actual floor location must be determined by transferring the object location onto walls in plan setup (dashed lines in plan).

3. Lines are then drawn from the station point to the plan wall locations found in 2 above, onward to the picture plane, and then onto the corresponding walls in the perspective drawing. Now, working on the perspective drawing, lines are drawn from the left vanishing point to the location where the wall projection (done in 2) meets the floor, and these lines are extended foward to the corners of the island. The height of the island is taken from the measuring line and extended using the vanishing points.

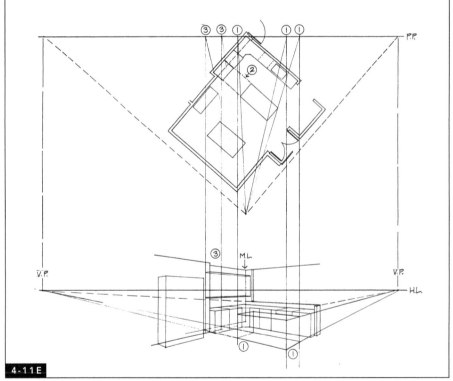

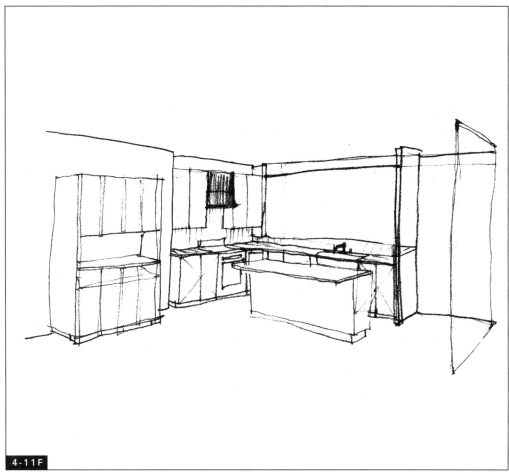

4-11F

FIGURE 4-11F
At this stage, a quick overlay sketch can be created to determine the quality of the perspective drawing and locate any problem areas.

FIGURE 4-11G

1. With the significant features completed, the plan is no longer necessary because most height and spatial relationships can be determined through use of the measuring line and vanishing points.

2. The location of the hood and cabinets above the stove is found by drawing lines upward from the back corners of the stove to the upper cabinets (dashed line with arrows). These locations are brought forward through use of the left vanishing point and then drawn on the front face of the upper cabinets.

3. To finalize the details of the freestanding buffet, dimensions are found on the measuring line, brought "behind" the buffet, and extended using the left vanishing point.

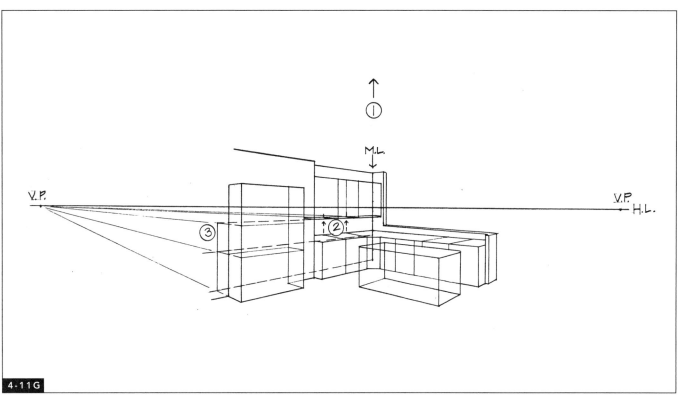

4-11G

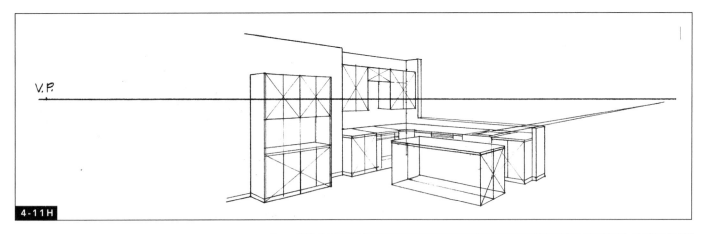

4-11H

FIGURE 4-11H
Using diagonal division, various details can be considered and drawn in place.

FIGURE 4-11I
Additional design elements can be estimated or measured.

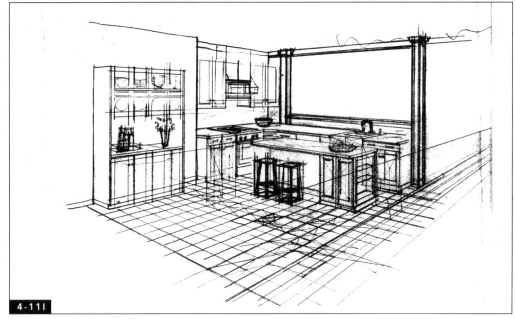

4-11I

FIGURE 4-11J
The final clean version of the drawing. Steps involved in rendering this drawng can be found in Figures C-25a and C-25b.

4-11J

PREPARED PERSPECTIVE GRID CHARTS

Prepared perspective charts are used by many designers and design illustrators. Charts are popular owing to their ease of use and speed of drawing construction. Many designers and illustrators use only prepared charts in the construction of perspective drawings.

The charts provide a perspective framework including horizon line, location of viewer, cone of vision, vanishing points, and measuring devices. This framework allows items to be located, measured, and drawn to appropriate vanishing points. Visual accuracy and the ability to draw ellipses and square-looking boxes are required in the use of prepared charts, just as they are in quick sketching. These skills are necessary because grids merely provide a perspective framework and measuring system — they do not do the drawing for you.

Perspective charts are based on a set of given conditions. The location and height of viewer (and corresponding horizon line), vanishing points, cone of vision, measuring increments, and the overall visual emphasis of the space are all given within a particular chart. For this reason it is helpful to keep a set of

charts with varying views and spatial relationships for use in various projects. Generally perspective charts cover a huge area and must be manipulated and measured to define the space required in a drawing.

Because the charts contain hundreds of lines, they can be confusing and difficult to read. It is a good idea to use a variety of colored pencils on tracing paper overlays to define the space and record important elements. Elements that establish the space — such as the horizon line, vanishing points, vertical measuring lines, and wall, floor, and ceiling grid lines — can be transferred to tracing paper using various colors. With these elements and other useful notes recorded, the original grid can be removed and a customized grid created. The customized grid should be overlaid with tracing paper and kept for future reference.

Grid charts are useful, relatively quick, accurate, and adaptable. Because one chart will not work for all projects, a series of charts is worth having. And, as discussed, all projects require that the grid be manipulated or customized to some degree, which can be confusing, especially for beginners. Figure 4-12 is an

FIGURE 4-12
A prepared perspective grid chart.

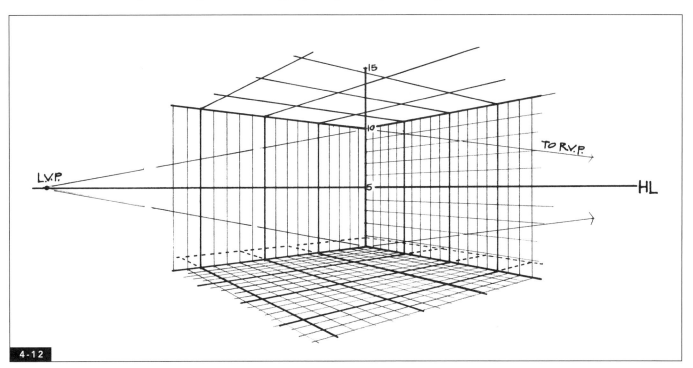

FIGURE 4-13A
The prepared chart customized for a particular project, the Royal Pavilion, Brighton, England. Drawing by Leanne Larson.

example of a prepared grid. Figures 4-13a–4-13h are a sequence of drawings using a prepared grid (see Figures C-28a and C-28b for color renderings of this drawing). See Figures C-37a and C-37b for drawings based on a grid used by a professional illustrator. A simplified grid that can be copied and used for constructing drawings can be found in Appendix 5.

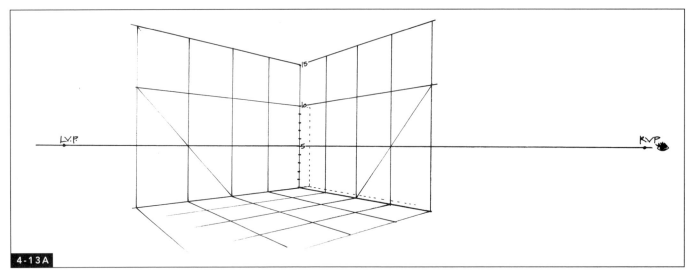

4-13A

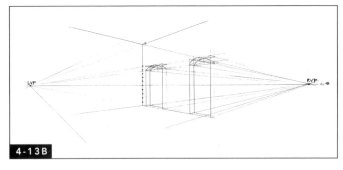

4-13B

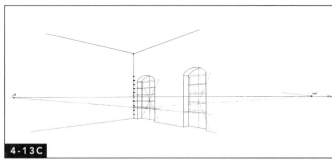

4-13C

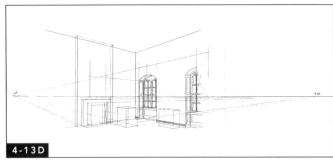

4-13D

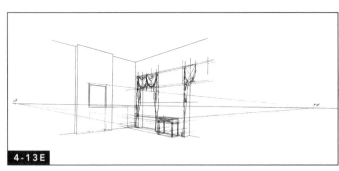

4-13E

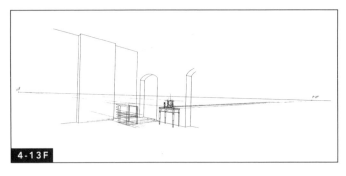

4-13F

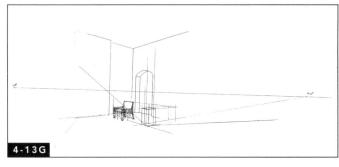

4-13G

4-13H

FIGURES 4-13B – 4-13H
The sequence of drawings prepared with the use of a grid, leading to a final line drawing of the Royal Pavilion, Brighton, England. (See Figure C-28b for a color rendering of this drawing.) Drawings by Leanne Larson.

PERSPECTIVES TRACED FROM PHOTOGRAPHS

Photographs can be traced to form a perspective framework. This method is especially useful in renovating existing space where a photograph of existing conditions is used. This method requires that a photograph be taken from the desired vantage point. In this situation it is necessary to be careful that the photograph is clearly taken from a one-point or two-point perspective vantage point. Once the photograph is processed, it can be enlarged, if necessary, on a photocopying machine. The enlargement is then overlaid with tracing paper, and the drawing can be constructed. Figure 4-14 is a quick reference of this method.

If the photograph is taken with the primary wall parallel to the camera lens (picture plane), a one-point perspective view is generated. The drawing in this case is constructed with one vanishing point located on the horizon line. This is done by tracing over the lines that form the floor and ceiling lines (or any series of major perspective lines). The location where these lines converge is the vanishing point.

A horizontal line is drawn through the vanishing point, and this serves as the horizon line. It is useful to check this location by tracing perspective lines from an additional object in the space and making sure they converge at the same vanishing point. With the vanishing point and horizon line noted, new or proposed design elements can be sketched into the space. Items to be retained in the proposed design can simply be traced from the photograph. Figure 4-14 illustrates this process.

Two-point perspectives can be drawn from photographs that show the two main walls or elements as oblique to the camera lens (picture plane). The system is similar to that used in one-point tracing, except for the fact that two vanishing points must be located and placed on the horizon line. Most often, the correct vanishing point can be located by tracing the left floor and ceiling lines (or the corresponding lines of some significant object) to a point of convergence. The left vanishing point is estimated by tracing the right floor and ceiling lines (or the corresponding lines of some significant object) to a point of convergence.

A horizon line is created by drawing a horizontal line connecting the right and left vanishing points. It is imperative that the horizon line link the two vanishing points with a single

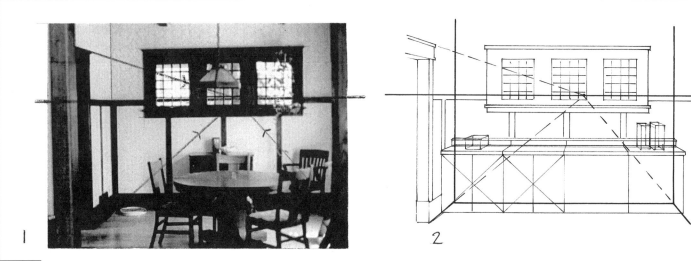

4-14

FIGURE 4-14
Quick reference: tracing from photographs.

1. **This photograph sets up a one-point view of the interior because the back wall is parallel to the picture plane (camera lens). Trace over the lines that form the walls and ceiling; these will lead to a single vanishing point. Draw a horizontal line through the vanishing point; this is the horizon line.**

2. **New or proposed items are drawn using the vanishing point and the horizon line.**

3. **Trace items that will be retained from the photographic image. Add entourage elements such as plants, figures, or fixtures.**

horizontal line. With the two vanishing points and horizon line located, proposed changes can be sketched into the drawing. All elements to be retained in the proposed design may be traced into the drawing. Figure 5-15 is a complex drawing created by tracing existing elements from a photograph.

Generally photographs taken of existing spaces include a number of interesting background and foreground elements. Human figures, plants, and details of daily life are often captured in photographs. These elements can be traced into the drawing to add interest and liveliness. Students often remove these items, creating lifeless drawings.

Photographic slides or transparencies also may be traced to create a perspective framework system. This is done by projecting a slide onto a screen or wall and following the same procedures described for photographic tracing.

Students are sometimes reluctant to trace perspective drawings from photographic images because it could be considered plagiarism. If, however, the photographs provide *only a perspective framework* for new and original design ideas, plagiarism is not an issue. Clearly, plagiarism is involved when a drawing done by

another individual is traced without credit given or if a design is lifted in totality and traced. Many professional illustrators and renderers keep a huge file of photographs of human figures, furnishings, and other elements to be traced into drawings. A light table makes any job of tracing very easy.

Digital cameras can be used to good effect in the creation of perspective drawings based on photographs. Existing conditions can be photographed and quickly downloaded for viewing on a monitor, with no need for photographic processing. Most digital cameras come with software that allows for image organization and manipulation, and in some cases easy importing onto the Web. Black-and-white as well as color images can be printed quickly and drawn on for creation of presentation sketches. Image files can also be imported into programs such as Adobe Photoshop®, Adobe Photoshop Elements®, or Adobe Illustrator® for further treatment and image manipulation. Figures 4-15a to 4-15c depict perspective drawings that have been manipulated using Photoshop Elements; Figure 4-16 is an elevation that has been enhanced using Adobe Illustrator.

4-15A

4-15B

4-15C

FIGURES 4-15A, 4-15B, 4-15C
A hand-drawn and rendered image
(see Figures 4-4a – 4-4d) was
scanned and manipulated to
include various signage options;
various filters were then applied.
Software: Adobe Photoshop Ele-
ments™.

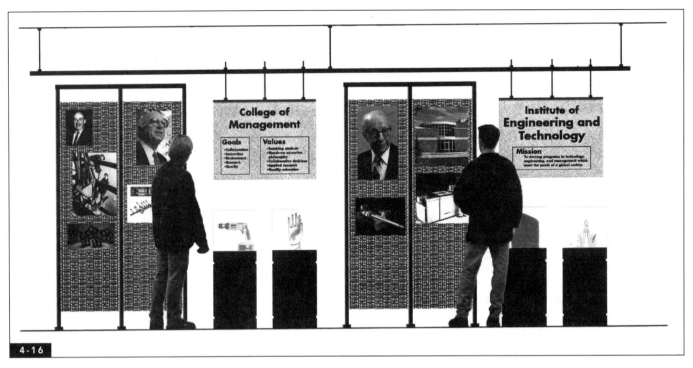

FIGURE 4-16
Computer-generated image using hand-drawn elements manipulated with Adobe Illustrator™. Drawing by Cory Sherman and the author.

COMPUTER-GENERATED IMAGERY

Increasingly architectural and interior designers are using CADD in the creation of paraline and perspective drawings — these are called three-dimensional models by some. As previously mentioned, some software allows CADD-generated orthographic projections to be converted easily into three-dimensional views. In other cases the three-dimensional image is built without first generating orthographic drawings. As with many CADD programs, often three-dimensional drawing programs are difficult to learn to use. Yet once the data are correctly entered, various three-dimensional views are easily generated and changes are made with great ease. The location and height of the viewer are easily changed, allowing a range of drawings to be created.

CADD-generated three-dimensional images are highly accurate and provide great flexibility because changes can be made quickly. The software ranges a great deal in price and sophistication, but rapid advances in CADD technology promise lower costs and greater sophistication in the future. CADD is currently used by designers in all areas of practice, from library design to kitchen and bath renovation. With future advances and refinement CADD-generated imagery will continue to revolutionize interior design practice. Figure 4-17 is a computer-generated perspective drawing. Figure 4-18 is a drawing done using AutoCAD that has been enhanced by hand. Figures 4-19a and 4-19b are hand-drawn and computer-generated images for a student project.

Many CADD three-dimensional views are generated as wire-frame models, which are representations of objects consisting of multiple boundary lines. Wire frames look similar to hand-drawn perspective sketches, with construction lines running in all directions. Some of these lines can be hidden to more clearly depict an environment. Even so, wire frames can look somewhat unnatural because items often do not appear as true three-dimensional solids until they are rendered. Although most three-dimensional modeling programs allow for quite a range of views of a given space, occasionally it is difficult to obtain the exact view desired. In cases such as this the image can be drawn over by hand to manipulate the view (see Figure 4-18).

4-17

FIGURE 4-17
An AutoCAD-generated perspective
drawing of the project featured in
the professional case study (see
Figures C-77 to C-86). Design and
drawing by Meyer, Scherer &
Rockcastle Ltd.

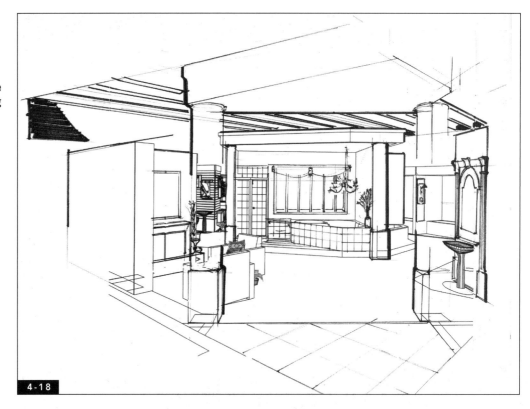

4-18

In CADD-generated three-dimensional views, rendering is often handled as a second step in the drawing process, much as it is in hand drawing. The most elegant rendering of surface materials, color, value, and shadow is done with sophisticated software. Much of this software requires that the CADD-generated three-dimensional view be imported into the secondary rendering application. CADD-gener-ated three-dimensional views can also be animated and used in multimedia presentations.

In current practice the largest and most specialized firms are using the most sophisticated three-dimensional computer imaging. Many small and medium-size firms employ some type of computer-generated three-dimensional imagery or hire professional computer illustrators on a project-by-project basis.

REFERENCES

Ching, Frank. *A Visual Dictionary of Architecture*. New York: John Wiley & Sons, 1995.

———. *Architectural Graphics*. New York: John Wiley & Sons, 1996.

Drpic, Ivo. *Sketching and Rendering Interior Space*. New York: Whitney Library of Design, 1988.

Forseth, Kevin, and David Vaughn. *Graphics for Architecture*. New York: John Wiley & Sons, 1980.

Hanks, Kurt, and Larry Belliston. *Rapid Viz*. Los Altos, Calif.: William Kaufman, 1980.

Leggit, Jim. *Drawing Shortcuts*. New York: John Wiley & Sons, 2002.

McGarry, Richard, and Greg Madsen. *Marker Magic: The Rendering Problem Solver for Designers*. New York: John Wiley & Sons, 1993.

Pile, John. *Perspective for Interior Designers*. New York: Whitney Library of Design, 1985.

Porter, Tom. *Architectural Drawing*. New York: John Wiley & Sons, 1990.

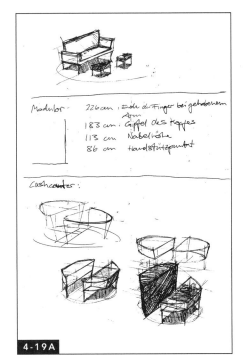

4-19A

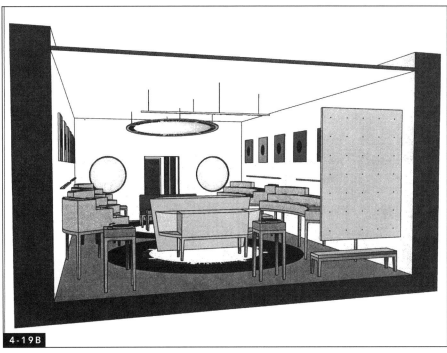

4-19B

4-19C

FIGURE 4-19A
Preliminary sketches of details for a retail project were created by hand. Design and drawings by Dirk Olbrich.

FIGURE 4-19B, 4-19C
The final design presentation, based on elements sketched in Figure 4-19a, was created in 3-D StudioVIZ. Design and drawings by Dirk Olbrich. Figures C-42a and C-42b are color studies for this project.

5 RENDERING

INTRODUCTION TO RENDERING

In the world of architecture and design the term RENDERING is used to describe the visual enhancement of drawings through the use of value and/or color. Rendering visually enhances drawings, making them more easily understood and allowing for greater visual communication in design presentations. Rendering is often done to convey depth and to allow a two-dimensional drawing surface to appear more three-dimensional, thus revealing the material qualities of forms.

Because it can help clients understand a project, rendering is useful as a means of communication. However, some project budgets and schedules do not allow time for highly detailed renderings, whereas other projects require extensive detailed rendering. This means that projects have different presentation parameters, requiring a range of rendering skills—from quick and loose to accurate and refined.

The level of rendering is also influenced by the phase of the design process in which the presentation takes place. For example, during the preliminary stages of design it is wise to keep renderings loose and sketchy to avoid having the project pinned down prematurely. It is best to consider carefully the audience and purpose before beginning the actual rendering.

Many students approach rendering with fear and lack of self-confidence. However, an understanding of basic rendering concepts and techniques can allow designers and students to enhance a visual presentation significantly. There are dozens of rendering techniques, materials, and tools available. Practice, study, and the use of reference material can help designers to develop a personal system of rendering.

This chapter is an overview of rendering covering some basic concepts, materials, and techniques. Orthographic drawings are rendered differently than perspective drawings and, for that reason, are covered separately in this chapter. Paraline drawings are rendered in a manner similar to perspective drawings and are discussed with them.

RENDERING AS ILLUMINATION

The most important thing to understand about rendering is that, regardless of style, it introduces qualities of illumination to a drawing. This means that good rendering introduces light into a drawing, making it appear more natural and creating the illusion of three dimensions. Rendering requires consideration of the light source, or sources, found in the environment and the resulting value relationships. This is true for quick sketches and elaborate illustrations, for colored and noncolored renderings. The illumination in a rendering is perhaps its single most important aspect.

Simply stated, light falls on an object and illuminates its surfaces to varying degrees. The type of lighting, the location of the light source(s), and the object's material qualities all affect the manner in which the object is illuminated. Without consideration of the light source(s) and the related value relationships, renderings always look like something out of a child's coloring book.

As a light source illuminates an object, it creates varying degrees of light on the object's surfaces. Those areas that receive direct light become the light areas of the object. Shade occurs in those areas not receiving light directly. Shadows are created on the surfaces blocked from receiving light. These varying degrees of light and shade are referred to as VALUE. All good rendering is based on value relationships. Figure 5-1 illustrates light, shade, and shadow.

MATERIALS, MEDIA, AND TOOLS

The list of materials and tools used in rendering is long and continues to grow. Professional illustrators and renderers employ many methods, use a range of supplies, and generally have distinct personal preferences. An understanding of materials and techniques allows a designer to make wise decisions and work quickly. This means that a basic understanding of materials and media is important. In rendering there are no hard-and-fast rules — anything goes. Great rendering requires exploration and curiosity about how materials will work in a given situation. Figure C-1 depicts a range of rendering media, materials, and tools; Figure C-2 gives examples of various rendering surfaces and media.

Because there are no absolute rules in rendering, it is wise to do a good deal of casual research. Looking at good rendering, fine art, and illustration is essential. To this end books, periodicals, exhibitions, and visits to design firms are useful. Looking at what works in a successful painting or pastel drawing can

5 - 1

FIGURE 5-1
This cube is rendered to illustrate value. The top of the cube is light because it is receiving direct light from the light source. Shade (found on the sides of the cube) occurs in those areas not receiving light directly. Shadows are created on the surfaces blocked from receiving light. These varying degrees of light and shade are referred to as VALUE. All good rendering is based on value relationships. The front edge of the cube is called the LEADING EDGE and is drawn in white.

teach a great deal about how to work with color markers. Discussions with art supply store personnel can be valuable in acquiring information about paper, drawing surfaces, and other supplies.

PAPER AND DRAWING SURFACES

The type of paper or rendering surface used has a significant influence on the quality of the final product. Many designers limit themselves to working on tracing paper or vellum because these papers are commonly used throughout the design process and are available in design offices.

Tracing paper and vellum have slick surfaces and are transparent, allowing them to be overlaid and easily traced. Graphite pencils, ink pens, and colored pencils and markers are often used with success on tracing paper and vellum. Markers are not absorbed into the surface of these papers, so the color stays rather weak and tends to pool. This creates softer color renderings that often have a watercolor effect, which can be attractive. Colored pencil can be layered on top of marker on these transparent papers to enrich the color and define edges. Using a combination of white, beige/cream, and darker pencils for highlights and refinement can work particularly well. On tracing paper and vellum, white gouache works well for tiny areas of highlight.

MARKER or VISUALIZING PAPER is commonly used in advertising and industrial design and is excellent for rich marker renderings. Marker paper is less transparent than tracing paper or vellum but absorbs markers well (see Figures C-6 and C-7). Graphite, ink pens, colored pencils, and small amounts of paint (including gouache) can all work well on marker paper. Some heavier types of marker paper may be difficult to see through and require the use of a light table or taping onto a sunny window for tracing. Some types of marker paper can be photocopied and rendered. Pretesting of paper, photocopier toner, and marker compatibility is required. Figure 5-2 is a rendering on marker paper.

Plain BOND PAPER, used in standard office copying machines, is highly absorbent and can be used for rendering. Bond paper can be very messy because it soaks up marker dye, but when used with care it can create rich marker renderings. This paper also allows colored pencils to be layered over marker for clarity, crispness, and highlights. Rendering directly on bond photocopies is a fast, popular rendering technique that is becoming the standard in design offices. A word of caution: some marker base components can smear and dissolve copy toner, resulting in disaster. Pretesting of all materials to be used on bond paper copies is highly advised. Some plotter paper used for CADD-generated drawings shares the same qualities as bond paper.

Marker paper and bond paper allow for mistakes to be carefully cut out and reworked; problem areas can be replaced with new portions. In addition, objects with ragged, poorly rendered edges can be cleanly cut and placed on a new sheet of paper. This technique works particularly well with photocopies and is used a great deal in product rendering.

There are many types of nontransparent paper that are used in rendering. These papers require some method of image transfer. TRANSFER PAPER, available from art supply stores, is placed between the original image and the rendering surface; the image is then redrawn and, thus, transferred. A cheap alternative method involves drawing on the back of the original with a soft pencil. The original is then placed face up on the rendering surface, and the image is redrawn, causing it to transfer. With some types of paper, commercial photocopying machines are also effective in reproducing images.

A variety of nontransparent colored papers can work well for stylized, minimally rendered presentations. Canson™ paper and other types of pastel paper accept graphite, ink, marker, colored pencil, pastel, and small amounts of gouache. This type of colored paper works best when the color selected is used in great amounts in the final rendering. For example, an interior

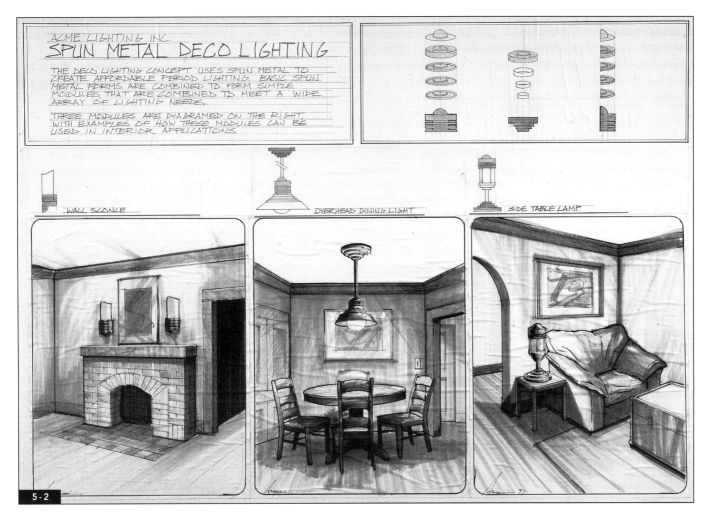

FIGURE 5-2
A rendering created on marker paper. Drawing and rendering by Michael Andreini.

with green slate used abundantly as a finish material can be rendered nicely on similarly green-colored Canson paper. With the appropriate paper color selected, only the highlights, darkest values, and shadows are rendered in, leaving the paper color to serve as the middle value of the rendering (see Figures C-38–C-41).

Many colored papers are highly textured on one side only. Colored pencils used on the highly textured side create a grainy look. Sometimes this is not desirable, so care must be taken in selecting the best side for rendering. Some types of colored paper can be photocopied, allowing for speed in the rendering process. However, tests should be run prior to rendering because copy toner does not adhere well to many types of colored paper.

Print paper used in diazo machines is also used for rendering. Because prints can be run quickly from an original, this method is highly efficient. Presentation BLUELINE, BLACKLINE, and sepia-toned prints are available at commercial blueprint shops and are easily rendered with marker and colored pencil. The choice of print paper is based on the colors used in the rendering. For example, a very warm rendering with a predominance of red, brown, or yellow is best rendered on brown- or black-toned print paper but is difficult to render on blue-toned paper. Large-format photocopying machines are increasingly replacing blueprint machines in popularity. Bond copies are highly absorbent, can offer rich renderings, and are commonly used in design offices for presentations.

Cheap brown KRAFT PAPER like the kind used for paper bags can also be used in rendering. Given the particular qualities of this paper, it should be used only in presentations where its earthy qualities are deemed appropriate. (Figures C-63a and C-63b are student presentations done on kraft paper.) When used for the right project this paper can work effectively. Kraft paper is highly absorbent and practically empties the dye out of a marker, which can be messy. Ink pen, colored pencil, and pastel work well on kraft paper to define edges and create highlights. Generally this type of paper can be used in photocopying machines.

A variety of specialized art papers and handmade papers can be used for rendering as well. These papers sometimes work in photocopying machines and are then rendered minimally for inclusion in a nontraditional presentation.

BRISTOL PAPER, BRISTOL BOARD, and ILLUSTRATION and MOUNTING BOARDS are, for the most part, highly absorbent and take marker very well. Many professional illustrators prefer illustration board for rendering. Bristol paper comes in a variety of weights, the thinnest of which work in photocopying machines. Illustration and some mounting boards are available in hot press (smoother, less tooth) and cold press (more textured, more tooth). Both hot and cold press boards absorb marker dye well. However, the texture of cold press products can create problems in detailed renderings. Colored pencils and ink pens can look unduly grainy on highly textured surfaces. Museum board is a beautiful, expensive, buttery soft board that comes in white, beige, gray, and black, is highly absorbent, and works well with colored pencil.

Drafting films are sometimes used in rendering. Generally these films are nonabsorbent and tend to pool marker dye and ink. Graphite and colored pencils are sometimes used on drafting film. Paint works well on plastic film but requires hours of practice to master.

WATERCOLOR PAPER is used in working with wet media such as watercolor paint. Watercolor paper is available in hot or cold press, in finishes that range from smooth to very rough, and in various weights. Heavier-weight paper is required in working without premounting the paper to a frame. Lighter-weight paper should be presoaked with water, stretched, and taped or stapled to a sturdy frame. Watercolor paper absorbs marker dye readily and can be worked with graphite, ink, colored pencil, acrylic and gouache paint, and just about anything else available commercially for mark making. Heavily textured watercolor papers are very difficult to use for detailed design renderings.

RENDERING MEDIA

A trip to an art supply store makes evident the huge selection of rendering media, from colored pencils to markers and paint. The available rendering media range in price and have advantages and disadvantages. This means that no one item does everything well. For this reason most renderings require the use of more than one medium, and many renderings require a little bit of everything.

Graphite pencils, lead holders, and mechanical pencils can be used in noncolored renderings. Pencils can be used for contour lines as well as texture, pattern, and material indication. Although pencil can be used to create subtle and beautiful original drawings and renderings, it does not reproduce as well as ink. This means that blueprints and photocopies of pencil renderings depicting variations of value and texture are often less clear than the originals. Deliberate individual pencil strokes reproduce far better than do those portions where the side of the pencil has been used to cover large areas. In cases where a rendering will be heavily reproduced, pencil may be a poor choice.

Ink used in refillable or disposable pens creates excellent line work that reproduces beautifully in both photocopying and diazo machines. Thus ink can be used successfully to create line drawings for reproduction and overrendering with colored media.

Unfortunately, using ink can be messy and time-consuming. Before ink dries, it can smear and ruin an original. Therefore, it is wise to take care with ink drawings and use ink only as the final step in drawings that have been fully drawn with guidelines in graphite, non-photo, or nonprint pencil. Inking triangles with raised edges are also helpful.

Refillable technical pens in varying widths are available, as are disposable ink pens. Refillable pens produce the finest quality of line, but they require cleaning and proper maintenance. Disposable ink pens are less consistent in terms of line quality, yet are preferred by some because they do not require cleaning or maintenance. Fine-point markers and various forms of felt-tip pens can be used to create excellent ink renderings. Disposable technical pens are useful in creating line drawings, whereas felt-tip ink markers work well on colored renderings to define edges.

There are three types of COLORED PENCILS: wax-based, oil-based, and water soluble. I find the wax-based the most useful in rendering. In my experience, Berol Prismacolor™ wax-based pencils are the easiest to render with. Colored pencils can work well alone, although for rich color buildup they must be layered or manipulated. See Figure C-3 for examples of colored pencil color manipulation. Without layering, colored pencils can look grainy because the pencil often works only on the top surface of the paper, allowing little valleys to stay uncolored. Underlayering warm colors with deep red pencil and cool colors with indigo blue pencil can diminish the grainy look.

A variety of solvents can be used to decrease the grainy quality of pencil renderings. One of the best is rubber-cement thinner, which is toxic and emits vapors that can cause serious health problems. Use rubber-cement thinner in an appropriate manner, and follow the warning instructions carefully. In using this solvent, a small amount is placed on a cotton swab and applied on top of colored pencil — in a well-ventilated space.

An alcohol-based colorless blender marker is an alternative pencil solvent that poses fewer health hazards. The colorless blender can be applied over the surface of the colored pencil area and worked back and forth, loosening up the pencil.

Often when used alone and overworked, wax-based pencils can produce a buildup of wax. This makes the area look shiny, overdone, and amateurish. The solution to this shiny buildup is to apply a layer of color or gray marker before any pencil touches the paper. The marker functions like a paint primer and allows the surface to accept pencil better. This works well when done with subtle shades of the object color or light values of gray. Coating paper with acrylic gesso also adds a primer coat for pencil renderings.

The appearance of colored pencil rendering varies greatly according to the type and texture of paper used, thus creating a need for experimentation. In addition, the way the pencil is held and the stroke used produce different effects. When used to cover large areas, colored pencils are best applied with angled strokes. Using strokes of roughly 45 degrees is less tiring and produces an attractive rendering. Sharp pencils have a greater surface area and cover large areas rapidly. Pencils also must be kept very sharp when used to define edges and outline objects. In creating outlines or definition, the use of a metal or plastic straightedge is required.

Pencils can be used over marker renderings to enhance color and define shape and value. A sharp white or light-colored pencil works well to clean up messy edges of marker rendering. To create subtle color variations, colored pencil pigment can be chipped away from the pencil using a blade and applied by rubbing onto the drawing surface with a tissue.

ART MARKERS, also called STUDIO MARKERS, are filled with transparent dye in an alcohol or xylene base solution. Xylene-based markers last longer and are considered by some to have better color rendition. Unfortunately, xylene-based markers produce fumes that can cause health problems. For this reason, some schools, institutions, and design firms have policies prohibiting the use of xylene-based art supplies.

Alcohol-based markers have recently improved greatly and are now widely used. Unfortunately, alcohol-based markers tend to dry up quickly and do not last long. Denatured alcohol or 91 percent alcohol solution can be used to revive markers. Marker tips can be removed and an alcohol solution placed in the marker body, or the marker can be placed (open) with the tip in an alcohol solution. Because they dry up quickly, alcohol-based markers should be tested prior to application on a final rendering; this prevents unwanted streaks and poor color matches.

There are numerous brands of high-quality art markers currently available. Many designers and illustrators have distinct personal favorites. Others tend to mix and match brands, based on availability, price, and color selection. Many of my students prefer Pantone Tria™ markers by Letraset™ because they have three tip sizes, produce good color rendition, and are refillable. Tria markers also make use of a chisel point for the marking tip, which works well in rendering nonorganic forms and in using a straightedge for marker application. Prismacolor brand markers have a true range of warm and cool grays and come with a rendering tip that is a modified chisel point, which works well for rendering organic forms and working freehand.

Markers are a popular rendering medium because they are quick to use, do not require extensive setup or cleaning time, and come in an enormous range of colors. However, markers can be difficult to master because they are difficult for beginners to control. Moreover, marker color must be manipulated to portray value, texture, and material qualities successfully.

When possible, marker strokes should be applied against a straightedge. Do not use metal or plastic edges for applying marker color because it smears and causes problems. The best straightedge for marker application is a strip of mat or illustration board.

Marker color is usually layered or touched up with additional media to properly render value and color. A single marker color can be applied in layers to create value contrast. Gray marker as well can be layered under the appropriate color to create value or enrich color. Col-

ored pencil, pastel, and small quantities of paint can be layered over marker color to create value contrast or tune up color. See Figure C-4 for examples of marker color manipulation.

Regardless of the method used, marker color must be manipulated to reveal form. The most common mistake in marker rendering is neglecting to manipulate marker color and, in so doing, creating "coloring book" images that appear amateurish. Often marker color is too intense for use in interior perspectives. One method for softening marker intensity is to use colorless blender to pick up the marker dye and then apply it to the drawing surface. To do this, apply the marker to slick paper, "pick it up" with the colorless blender, and apply it to the rendering surface (Figure C-5).

DRY PASTELS (sometimes called chalk) work well as a complement to marker and colored pencil renderings. These pastels are dry and chalky in contrast to oil pastels. Dry pastels can be used to color an area quickly and can create light washes for highlights. One useful dry pastel technique involves using the edge of a blade to shave off portions of pastel, creating a pastel pigment dust. The pastel dust can be mixed with baby powder, making it easy to work. The dry pastel and baby powder mixture is then smoothed onto the rendering surface with tissue, cotton pads, or swabs over marker, or used alone to create washes of color. Pastels are also blended into a drawing with a finger, which works far better than simply drawing with a pastel stick. Pastels are available in pencil form; however, these lack the speed of application found with stick pastels.

Many of those involved in rendering enjoy the speed with which pastels can be employed. Dry pastels work well on colored paper as a primary rendering medium but are best used in less detailed renderings. Large areas of pastel can be applied neatly when worked against removable tape or sticky back as a masking agent. It is easy to erase or brush pastels from a drawing surface. This makes pastels a far more forgiving medium than markers. Finished pastel drawings require the application of fixative spray to keep them in place. This can cause problems in renderings done with markers because fixative can remove marker dye. However, special marker fixative is available.

WATERCOLORS, transparent water-based paints used by many professional illustrators and artists, can be used to create beautiful renderings. However, they are difficult and extremely time-consuming to use. A good deal of practice and experimentation is required in developing watercolor painting skills. Students interested in watercolor rendering are well advised to enroll in a watercolor painting course; information gained there can be used in rendering.

Watercolor rendering requires special tools such as brushes, high-quality paper, and mounting board. Because it is time-consuming, watercolor rendering is not often used for preliminary or schematic presentations but is instead used in final design presentations.

GOUACHE is an opaque water-based paint. When used straight from the tube, it appears opaque; when mixed with water, it can become somewhat transparent. Professional illustrators and renderers use gouache to create rich, realistic renderings. However, like watercolors, gouache painting is time-consuming and requires special skills and equipment. Because it is water-based and is often mixed with water, gouache should be applied only to heavier papers. White or light-colored gouache can be used to create highlights and glints on marker, ink, and pencil renderings. This is best done by mixing white gouache with a small amount of water and applying it to the drawing surface with a fine paintbrush. The gouache should be applied with great care in extremely small quantities only. When applied improperly, white gouache can appear unnatural and seriously distract from a rendering. It is advisable for students to keep a small tube of white gouache, as well as a very fine paintbrush, on hand for painting tiny highlights into some renderings.

An AIRBRUSH is a system that actually propels paint or dye onto a drawing surface. In standard airbrush systems a compressor, hose, and spray gun combine to propel the pigment. Airbrushes produce dazzling, sophisticated images with an amazing range of hue and value. Standard airbrush systems are expensive and require lots of practice. A great deal of setup and cleanup time is required for airbrush use.

There are airbrush attachments that can be purchased for use with markers. These are less costly and require less preparation time than traditional airbrushes. Marker airbrush attachments require plenty of practice and generally involve masking off large areas of a drawing. I have found them to produce inconsistent results.

Many renderings combine various forms of media. It is common to see renderings created with marker, colored pencil, a bit of pastel, ink, and tiny areas of paint. The combining of media limits weaknesses and takes advantage of strengths. Some designers create renderings that are collages of a variety of materials and media and come from a range of sources (see Figure C-8). Some collages make use of computer-generated images combined with hand-drawn images.

Other successful collages are hand rendered, with the exception of photographs of human figures and entourage elements. For the most part these collages create nontraditional renderings that may not be appropriate for all projects. With the audience and project carefully considered, nontraditional collage-type renderings can successfully communicate conceptual as well as spatial issues.

RENDERING ORTHOGRAPHIC PROJECTION DRAWINGS

Rendering orthographic projections helps to reveal the material qualities of the design and indicate relative depth. Because orthographic views are by nature flattened views, they often require rendering as a means of graphic enhancement. With the appropriate enhancement, orthographic views can be used successfully in design presentations. This is fortunate, because orthographic views are created on most projects and are therefore readily available for use in design presentations. For this reason, rendered orthographic views are commonly used for presentations made throughout the design process. Orthographic projections are faster and easier to render than perspective drawings.

The best way to begin a rendered plan, section, or elevation is to create a clean original drawing. For the final rendering to have clarity, complex dimensions and confusing notes should be omitted. Items such as ceramic tile and certain simple textures may exist on the original drawing or can be drawn in as part of the rendering process.

The key to rendering is to consider light, and this is most easily accomplished in orthographic projections by adding shadows. If time allows, additional value contrast, materials, and color rendition can be included in the rendering. Including shadows helps to reveal height and can provide the contrast necessary to enhance the drawing. There are a number of methods for determining shadow location and

length; most of these are overcomplicated. Quite often, shadows can be simplified and estimated with few ill effects.

SIMPLIFIED SHADOWS IN PLAN DRAWINGS

There are two simple systems for estimating shadows in plan drawings. One system employs a consistent shadow orientation for the entire plan. Typically this simplified system employs a 45-degree diagonal direction for the light source. Each element and object in the entire plan receives a shadow cast by the same 45-degree light source. Shadows are drawn adjacent to each form in plan at a 45-degree angle, using a standard 45-degree triangle. The length of each shadow is estimated based on the relative height of each form. This method is simple and creates an easy-to-read plan (Figure 5-3).

Another shadow estimation system involves creating shadows that are cast by the variety of light sources found in the environment. The locations of windows, skylights, and electric light sources are used to cast 45-de-

FIGURE 5-3
A floor plan with simplified shadows, all cast at a consistent 45 degrees.

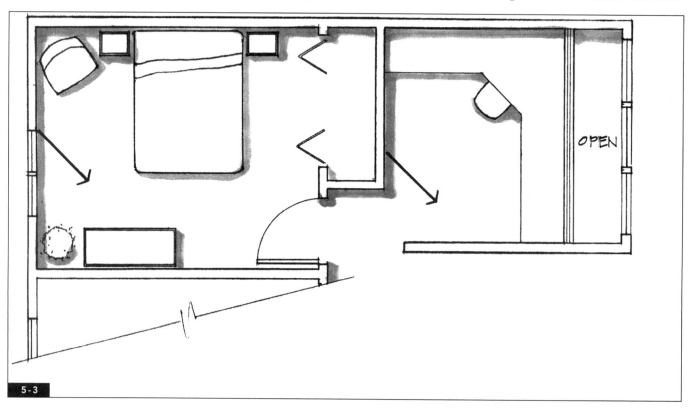

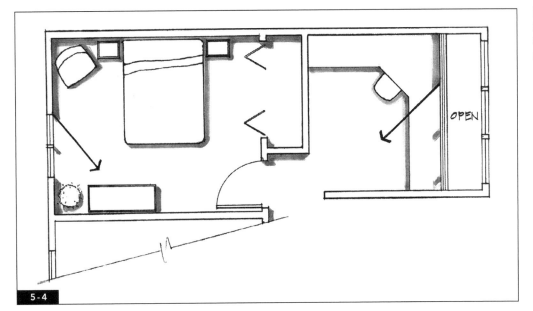

gree shadows. This system creates shadows that vary from room to room, relative to the natural and electric light sources. Shadows are cast at 45-degree angles (using a 45-degree triangle), based on the location of the light source. Shadow length is estimated relative to height. This variable shadow system creates dramatic effects that help to indicate window locations (Figure 5-4). However, plans employing this system require more time, and complex plans can be visually confusing.

SIMPLIFIED SHADOWS IN ELEVATION AND SECTION DRAWINGS

Shadows enhance elevations and sections. In these drawings they can be used to indicate the relative depths and the forms of design elements. A simple technique is for shadows to be drawn in section and elevation as cast from top right to bottom left, following a 45-degree diagonal, allowing for the use of a standard 45-degree triangle.

In elevation, shadows are cast at 45 degrees with lengths determined by the relative depth of the object casting the shadow (Figure 5-5). Shadows drawn in elevation enhance a drawing but should generally be kept minimal in terms of length for purposes of graphic clarity. Where a dramatic rendering is required,

shadows can be drawn with great lengths to create interest. It is important to note that exterior elevations, unlike interiors, are often drawn with dramatic shadows because they are outdoors and receive large quantities of natural light.

Section drawings have shadows cast by cut elements such as the roof, floors, and walls. Generally the length of these shadows is varied, based on the distance from the cutline to the plane receiving the shadow.

FIGURE 5-5
An interior elevation with simplified shadows, cast at 45-degree angles.

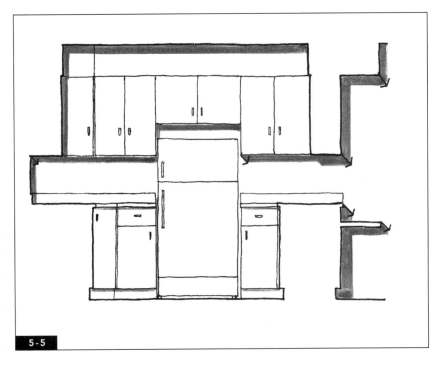

TEXTURE, PATTERN, AND MATERIAL QUALITIES

It is often useful to render the material properties of design elements in orthographic projection drawings. This is done by delineating the size and location, texture and finish of both building elements and furnishings. Rendering these elements in plan and elevation drawings is easier and less time-consuming than rendering in perspectives and paraline drawings. For this reason, it is not unusual to see professional design presentations that consist of rendered plans and elevations and nonrendered perspective drawings. When such elements are drawn successfully, many clients can distinguish material qualities quite well in rendered orthographic projections.

Rendering materials and finishes can be done quite simply, for example, with minimal line work and stippling used to indicate wood and ceramic tile. When necessary, great detail can be added to plans and elevations. There are some fairly standard conventions for rendering common finish materials in orthographic projection. See Figure 5-6 for examples of orthographic finish materials.

Regardless of the level of detail required for a given project, materials must be rendered in

FIGURE 5-6
Examples of rendered finish materials for use in orthographic projections. Note: These are not the standard symbols for use in construction documents.

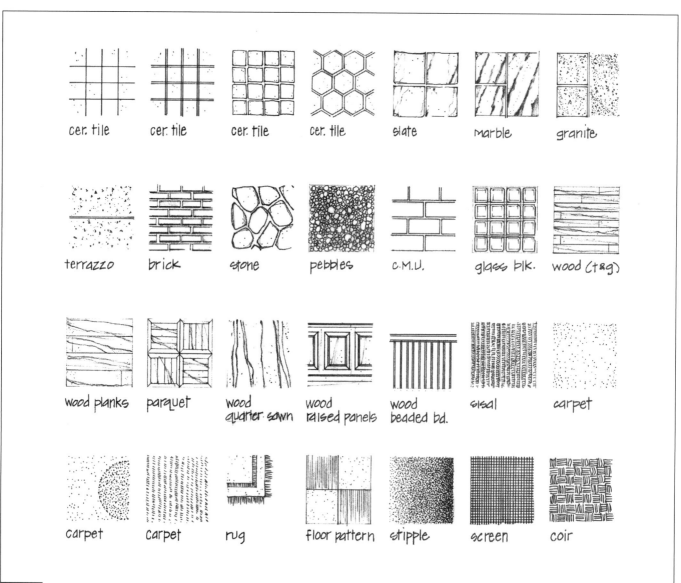

cer. tile   cer. tile   cer. tile   cer. tile   slate   Marble   granite

terrazzo   brick   stone   pebbles   C.M.U.   glass blk.   wood (t&g)

wood planks   parquet   wood quarter sawn   wood raised panels   wood beaded bd.   sisal   carpet

carpet   carpet   rug   floor pattern   stipple   screen   coir

5-6

scale and with some indication of texture or surface finish. For example, the most minimally rendered plan should show properly scaled tile locations, wood floors in scale with a slight graining pattern, and minimal stippling for carpet locations. The indication of surface finishes in proper scale allows the plan to indicate accurately the finish material sizes and locations.

When in doubt about the rendering of a particular material, it is best to carefully examine the actual material and render an abstraction of what is visible. For example, no convention exists for rendering a speckled rubber floor tile. This particular tile can be rendered

only through examination of its visual qualities. Are the speckles large or small? Are the speckles in a contrasting color? Are they random or in a particular pattern?

Some designers prefer spare, minimally rendered orthographic projections, whereas others prefer a detailed, rather busy style of rendering. This is certainly a matter of taste or personal style. Regardless of personal style, however, renderings of orthographic projections must be drawn in scale and should accurately reflect proportion and true material qualities. Figures 5-7, 5-8, and 5-9 are orthographic projections rendered with line work, stippling, and shadows.

FIGURE 5-7
Floor plan rendered using lines, stipples, and shadows (tone).

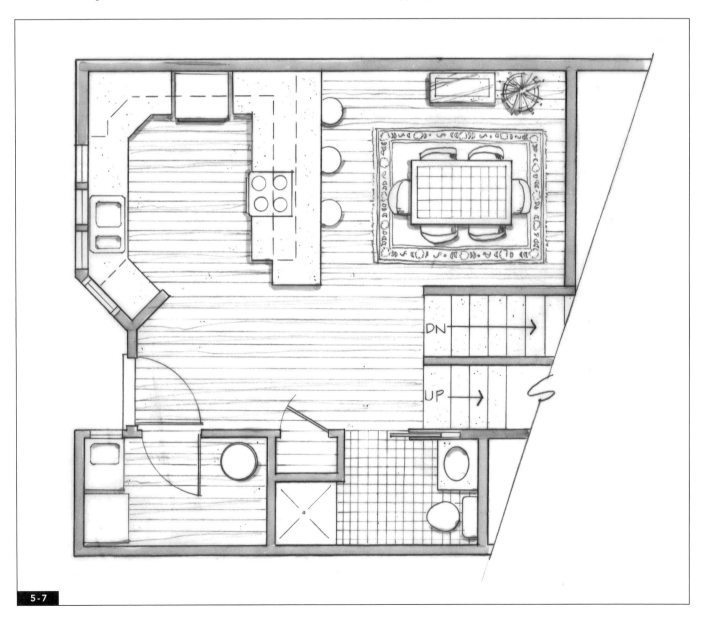

5-7

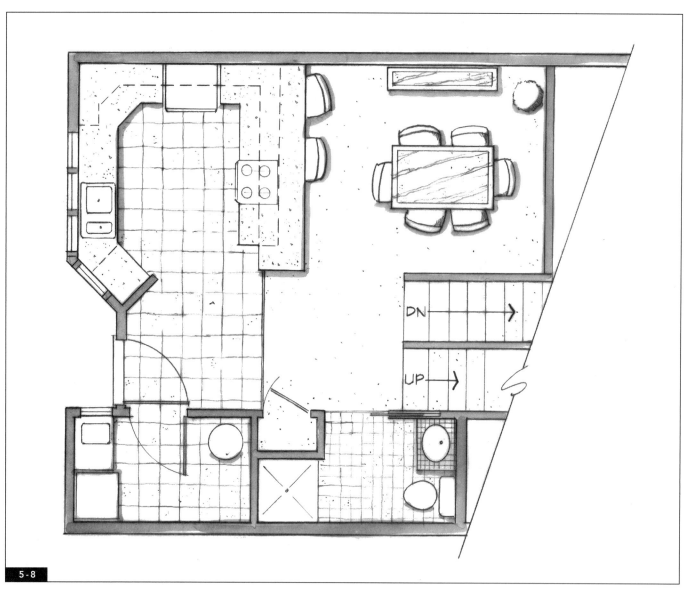

FIGURE 5-8
Floor plan rendered using lines, stipples, and shadows (tone).

FIGURE 5-9
Interior elevation rendered with disposable ink pens and marker.

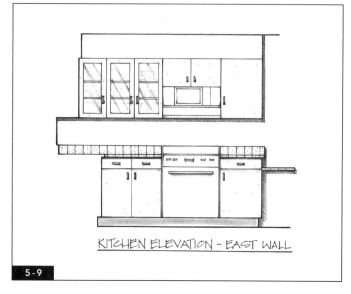

KITCHEN ELEVATION - EAST WALL

Generally, accurate visual assessment of materials is a key to successful rendering. In some cases, certain materials simply cannot be rendered in the time allowed, so a legend system can be used to delineate material locations.

COLOR-RENDERING PLANS, SECTIONS, AND ELEVATIONS

Prior to beginning any color rendering, a designer should consider the amount of time available and the nature of the project. Project phase, type of project, and the presentation audience are important factors in the selection of a color rendering style. All factors must be considered and the most appropriate media chosen. Color rendering requires a working knowledge of color theory; some basic color information can be found in Appendix 3.

Color rendering can greatly enhance plan, elevation, and section drawings. The quickest method calls for creating a photocopy or print of an original line drawing and rendering on the copy with pencil, marker, pastel, or a combination of these media (see Figures C-9a–C-23). Another quick method involves the use of white or colored tracing paper laid over drawings and washed with colored pencil, ink, or washes of marker.

In working on bond copies and print paper, shadows can be rendered into the print with gray markers before the application of any colored marker or pencils. Areas that are to appear much darker in value should also be laid in gray marker prior to the application of color media. With shadows and darker values applied, marker color, pencil color, or pastels may then be used to create the desired hue. Because rendering on bond and print papers is quick and relatively easy, they are often used for design presentations, such as those made in the schematic design phase of a project. Figures C-9a through C-12b show the steps in rendering bond paper copies of plans and elevations.

Some varieties of colored paper can be photocopied and rendered. The color of paper selected will be predominant in the final rendering, and this should be considered. For example, selecting a paper color that is the middle value of a predominant color in the design allows one to render only shadows, dark values, and highlights into those areas (see Figures C-40 and C-41).

In some cases, when little time is available, orthographic drawings can be spot rendered; this means that only a small portion (usually circular) of the drawing needs to be rendered accurately to indicate the materials used throughout the project (Figure C-13a). This technique is effective when the spot that is rendered clearly depicts the range of materials used in the project.

Another time-saving method involves using the correct color in a particular area and defining elements accurately in part of that area. For example, a large tile area can be indicated by applying the correct marker to the entire tiled portion, with only a limited number of tiles outlined in pencil, ink, or marker to show the tile size and shape (Figure C-13b). This allows the rendering to communicate material locations with a limited amount of detail work. This method must be accompanied by clear verbal communication to allow clients to understand material locations.

TECHNIQUES AND TIPS

All rendered orthographic projections require shadows. Shadows should be considered prior to rendering, and a shadow plan should be created with each shadow located. Shadows can then be rendered in colored pencil, ink, or marker.

Because they can remove ink and colored pencil, markers should generally be used for a base coat. This means they should be applied before the use of ink or colored pencil. However, when necessary, light markers and colorless blenders can be used to remove areas of pencil that have become too waxy.

Plans, elevations, and sections require that large areas of marker be applied in deliberate strokes with a straightedge. Large areas of carpet or wood flooring should be applied with the lightest marker color possible, applied with a straightedge.

Additional layers of marker can be applied to tune up marker color and to add nuances where required. In rendering natural materials such as wood and stone, marker color should vary slightly; this requires going over particular areas with a second application of marker.

Unsuccessful marker renderings of orthographic projections generally suffer from one or more of the following: strokes not created with a straightedge, marker color that is too intense, lack of value contrast (no highlights or dark values), or a combination of these flaws.

Colored pencil is often applied over gray or colored markers to add highlights, intensify dark areas, and enrich color. Marker color alone is often too intense for use in interior renderings and requires the addition of colored pencil to soften and subdue the color.

Unsuccessful colored pencil renderings often suffer from heavy-handed use of a single color, pencil strokes that are all over the place, unsharpened pencil points, or a combination of all three.

RENDERING PERSPECTIVE DRAWINGS

Rendering perspective and paraline drawings is often more difficult and time-consuming than rendering orthographic projections. This is due to the complex nature of perspective drawing. Light, shade, and shadow must be rendered in perspective drawings. Moreover, the surfaces of objects recede toward vanishing points, creating complexity in rendering colors and materials. However, rendering adds richness, interest, and reality to perspective drawings, allowing for successful visual communication.

Rendered perspectives can help the proposed design to become real to a client and are thus excellent sales and communications tools. For this reason rendered perspectives are often used in formal final design presentations. There are many perspective rendering techniques, varying from those that can be accomplished quickly to those that require days for completion.

The time and budget constraints of a project influence the rendering method selected. When scheduling and budgets allow, professional illustrators may be hired to create highly detailed or dramatic renderings. Quickly drawn perspectives rendered with value and almost no color may be used on some projects. Sometimes minimally rendered black-and-white perspective drawings are used in tandem with rendered floor plans because they can be produced quickly. Because projects vary in terms of design fees and schedules, it is useful to be aware of a range of rendering techniques and basic perspective rendering concepts.

All rendering requires that the source of light and its influence on the environment be considered. In perspective rendering, however, light and its relationship to the object(s) rendered must be considered above all else. What is the light source or sources? How do the rendered materials react in relationship to the light source? Every stroke of the marker or pencil is actually determined by the relationship of light to the object.

Understanding the relationship of light, value, and shadow on basic forms in perspective is required for successful perspective rendering. The cube, cylinder, sphere, and cone are basic shapes that are found in combination in more complex objects. Learning to render these basic shapes in a variety of noncolor media is a useful preparation for the eventual rendering of color and materials. The basic shapes are most easily rendered with a light source above and slightly to the right or left. The light source in this position creates three distinct values — light (1), medium (2), and dark (3) — and a cast shadow (4). Figure 5-10 illustrates this light source setup in relation to a variety of simple forms.

In this light-source setup, the top surface of a cube receives the most light (value 1), followed by the side closest to the light source (value 2). The side farthest from the light source receives the least light and is darkest (value 3), and typically the cast shadow (4) is adjacent to the darkest side (see Figure 5-10).

5-10

A cylinder with this lighting setup has its top surface rendered as the lightest (value 1). Light curves around a curving surface, creating levels of value contrast that also curve around the cylinder. On a simplified nonreflective cylinder, the portion of the cylinder closest to the light is rendered with the medium value (value 2) and the portion farthest from the light source is rendered the darkest value (value 3). The shadow (4) is generally located on the surface next to the darkest portion of the cylinder (see Figure 5-10).

FIGURE 5-10
The basic shapes are most easily rendered with a light source above and slightly to the right or left. The light source in this position creates three distinct values — 1, light; 2, medium; 3, dark; and a cast shadow (4).

Cylinders are frequently drawn in a more complex manner because they often pick up reflective light, causing a dark reflection next to the medium value of the cylinder, as well as a light reflection on the dark value. This is the case when rendering highly reflective material such as metal. The portions of the cylinder farthest from the light source, which recede from the viewer, also receive medium to dark values. The location of the darkest value on a cylinder, cone, or sphere is called a CORE. Cores often have a thin reflected highlight immediately next to them.

A sphere with the described lighting setup has its top portion rendered as lightest (value 1), and as the surface curves away from the light source, values are blended in a range from medium (value 2) to dark (value 3). The shadow (4) is generally found on the surface next to the darkest portion of the sphere. Generally values are rendered into a sphere with curved strokes that follow the form of the sphere. Often a bright highlight can be found toward the top portion of the sphere in the location of the lightest value. The darkest portion, or core, of a sphere is sometimes rendered with a narrow adjacent highlight on reflective surfaces (see Figure 5-10).

A cone is rendered with the portion closest to the light source lightest (value 1), with adjacent areas of the cone rendered darker (value 2 and ranging to almost value 3); the portion of the cone farthest from the light receives the least light and is darkest (value 3). A shadow is most often found on the surface next to the darkest value of the cone. A cone with a reflective surface is rendered with the core, or darkest portion, adjacent to a highlight indicating surface reflection (see Figure 5-10).

It is essential to be able to render these basic forms with a minimum of three values plus a shadow. Complex, detailed rendering requires more value contrast to illustrate more complex lighting situations. However, creating a minimum of three values plus a shadow often allows a rendering to be visually successful.

RENDERING SHADOWS IN PERSPECTIVE DRAWINGS

In quick sketch renderings fewer values than the three discussed can be used in combination with rendered shadows. When time is scarce, a drawing can be slightly rendered by the inclusion of shadows only. There are a variety of methods of shadow construction, most of which are rather confusing and overtechnical. The important

FIGURE 5-11
Quick reference: simple parallel shadow construction. Construct shadows by selecting an angle formed by the light source and using this angle consistently to create triangles at appropriate corners of the object. The bases of the triangles are then connected to one another to form the shadow.

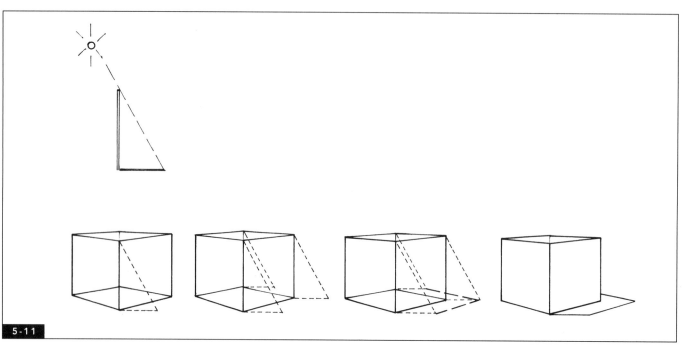

5-11

things to remember about shadows in perspective renderings are that shadows are absolutely necessary, especially on floor surfaces; shadows should be handled in a consistent fashion throughout the rendering; and shadows need not be absolutely technically accurate to work well. Although shadows are necessary, they can be simplified and minimized for ease of rendering.

The easiest method of shadow construction employs sets of parallel lines that are cast as the bases of triangles. Shadows are constructed by selecting an angle formed by the light source and using this angle consistently to create a triangle from each corner of the object. The bases of the triangles are then connected

to each other to form the shadow (Figure 5-11).

More dramatic shadows can be created by the use of a shadow vanishing point. This method requires that the light source be located somewhere above the horizon line. A shadow vanishing point is then plotted directly below the light source, on the horizon line. Lines are drawn from the light source through the top corners of the object. Lines are then drawn from the shadow vanishing point through the bottom corners of the object. These two sets of lines form the shadow location. The lines determining the length of the shadow are drawn by connecting the two sets of lines as shown in Figure 5-12.

FIGURE 5-12
Quick reference: shadow construction with a shadow vanishing point (S.V.P.). Decide on the location of the light source (L.P.). Plot a shadow vanishing point (S.V.P.) directly below the L.P. on the horizon line. Draw lines from the L.P. through the tops of the appropriate corners. Draw lines from the S.V.P. through the bottoms of the appropriate corners of the object. The lines determining the length of the shadows are drawn by connecting the two sets of lines (in this case the two sets of dashed lines where the tic marks are).

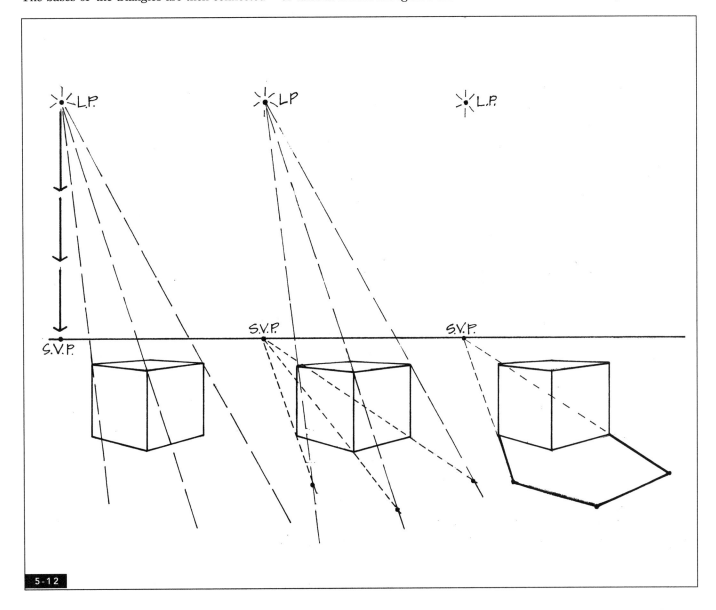

5-12

RENDERING PERSPECTIVE DRAWINGS WITHOUT COLOR

Most current reference books on rendering focus a great deal on colored perspective drawings. It is useful, however, to learn to render without color, because such renderings are quick and help one to develop an understanding of value.

In noncolored renderings the type of marks made must be appropriate to the surfaces being rendered and the rendering style. For example, carpet is best rendered with stipples or tiny irregular strokes, whereas polished metal is best rendered with gray markers or ink washes. Messy scribbles and hatch marks look best on quick freehand renderings. Detailed, refined renderings require lines drawn with tools. The use of varying line weights can quickly define and enhance a drawing. This is particularly true in outlining and defining the overall form of an object.

The way the edges of an object are outlined can greatly enhance the graphic quality of a quick rendering. The edges of an object that lead toward the viewer are called LEADING EDGES. Leading edges are generally kept very light in line weight and are sometimes drawn in white pencil or gouache. The edges of an object that recede away from the viewer are sometimes called RECEDING EDGES. Receding edges can be drawn in a very bold line weight to readily define the form of an object. The use of varying line weights to delineate leading and receding edges can greatly enhance a rendering. Figures 5-13 and 5-14 illustrate the use of leading edges. Occasionally the quality of the line work employed creates a focal point in the drawing that serves to enhance the entire composition (see Figure 5-15).

The best way to ensure that value and shadow relationships are included in every rendering is to create a value study prior to beginning the actual rendering. To create a value study, take a copy of the perspective line drawing and mark the values that will be rendered in each area. Shadows and highlights should be included (Figure 5-16a).

The three values and the shadow can be created without the introduction of color by using graphite pencils, ink pens or washes, markers, pastels, gray markers, or gray or white pencils. The values can be created using lines, scribble marks, hatching and cross-hatching, stippling, and shading by using the side of a pencil on edge. Marks made in ink will allow the best reproduction (Figures 5-16b and 5-16c).

Perspective drawings rendered with gray markers can work well in design presentations when combined with material sample boards or colored orthographic renderings. In addition, creating gray marker renderings can teach design students a great deal about value and marker application. For this reason, students should practice rendering with gray markers.

Gray marker renderings require that markers be applied with accurate and deliberate strokes. In most renderings the tops of horizontal surfaces are rendered in the lightest

FIGURE 5-13
Leading and receding edges.

1. The edges of an object that lead toward the viewer are called LEADING EDGES; these edges are generally kept very light in line weight (a). The edges of an object that recede away from the viewer are called RECEDING EDGES (b); these can be drawn in a very bold line to define the form of the object.

2. As lines recede, they can become bolder (c).

3. The use of leading and receding edges can quickly enhance a drawing.

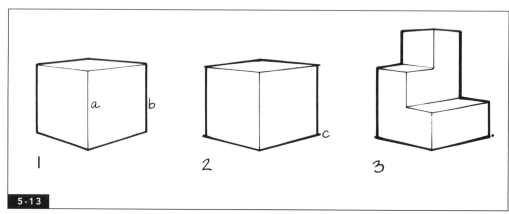

5-13

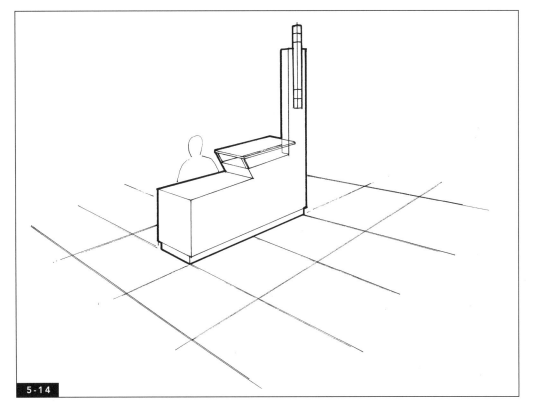

FIGURE 5-14
This clean line drawing of an information desk employs leading and receding edges. (Figure 3-19 shows the steps involved in constructing this drawing.)

5-14

FIGURE 5-15
This drawing of the proposed renovation of a Victorian residence employs leading and receding edges. In addition, the dramatic use of bold line work in the foreground archway creates an inviting composition. Note: this perspective was sketched from a photograph. The lines on the floor indicate tape that was placed at one-foot increments on the floor during photography; these locations were later used as proportional markers. Drawing by Jack Zellner.

5-15

FIGURE 5-16A
A value study is an important first step in rendering a perspective drawing.

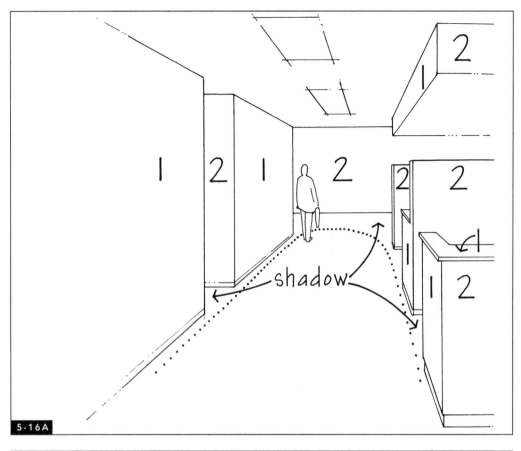

5-16A

FIGURE 5-16B
Value relationships can be rendered using lines and stipples. In this drawing the back wall was rendered in a value darker than the other walls.

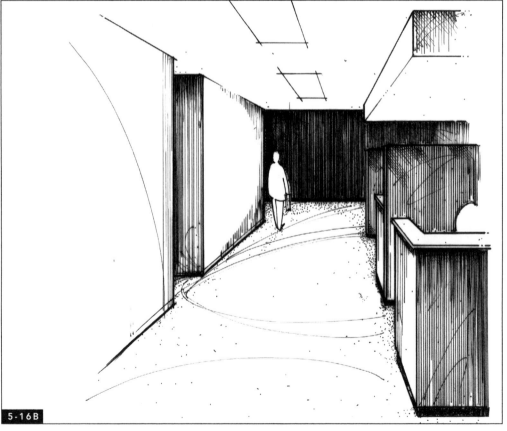

5-16B

FIGURE 5-16C
Value relationships can be rendered using scribbles.

5-16C

value, using very small amounts of marker. These lightest areas can have marker applied in circular strokes that are nondirectional. Also on these lightest surfaces, light gray marker (10 to 20 percent gray) can be applied vertically or at an angle representing light reflection. For light surfaces a dusting of gray pastel mixed with powder can be applied.

Floors and walls of interior perspectives require special consideration concerning marker application. It is easiest to render walls by applying marker strokes vertically with a straightedge (see Figure 5-17a). It is difficult to apply marker strokes horizontally or aiming toward a vanishing point because the lines will overlap and distort the perspective.

A quick look at any floor surface will reveal many shadows, values, and highlights. No floor surface can be rendered by the application of a single marker layer applied consistently — this will look amateurish. Reflective and polished floors must be rendered with a range of lights, darks, and highlights (Figure

5-17b). Carpet must be rendered with a range of values, or it will appear flat and artificial.

Walls in most environments receive varying amounts of light, so to work well in a rendering, walls must vary in value. Typically in one-point perspective the rear wall can be rendered in a medium value with the two adjacent side walls rendered very light — or not rendered at all (Figure 5-17b). See Figures 5-18 a, b, c for additional information on one-point gray interior renderings. In two-point perspective, walls should vary in value to indicate light-source locations (Figures 5-19 and 5-20). Depending on the locations of the light source(s), a single wall plane may have variations in value. For example, those walls with accent lights or sconces may be very light at the sources of light and become darker as they recede from the light sources.

Gray marker renderings are useful study tools and can be used in design presentations. Special care must be taken in these renderings to create value contrast, to include shadows,

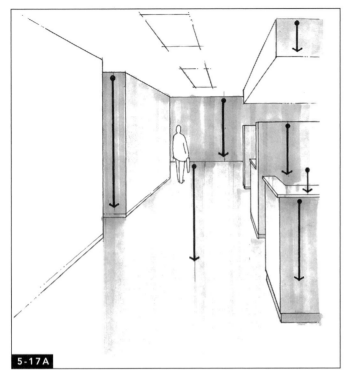

5-17A

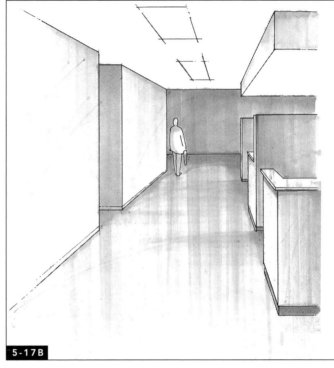

5-17B

It is useful to apply marker with a straightedge. Markers used on wall and floor surfaces are often applied with a vertical stroke for the first layer; secondary layers can be applied freehand or with tools, depending on the desired effect.

and to use a range of values on floor and wall surfaces. Markers should be carefully applied, and strokes should relate to the structure, form, or direction of an object. With these aspects considered, gray marker renderings can serve a valuable purpose.

Most noncolored renderings are created using combinations of the media mentioned here. Ink line work can be used to create value and indicate receding and leading edges, as can stipples. Gray markers used with black ink and gray and white colored pencils can clearly reveal the material qualities of form. With the introduction of minimal amounts of color, these drawings can be greatly enhanced.

COLOR-RENDERING INTERIOR PERSPECTIVES

Adding color to renderings enhances design communication. It is best to think of color rendering as existing on a continuum, progressing from lightly rendered to fully rendered. Project constraints and the materials used often dictate the level of finish a color rendering will have. As with all aspects of design presentation, the designer must consider the audience, the con-

ceptual issues, the phase of the design process, and the amount of time available. Color rendering requires a working knowledge of color theory; basic color information can be found in Appendix 1.

Colored renderings generated in the schematic phase of a project should reflect the preliminary nature of the presentation. This means that renderings created for schematic design presentations often hint at the color, finish, and design details of a project. Renderings created for a final design development presentation may be far more refined to allow for communication of details and actual material finishes (Figure C-87). Some designers prefer that renderings retain a sketchlike quality so as to reflect the conceptual nature of the project. Others use only highly detailed realistic renderings to fully communicate project design and to eliminate guesswork by the client.

Regardless of the level of finish, most renderings require that a color and value study be completed prior to the final rendering. To create a color and value study, take a copy of the perspective line drawing and mark the values, shadows, and highlights that will be rendered

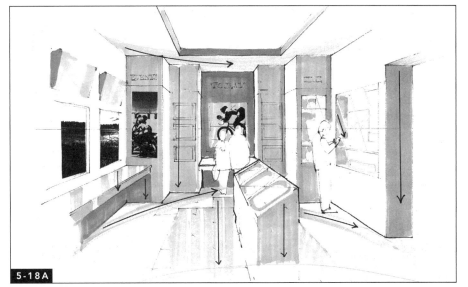

FIGURE 5-18A
The first step in the creation of this drawing is the application of cool gray markers of varying values in the directions indicated by the arrows.

FIGURE 5-18B
The finalized drawing includes additional layers of gray markers applied freehand, the application of black ink (Sharpie® pens and Staedtler Pigment Liner® in various line weights), and the use of Liquid Paper® "white-out" pen for highlights and reflections.

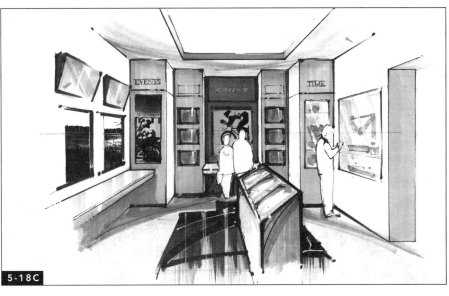

FIGURE 5-18C
A second drawing was created in a manner described in 5-18a and b; however, this version makes use of darker marker values, especially for the flooring materials.

FIGURE 5-19
This gray marker interior study was completed in 20 minutes using marker paper and gray markers. Drawing and design by Jack Zellner.

in each area. Colors must be fully tested on the study prior to beginning the final rendering (see Figures C-28a and C-28b).

Minimally colored perspectives work well when time is limited, when the actual materials have not been finalized, or when one or two hues are predominant. This method is sometimes referred to as "underrendering," which allows for the introduction of color yet only hints at actual materials. See Figures C-34, C-36, and C-37b.

Shadows are rendered in color in a variety of ways. Shadows often contain the color of their surface in a very dark value. In addition, the color of the object casting the shadow can be subtly washed into the shadow. Shadows are often created by applying warm gray (for warm colors) or cool gray (for cool colors) marker to the appropriate location prior to the application of colored marker or colored pencil. In very soft colored pencil renderings shadows can be created in pencil in the surface

color, in a complementary color, or in gray (Figure C-29 is a soft colored pencil rendering).

COLOR MOVEMENT is another key aspect of color rendering. Color movement is based on the idea that light and color bounce around in the environment. Capturing the reflection of light and the movement of color makes renderings appear rich and interesting. Objects and surfaces should never be rendered in just one color of marker; instead they should have additional color washed or dotted into them. For example, a red apple sitting on a wood table will bounce a bit of red onto the table surface, and an adjacent wall may also pick up a dot of red from the apple. Because green is the complement of red, a bit of green can be washed into the apple and dotted onto the table as well (see Figure C-87).

A simplified method of creating color movement requires that when a color is used on a surface, that same color is washed or stippled into a minimum of two additional surface

5-20

locations. Incorporating movement of color is a bit strange at first, but it is a useful rendering trick. Objects sitting close to one another actually wash each other with color, and this color movement must also be considered in rendering.

Along with color movement, renderings require COLOR VARIATION. A hue such as green should be rendered with variations of that hue, not with one layer of forest green marker. Of course, creating value contrast does to some extent create value variation. However, hues should be varied to communicate the actual inherent variation of color found in many materials. Wood floors, for example, have variety owing to graining patterns and actual variations in hue from board to board. Plants have leaves with a range of hues and values; new leaves appear bright and fresh, older leaves become yellow or brown. This type of natural variation in hue must be communicated in renderings. This means that it is not advisable to

use any single color of marker for any natural surface — it always looks unnatural.

Color variation can be used to create a focal point in a drawing as well. The focal point of a drawing may contain richly rendered colors. As the surfaces recede from the focal point, they can fade away. This technique creates a lively rendering; it also highlights important points and requires less rendering time.

Interior perspective renderings are complex and vary greatly in technique. It is important to note that there is no single way to render any particular material or setting. The way items are rendered must reflect design intent. For this reason rendering requires the use of extensive reference material. A clip file (or reference file) with hundreds of images of figures, surfaces, materials, plants, and entourage elements is fundamental. It is by examining images that one can render them in a manner appropriate to the project. Professional illustrators keep vast reference archives containing everything from

FIGURE 5-20
This gray marker rendering was created using gray markers and a small amount of white pen (for the light fixture) on marker paper. Drawing and design by Kristy Bokelman.

gardening catalogs to plumbing supply catalogs. Sometimes appropriate images can be enlarged and photocopied to reveal value and shadow relationships.

TECHNIQUES AND TIPS

The actual marker strokes used in color rendering interior perspectives should follow the form of an object or be applied with diagonal or curved strokes, indicating highlights and shadows. It is often best to apply marker strokes vertically for walls and floors.

Unsuccessful marker renderings most often suffer from inappropriate use of color and poor marker application. Marker color should not be overpowering; for the most part, it should be subdued and enriched by colored pencil and color movement. Many colored markers are far too intense to be used on large areas of renderings without blending, manipulation, or "tuning up" with pencil or pastel.

Colored pencil and ink can be used to create profile lines and define edges on marker renderings. White gouache and dry pastels can tone down marker color and create highlights and glints. These are applied over the desired layers of marker.

Highly detailed colored perspectives are not used in every design project, but they are used when the project and client can benefit from them. Highly detailed color renderings are often created by professional illustrators. However, the tools and techniques used by illustrators and designers can also be employed by students in the creation of in-process design renderings. These renderings can be used throughout the design process as communication tools. Figures C-24a–C-26b are perspective renderings with step-by-step instructions. Figures C-27 and C-31–C-37b present a range of perspective renderings created by students and professionals.

As with all presentation methods, rendering and color rendering can be used to explore and communicate. Increasingly computers are used in rendering to create two-dimensional images and multimedia presentations. A range of rendering and illustration software is employed in the creation of digital images. The most realistic computer-generated renderings employ multiple software applications, allowing for sophisticated color, material, and lighting rendition. Figures C-42a–C-49 are various examples of computer-generated images.

REFERENCES

Doyle, Michael. *Color Drawing,* 2nd ed. New York: John Wiley & Sons, 1999.

Drpic, Ivo. *Sketching and Rendering Interior Space.* New York: Whitney Library of Design, 1988.

Forseth, Kevin, and David Vaughn. *Graphics for Architecture.* New York: John Wiley & Sons, 1980.

Green, Gary. *Creating Textures in Colored Pencil.* Cincinnati, Ohio: North Light Books, 1996.

Hanks, Kurt, and Larry Belliston. *Rapid Viz.* Los Altos, Calif.: William Kaufman Inc., 1980.

Linn, Mike. *Architectural Rendering Techniques: A Color Reference.* New York: John Wiley & Sons, 1985.

McGarry, Richard, and Greg Madsen. *Marker Magic: The Rendering Problem Solver for Designers.* New York: John Wiley & Sons, 1993.

Porter, Tom. *Architectural Drawing.* New York: John Wiley & Sons, 1990.

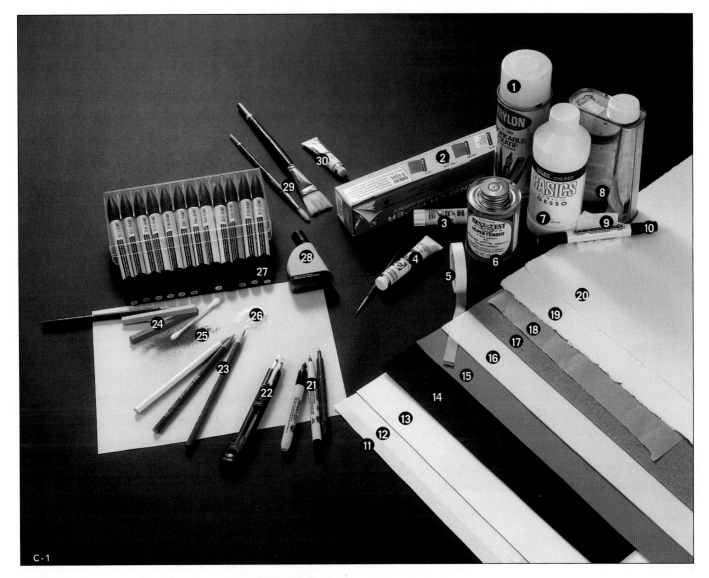

C-1

FIGURE C-1
Rendering media, materials, and tools.

1. Spray fixative
2. Transfer paper
3. Glue stick
4. Gouache and brush
5. Removable tape
6. Rubber cement
7. Acrylic gesso
8. Rubber cement thinner
9. Cotton pad (for use with thinner and pastels)
10. Marker blender
11. Vellum
12. Marker paper
13. Illustration board
14. Black mounting board
15. Canson™ paper
16. Museum board
17. Handmade paper
18. Kraft paper
19. Watercolor paper (hot press)
20. Watercolor paper (cold press)
21. Ink pens
22. Snap-off cutter
23. Colored pencils (wax-based)
24. Dry pastels
25. Pastels scraped into powder
26. Baby powder (for use with pastel powder)
27. Studio markers
28. Marker refill
29. Watercolor brushes
30. Watercolor paint

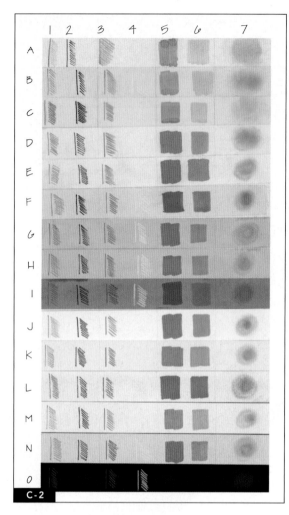

FIGURE C-2
Matrix showing examples of various
rendering surfaces and media.

1. Graphite
2. Ink
3. Wax-based colored
   pencil (color)
4. Wax-based colored
   pencil (white)
5. Studio marker (colored)
6. Studio marker (gray)
7. Dry pastel (powder)
A. Vellum
B. Trace paper
C. Drafting film
D. Marker paper
E. Bristol paper

F. Blueline diazo print
   paper
G. Canson™ paper
   (textured side)
H. Canson™ paper
   (smooth side)
I. Kraft paper
J. Bristol board
K. Museum board
L. Watercolor paper
   (cold press)
M. Illustration board
   (hot press)
N. Mat board
O. Black mounting board

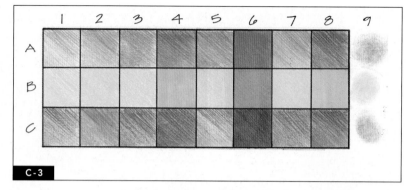

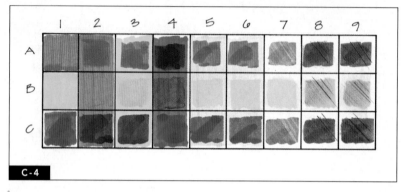

FIGURE C-3
1. Nothing applied to alter pencil
2. Marker blender applied over pencil
3. Gesso applied under pencil
4. Warm gray marker under pencil
5. Cool gray marker under pencil
6. Red marker under pencil
7. Yellow marker under pencil
8. Blue marker under pencil
A. Red-orange colored pencil (wax-based)
B. Yellow colored pencil (wax-based)
C. Blue colored pencil (wax-based)

FIGURE C-4
Examples of marker color manipulation.
1. Nothing applied to alter marker
2. Red marker applied under colored marker
3. Yellow marker under colored marker
4. Blue marker under colored marker
5. Warm gray marker under colored marker
6. Cool gray marker under colored marker
7. White colored pencil over colored marker
8. Gray colored pencil over colored marker
9. Complementary colored pencil over
   colored marker
A. Red studio marker
B. Yellow studio marker
C. Blue studio marker

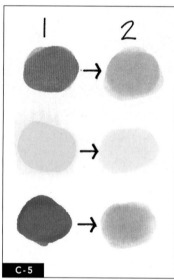

FIGURE C-5
Special blender markers can be
used to pick up an intense color
(1) and apply it to the drawing
surface (2).

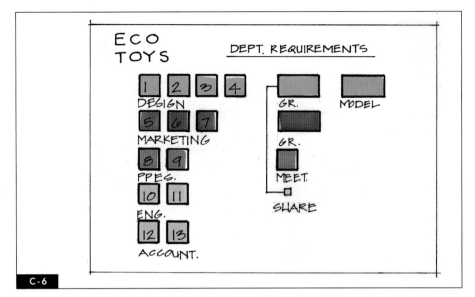

FIGURE C-6
Colored program analysis graphic (see Chapter 2). Marker and ink on marker paper.

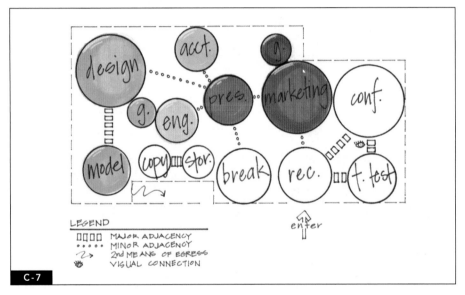

FIGURE C-7
Colored bubble diagram (see Chapter 2). Marker and ink on marker paper.

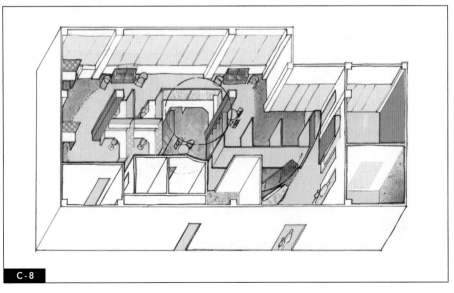

FIGURE C-8
Collage axonometric rendering. Mixed media on bond paper.

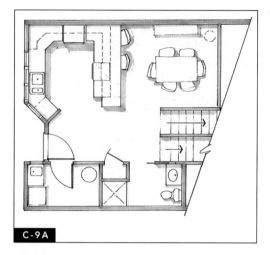

C-9A

FIGURE C-9A
The first step in rendering floor plans on bond paper is the application of gray markers to shadow locations.

FIGURE C-9B
The second step in rendering floor plans on bond paper is the application of colored markers (using a straightedge). It is best to use subdued marker color to give mere indications of color and texture.

FIGURE C-9C
The final step in rendering floor plans on bond paper is "tuning up" color by adding multiple layers of colored marker and colored pencil. When tuning up color, markers may be applied freely without the use of a straightedge. Shadows are enhanced with washes of colored pencil.

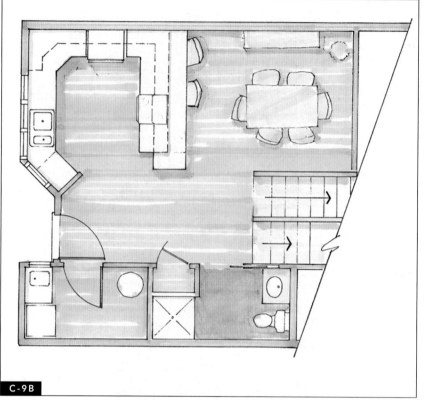

C-9B

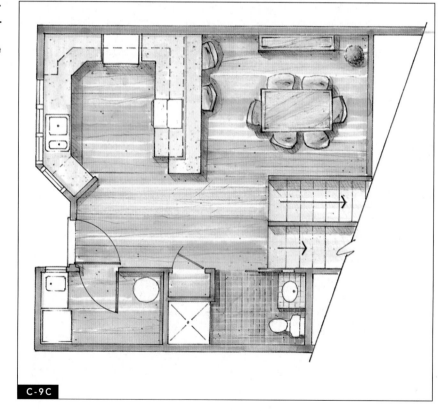

C-9C

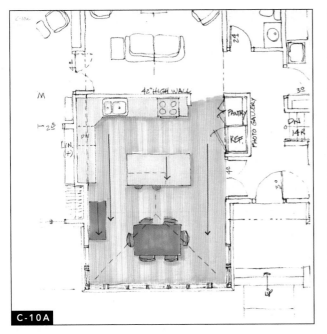

C-10A

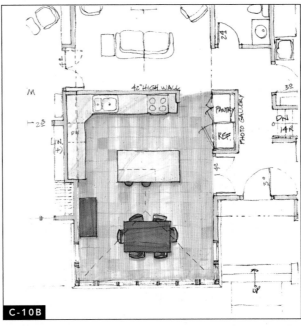

C-10B

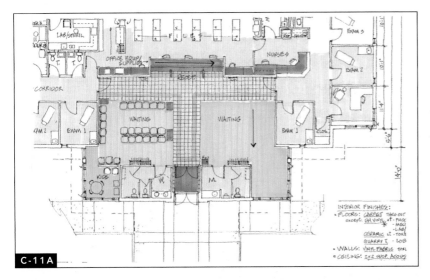

C-11A

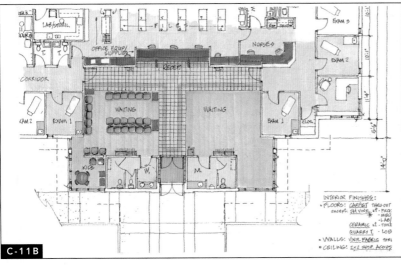

C-11B

FIGURE C-10A
The first steps in rendering this floor plan on bond paper involved laying in shadows and general material hues using a straight-edge for marker application in the direction shown. Design and line drawing by Court-ney Nystuen.

FIGURE C-10B
The final steps in rendering this floor plan on bond paper involved tuning up hues and adding variety to the limestone floor tiles so that they illustrate the variety inherent in the material.

Colored pencil was added to floor, table-top, and chairs. A rendered perspective drawing of this kitchen can be found in Figures C-25a and C-25b. Design and line drawing by Courtney Nystuen.

FIGURE C-11A
The first steps in rendering this freehand floor plan drawn on bond paper involved laying in shadows and general material hues using a straightedge for marker appli-cation in the direction shown. Note: Because the carpet shown is to be lighter than the final chair color, marker is applied right over chairs to save time and keep things tidy. Design and line drawing by Courtney Nystuen.

FIGURE C-11B
The final steps in rendering this floor plan involved tuning up hues and adding green and orange marker to the chairs as well as blue colored pencil to dark portions of green chairs.

FIGURE C-12A
Rendering a plotted AutoCAD drawing is similar to working with hand-drawn plans. The first steps in rendering here involved laying in shadows and general material hues. Because the flooring shown is to be lighter than the final chair, table, and bar colors, it was possible to apply marker right over furniture locations to save time and keep things tidy. AutoCAD drawing by Randi Lee Steinbrecher.

FIGURE C-12B
The final steps in rendering this floor plan involved applying marker color to the furnishings as well as inconsistent marker treatment of the tiles. Also, orange Prismacolor pencil was applied on top of gray marker to create the bar stool color. Note that plants are best rendered in a range of green hues.

FIGURE C-13A
Spot rendering is a time-saving technique allowing for a small descriptive area to be fully rendered (bond paper, marker, colored pencil).

FIGURE C-13B
Time is also saved by washing large areas with the appropriate colors and detailing only portions of each material (bond paper, marker, colored pencil).

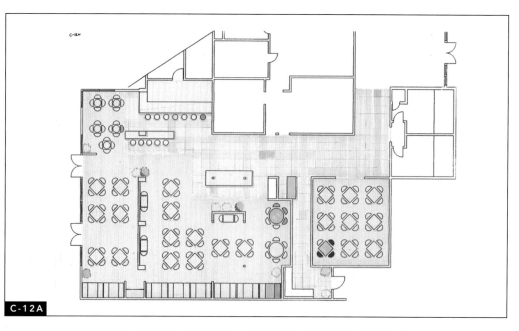

C-12A

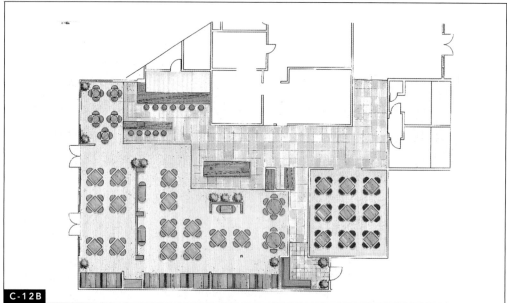

C-12B

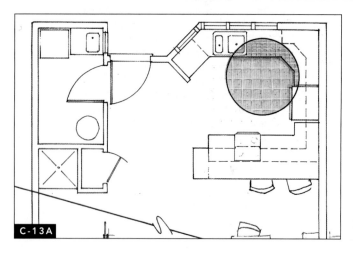

C-13A

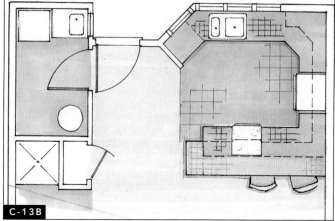

C-13B

C-14A

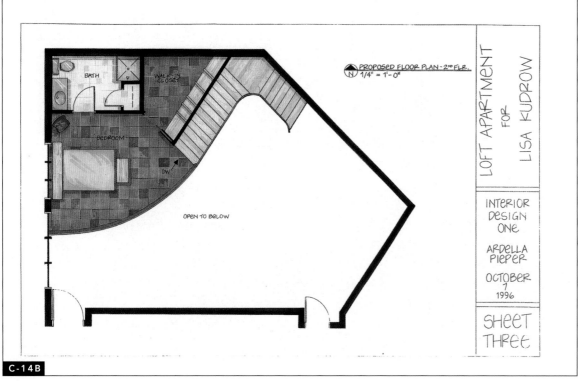

C-14B

FIGURES C-14A, C-14B
Student design-development presentation rendering on bond paper with marker and colored pencil. Design and rendering by Ardella Pieper.

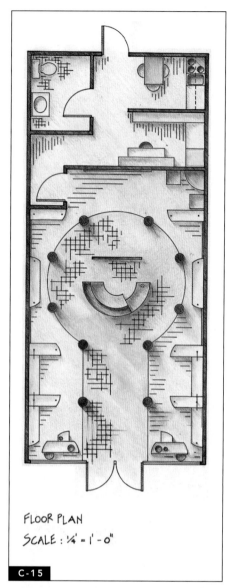

FLOOR PLAN

SCALE : ¼' = 1'-0"

C-15

FIGURE C-15
Rendered plan for use in preliminary student presentation. Colored pencil on bond paper copy. Design and rendering by Martina Lehmann.

FIGURE C-16
Rendered plan for use in preliminary presentation. Pastel, marker, and ink on printed bond paper copy. Design and rendering by Smart and Associates.

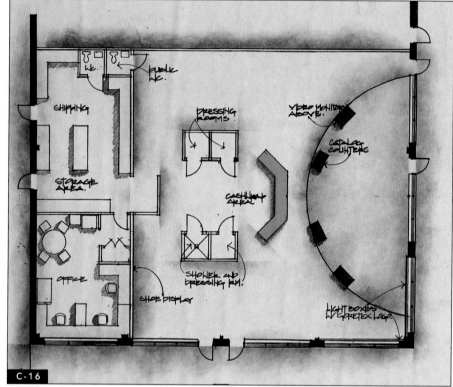

C-16

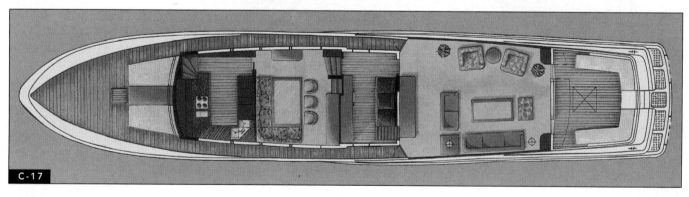

C-17

FIGURE C-17
Rendered floor plan for a yacht project. Marker and colored pencil on marker paper, mounted on Canson paper. Design and rendering by Mercedes Thaver.

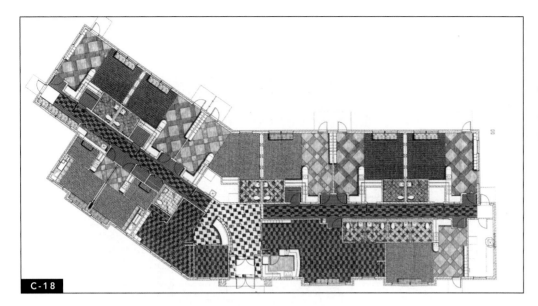

FIGURE C-18
Floor plan rendered using Photoshop software. This image was created by scanning an AutoCAD drawing and the actual materials to be used, and adjusting for scale. Photoshop was then used to render the desired materials into the appropriate locations. Design and drawing by TKDA, Engineers, Architects, Planners.

KITCHEN ELEVATION - EAST WALL

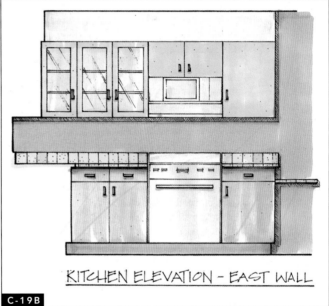

KITCHEN ELEVATION - EAST WALL

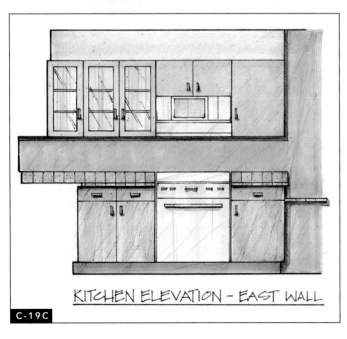

KITCHEN ELEVATION - EAST WALL

FIGURE C-19A
The first step in rendering elevations on bond paper is the application of gray markers to shadow locations.

FIGURE C-19C
The final step in rendering elevations on bond paper is tuning up color by adding multiple layers of colored marker and colored pencil. When tuning up color, markers may be applied freely without the use of a straightedge.

FIGURE C-19B
The second step in rendering elevations on bond paper is the application of colored markers (using a straightedge). It is best to use subdued marker color, to give mere indications of color and texture, and to avoid overly dark or intense marker color.

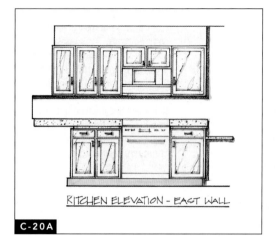

RITCHEN ELEVATION - EAST WALL

C-20A

FIGURE C-20A
The first step in rendering elevations on bond paper is the application of gray markers to shadow locations.

FIGURE C-20B
The second step in rendering elevations on bond paper is the application of colored marker (using a straightedge). It is best to use subdued marker color, to give mere indications of color and texture, and to avoid overly dark or intense marker color.

FIGURE C-20C
The final step in rendering elevations on bond paper is tuning up color by adding multiple layers of colored marker and colored pencil. When tuning up color, markers may be applied freely without the use of a straightedge. Shadows are enhanced with washes of colored pencil.

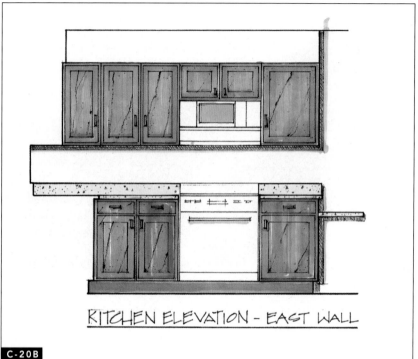

RITCHEN ELEVATION - EAST WALL

C-20B

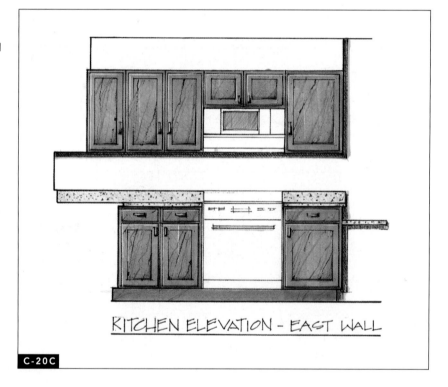

RITCHEN ELEVATION - EAST WALL

C-20C

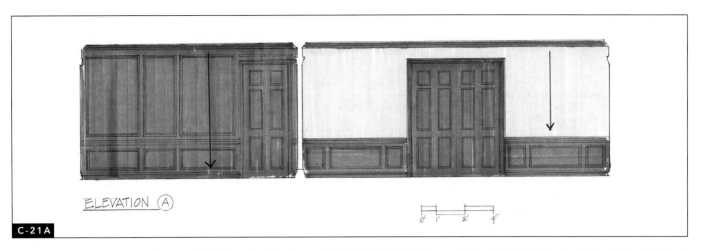

ELEVATION Ⓐ

C-21A

ELEVATION Ⓐ

C-21B

FIGURE C-21A
The first steps in rendering this elevation on bond paper involved laying in general material hues in values lighter than the final will depict. A straightedge was used for marker application in the direction shown.

FIGURE C-21B
The final steps in rendering this elevation involved tuning up hues by adding yellow marker used for the wall on top of the brown marker in the wood areas, bringing the composition together visually. Dark blue and white colored pencil were used to create highlights and shadowed areas for each wood panel. Black ink pens (Staedtler Pigment Liner) were used to punch some lines up in terms of weight.

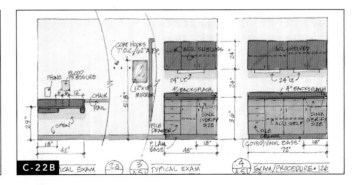

C-22A

C-22B

FIGURE C-22A
The first steps in rendering this hand-sketched elevation on bond paper involved laying in general material hues in values lighter than the final will depict. A straightedge was used for marker application in the directions shown. Note that because the wall color is lighter than the other elements, the marker used for the walls was applied everywhere as a base coat. Design by Courtney Nystuen.

FIGURE C-22B
The final steps involved using additional marker layers for the colored built-ins and trim, which was done freehand with some 45-degree strokes to indicate reflections. Dark blue Prismacolor pencil was used to outline and for shadowed areas. This finished drawing was meant for use with the plan shown in Figure C-11b.

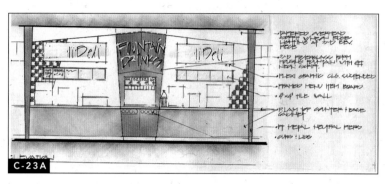

C-23A

C-24A

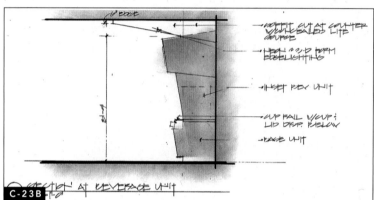

C-23B

C-24B

FIGURES C-23A, C-23B
Rendered elevation and section for use in preliminary presentation. Pastel, marker, and ink on printed bond paper copy. Design and rendering by Smart and Associates.

FIGURE C-24A
The first steps in rendering this one-point perspective on bond paper involved laying in general background material hues, in values lighter than the final will depict. A straightedge was used for marker application in the direction shown. Simple shadows were laid in with warm gray marker.

FIGURE C-24B
The next steps involved using additional markers layers for the purple wall, yellow chairs, flooring, and wood furniture. Horizontal blue marker strokes were applied in the rear hallway area.

FIGURE C-24C
The rendering was completed with the application of more gray marker in the background areas, orange Prismacolor pencil for fruit and artwork, gray marker applied as random reflections, and a good deal of black ink for outlines of all objects.

C-24C

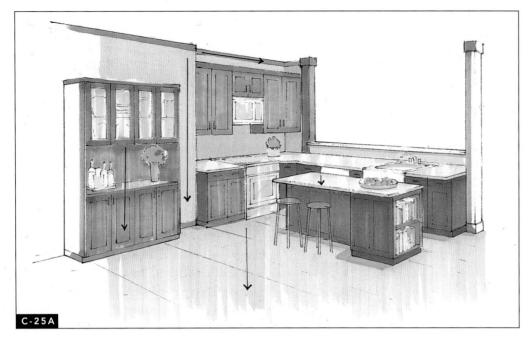

FIGURE C-25A
The first steps in rendering this two-point perspective on bond paper involved laying in general background material hues in values lighter than the final will depict. A straightedge was used for marker application in the directions shown. Large areas of white space were left in the countertop areas to indicate a highly reflective surface. Simple shadows were laid in with warm gray marker. Residence designed by Courtney Nystuen.

FIGURE C-25B
The next steps involved using additional marker layers for the wood, with contrast between light and dark surfaces given special attention. Additional blue and green marker was applied to plants, decorative elements, and books. Additional buff-colored marker was applied in various directions on the floor to depict reflections. White correction pen was used for reflections at the leading edges of countertops and faucets. Black ink and white Prisamcolor pencils were used to depict leading and receding edges. Residence designed by Courtney Nystuen.

C-26A

FIGURE C-26A

The first steps in rendering this two-point perspective on bond paper involved laying in general background material hues in values lighter than the final will depict. A straightedge was used for marker application in the directions shown. The top surfaces of the sofa and floor were left blank to prepare for the use of dry (chalk) pastels. Simple shadows were laid in with warm gray marker on the floor, while the wall surfaces received cool gray markers.

C-26B

FIGURE C-26B

The next steps involved using dry (chalk) pastels for the orange flooring and top areas of the couch (lighter blue areas) as well as the pillows. The orange pastel was applied freely and then erased as required for the floor; the same was done with the blue on the window. Blue and orange pastels were also washed into the bookcase, small vertical areas of the lamp, and the white rug. Black pens in varying widths were used for leading and receding edges.

C-27

FIGURE C-27

Demonstration drawing created using steps similar to those followed in Figures C-26a and C-26b. This drawing makes use of a good deal of white correction pen for highlights and bold black ink outlines.

C-28A

FIGURE C-28A
A color and value study on bond paper and marker, a helpful step in successful rendering.
Project: Period interior, Royal Pavilion at Brighton, England. By Leanne Larson.

FIGURE C-28B
Final rendering on bond paper with markers and colored pencil.
Project: Period interior, Royal Pavilion at Brighton, England. By Leanne Larson.

C-28B

FIGURE C-29
Rendered perspective included in student design-development presentation, created primarily with colored pencils. Design and rendering by Jessica Tebbe.

FIGURE C-30
Rendered floor plan included in student design development presentation shown in Figure C-29. Design and rendering by Jessica Tebbe.

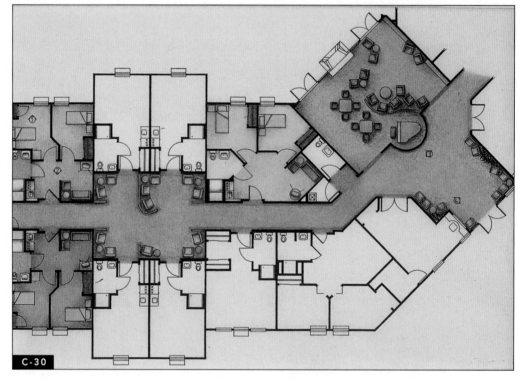

C-31

FIGURE C-31
Rendered perspective included in student schematic design presentation. Marker, colored pencil, and ink on Canson paper with bond-paper insert. Note that a small icon of the floor plan is included to indicate direction of view (cone of vision). Design and rendering by Ardella Pieper.

FIGURE C-32
Rendered perspective included in student schematic design presentation. Marker, colored pencil, and ink on marker paper with photograph under tracing paper used as an insert. Note that a small icon of the floor plan is included to indicate direction of view. Design and rendering by Anne Cleary.

FIGURE C-33
Rendered perspective and design details included in a student design-development presentation. Note that the floor plan is used as a project graphic in the title area. Marker, ink, and colored pencil on bond paper. Design and rendering by Kelly Urevig.

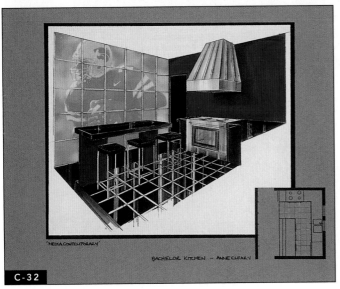

"MEDIA CONTEMPORARY"

BACHELOR KITCHEN — ANNE CLEARY

C-32

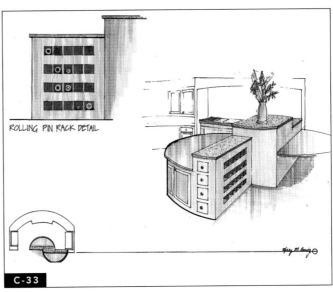

ROLLING PIN RACK DETAIL

C-33

FIGURE C-34
Drawing rendered on marker paper using markers only. The use of bold, strongly directional marker strokes enhances the drawing, which was completed in two hours (including the two-point perspective drawing). Design and rendering by Jack Zellner.

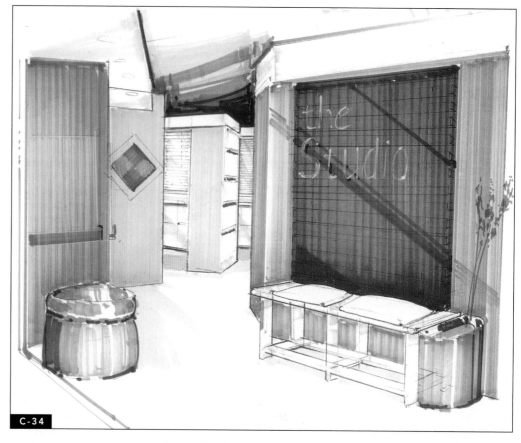

FIGURE C-35
Rendered perspective included in student design-development presentation. Marker and pencil on bond paper. Notice the vertical application of marker and portions of paper left blank to serve as highlights. Design and rendering by Susan Reische.

C-36

FIGURE C-36
This drawing is minimally rendered yet executed in a manner that makes it clear, dynamic, and highly useful as a presentation element. The entire drawing was completed in one hour on marker paper with markers and a Sharpie pen. Design and rendering by Jack Zellner.

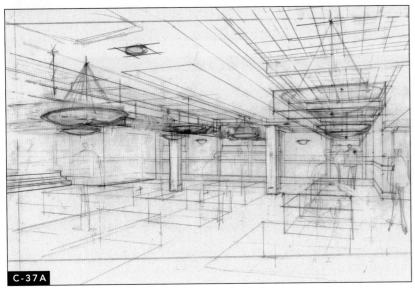

C-37A

FIGURE C-37A
Perspective rough-out using prepared grid. Notice that boxes are used as guides for drawing furnishings, fixtures, and architectural elements. Project: University Church of Hope, Minneapolis, Minnesota. Design by CNH Architects Inc. Drawing by Janet Lawson, Architectural Illustration.

C-37B

FIGURE C-37B
Final perspective rendering by a professional design illustrator. Marker on bond paper. This rendering is treated with minimal marker application, with excellent results. Project: University Church of Hope, Minneapolis, Minnesota. Design by CNH Architects, Inc. Illustration by Janet Lawson Architectural Illustration.

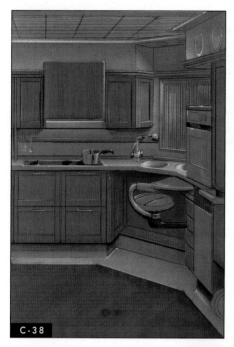

C-38

C-39

TAOS CABIN
NOOK AREA

FIGURE C-38
Drawing rendered on brown Canson paper with colored pencil and marker, applied mostly with the use of a straightedge. The color of the paper serves as the middle value range of the drawing. Marker is used for the darker values, with white pencil serving as the lighter values; a bit of green and orange have been added to perk up the drawing. Design and rendering by Jack Zellner.

FIGURE C-39
This drawing is rendered on brown Canson paper with marker used for the floor and wood areas and colored pencil for additional colored areas.

FIGURE C-40
Student design-development presentation using Canson paper, marker, and colored pencil. Design and rendering by Theresa L. Isaacson.

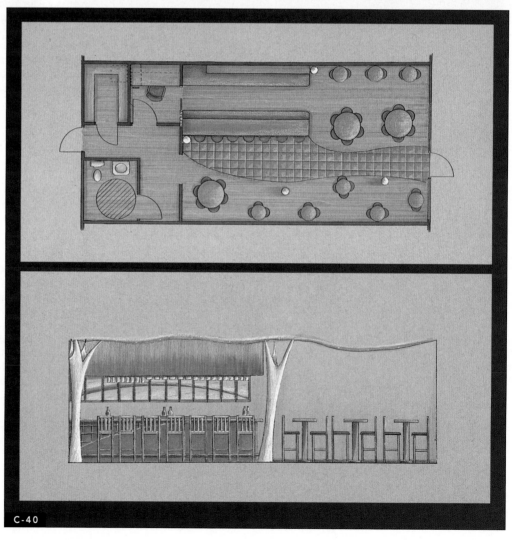

C-40

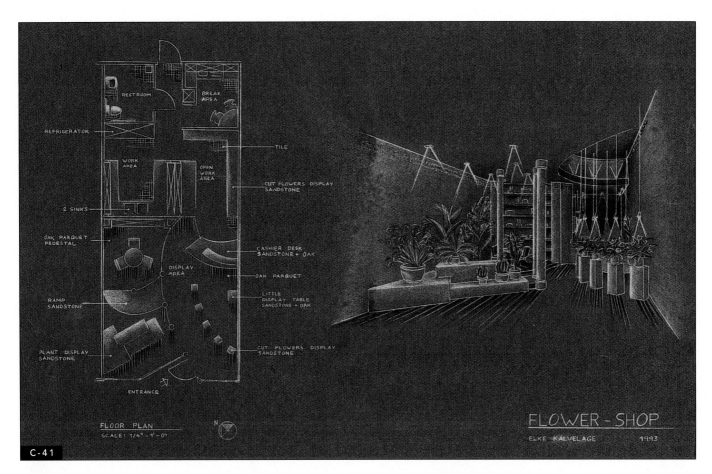

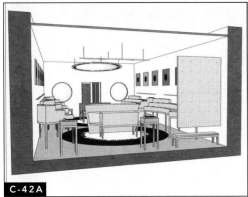

FIGURE C-41
Student design-development presentation using Canson paper, marker, and colored pencil. Design and rendering by Elke Kalvelage.

FIGURES C-42A, C-42B
AutoCAD-generated three-dimensional views serving as color studies. Design and drawings by Dirk Olbrich.

C-43

FIGURE C-43
Computer rendering of a worship space.
Software: Architrion™, Art-lantis™, Canvas™. By Aj Dumas, Minds Eye Design.

FIGURE C-44
Image taken from a professional multimedia design presentation. Project: New Headquarters Facility, Middle East. Software: AES™ (Architect/Engineer Software), 3-D Studio Max™R3, Photoshop™ 4.0, Autocad™ R12. By Ellerbe Becket, Minneapolis. Project team: Jerry Croxdale, Robert Herrick, Dave Koenen, Chris Mullen, Prasad Vaidya, Jeffrey Walden.

C-44

FIGURE C-45
Professional computer-generated image. Project: Wilsons, the Leather Experts. Software: FormZ™ (modeling) and Electric Image Animation System™ (rendering). Designed, computer modeled, and rendered by Craig Beddow, Beddow Design • Digital Architecture.

FIGURE C-46
Professional computer-generated image. Project: Wilsons, the Leather Experts. Software: FormZ (modeling) and Electric Image Animation System (rendering). Designed, computer-modeled, and rendered by Craig Beddow, Beddow Design • Digital Architecture.

FIGURE C-47
Professional computer-generated image (photo merge). Project: Wilsons, the Leather Experts. Software: FormZ (modeling and rendering), Adobe Photoshop (compositing and image manipulation).
Designed, computer modeled, and rendered by Craig Beddow, Beddow Design • Digital Architecture.

FIGURE C-48
Professional computer-generated image. Designed, computer-modeled, and rendered by Robert Lownes, Design Visualizations. Software: Autodesk VI24 and architectural Desktop 2.

FIGURE C-49
Professional computer-generated image. Designed, computer-modeled, and rendered by Robert Lownes, Design Visualizations. Software: Autodesk VI24 and Architectural Desktop 2.

FIGURES C-50A, C-50B
This model was constructed as part of a final design-development presentation for an exhibition-space project. Wood, plastic, paperboard, and metal. Design and model by Melanie Deeg. Photograph by Bill Wikrent.

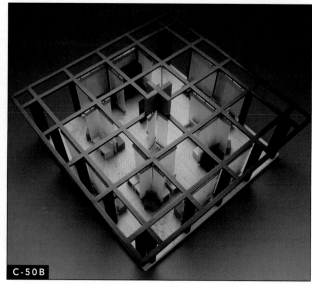

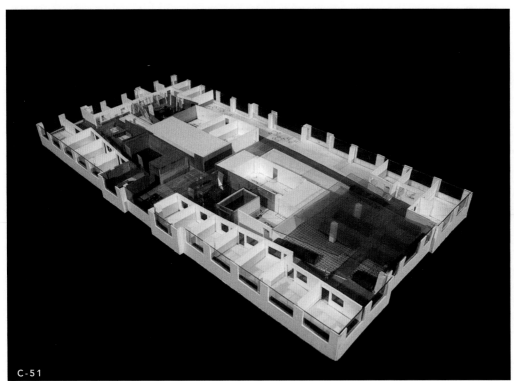

C-51

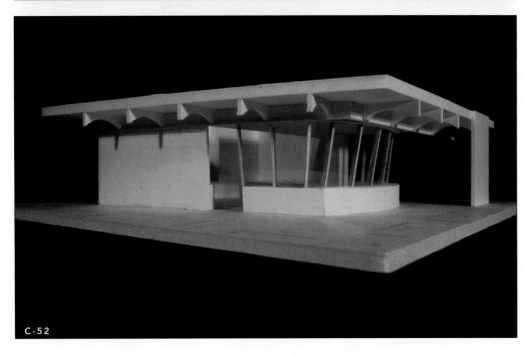

C-52

FIGURE C-51
Study model for a corporate head-
quarters. Foam board, plastic,
teak veneer, metal mesh, fabric.
Design and model by Meyer,
Scherer & Rockcastle Ltd.

FIGURE C-52
Detailed presentation model for a
corporate headquarters. Basswood. Design and model by
Meyer, Scherer & Rockcastle Ltd.

C-53A

THE PALMS
At Valley Royal, CA

C-53B

THE PALMS
At Valley Royal, CA

FIGURES C-53A, C-53B
Final presentation boards for a
hospitality project containing
drawings that are window matted
and samples that are surface
mounted, including actual plant
materials. Drawings for this presentation were mounted not with
spray adhesive but with limited
amounts of double-sided tape to
prevent warping.

FIGURE C-54
Professional presentation board
mounted on foam board with titles
on plastic label tape and hand-
drawn ink borders. Project: Laurel
Gardens of Avon, Avon, Conn. By
Arthur Shuster Inc.

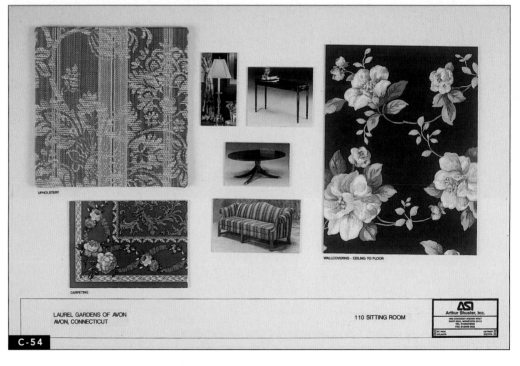

UPHOLSTERY

CARPETING

WALLCOVERING - CEILING TO FLOOR

LAUREL GARDENS OF AVON
AVON, CONNECTICUT

110 SITTING ROOM

Arthur Shuster, Inc.

C-54

FIGURE C-55
Professional presentation board mounted on foam board with titles on plastic label tape and hand-drawn ink borders. Project: Lourdes Nursing Home, Waterford, Mich. By Arthur Shuster, Inc.

FIGURE C-56
Conceptual design presentation exploring material culture. Constructed of found objects and paper mounted on wood. Photograph by Bill Wikrent.

FIGURE C-57
Conceptual design presentation for a hospitality project created using Photoshop Elements® with scanned vintage photographs, a scanned floor plan, and scanned fabric samples.

FIGURE C-58
Virtual sample board created using BlueBolt Network's online services.

FIGURE C-59
Virtual sample board created using BlueBolt Network's online services. This image incorporates the product shown in C-58.

FIGURE C-60A
Student final design presentation with samples mounted on photocopied Canson paper, rendered in marker. By Kelly Urevig.

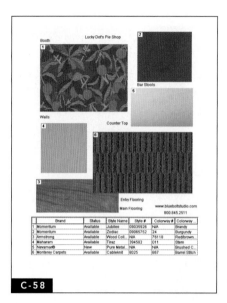

C-58

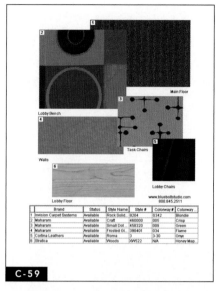

C-59

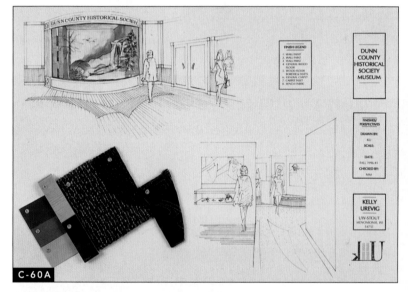

C-60A

FIGURE C-60B
Two portfolio pages making use of a grid format consistent with that of Figure C-60a. By Kelly Urevig.

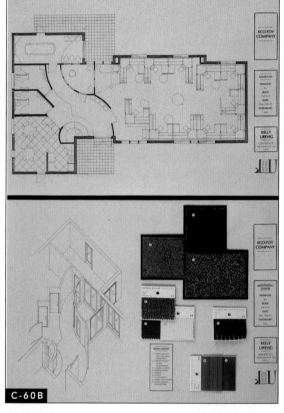

C-60B

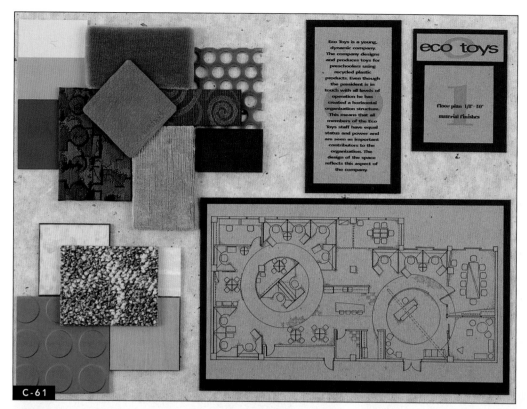

C-61

FIGURE C-61
Student final design presentation with samples mounted on hand-made paper; plan and text photocopied on kraft paper. By Ardella Pieper.

FIGURE C-62A
This presentation board has a translucent paper overlay containing the reflected ceiling plan and light-fixture information, which can be removed to reveal a floor plan underneath. By Anne Cleary. Photograph by Andrew Bottolfson.

FIGURE C-62B
This rendered floor plan is revealed when the overlay, shown in Figure C-62a is removed. By Anne Cleary. Photograph by Andrew Bottolfson.

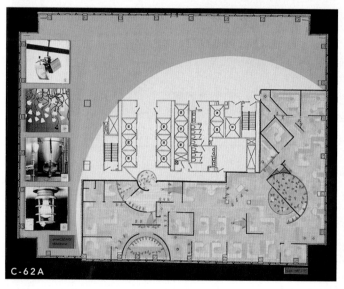

C-62A

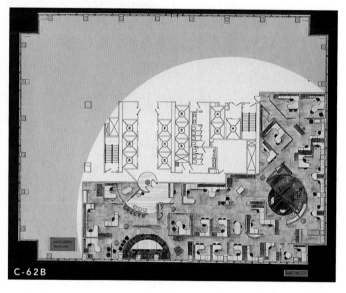

C-62B

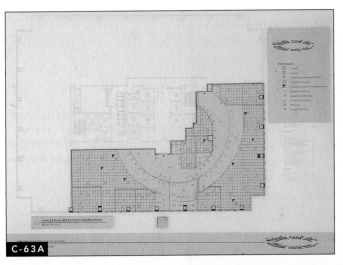

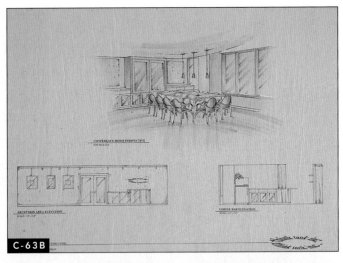

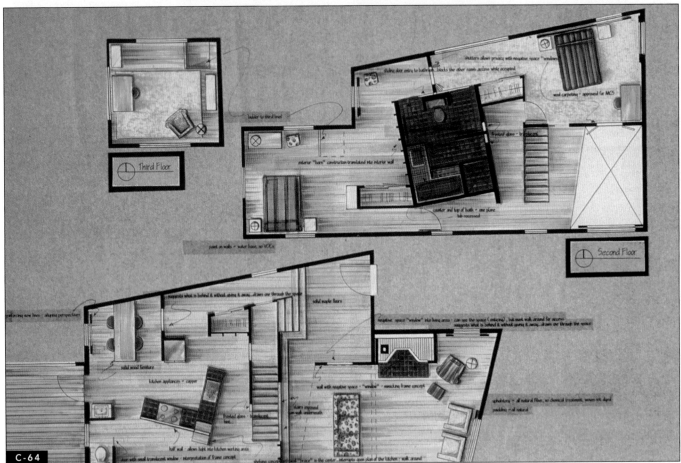

FIGURE C-63A
Presentation board with a translucent paper overlay containing a partial reflected ceiling plan (on kraft paper), which can be removed to reveal a floor plan underneath. By Daniel Effenheim. Photograph by Andrew Bottolfson.

FIGURE C-63B
Presentation board with drawings copied onto kraft paper, some of which are rendered. The board is one of many from the project shown in Figure C-63a. By Daniel Effenheim. Photograph by Andrew Bottolfson.

FIGURE C-64
These rendered floor plans were placed on exposed blueline diazo paper (blueprint paper); the board was then color copied. Kroy® tape titles were added to the board. By Anne Cleary. Photograph by Andrew Bottolfson.

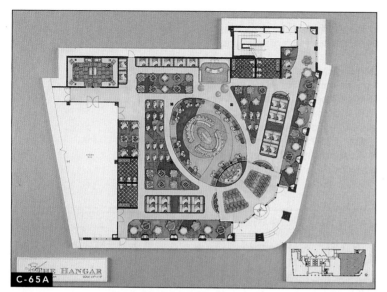

FIGURE C-65A
AutoCAD-generated floor plan with complex interior finish material relationships. Rendered with markers on bond paper mounted on silver paper board for a senior thesis project presentation. By Angela Skaare. Photograph by Andrew Bottolfson.

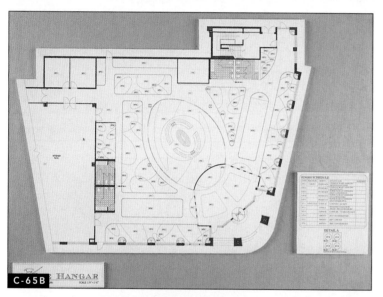

FIGURE C-65B
A finish plan and schedule to be presented together with the board shown in Figure C-65a. By Angela Skaare. Photograph by Andrew Bottolfson.

FIGURE C-65C
One in a series of material sample boards to be used together with those shown in Figures C-65a and C-65b. By Angela Skaare. Photograph by Andrew Bottolfson.

CASE STUDY 1
Designer Thom Lasley began his work on this project, a large multilevel museum facility, by creating preliminary "droodles" or design-doodles (Figures C-66a and C-66b). He sought to create order within the huge volume of space and to create an "experience of exhibits." This was accomplished by employing the concept of a game board as a design metaphor and ordering spaces as they would be in a dynamic city.

Lasley then worked with Harris Birkeland, a professional design illustrator, to clarify and communicate the design with colored preliminary conceptual sketches. Birkeland's sketches were used as a means of communicating the spirit of the design to the client early in the design process (Figures C-67–C-72).

Interior designer Jane Rademacher researched and selected a wide range of materials and finishes, which were presented on large dynamic boards (Figures C-73–C-76). The conceptual sketches, materials boards, and CADD-generated floor plans were presented together in preliminary conceptual design presentations. A preliminary CADD floor plan can be found in Appendix 6.

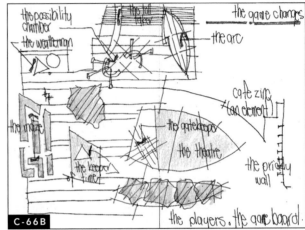

FIGURES C-66A, C-66B
Preliminary conceptual sketches ("droodles"), marker, colored pencil, and ink on watercolor paper. Drawings by Thom Lasley. Courtesy of Thom Lasley.

FIGURES C-67, C-68, C-69, C-70, C-71, C-72
Colored conceptual sketches, created in mixed media including marker paper, colored paper, markers, dry pastel, and white-out pen. Sketches by Harris Birkeland. Courtesy of Ellerbe Becket and the Science Museum of Minnesota.

C-68

C-69

C-70

C-71

C-72

FIGURES C-73, C-74, C-75, C-76 Presentation boards (Gator Board™). Boards prepared by Jane Rademacher; logos by the Ellerbe Becket graphic design staff. Photographs by Peter Lee. Courtesy of Ellerbe Becket and the Science Museum of Minnesota.

CASE STUDY 2

This project involved the design of a new corporate campus for 700 occupants. The client sought a design that was revolutionary in terms of work process and flexibility, was technologically advanced, and made use of environmentally responsible materials.

The designers sought to create elements of visual consistency that could be shared by the various buildings and at the same time create buildings with distinct identities. Project interior designer Lynn Barnhouse began the process with "inspiration boards" as a means of defining color identities for each building (Figures C-77 and C-78). Based on the inspiration boards and further study, preliminary materials boards were made and presented for each building (Figures C-79 and C-80), as were colored drawings (Figures C-81 and C-82). Later finalized materials boards were presented (Figure C-83).

Scale models were used to study interior spatial relationships as well as specialized furnishings and equipment (Figures C-84 and C-85); eventually full-scale mock-ups were created to study interior details. CADD-generated perspective views were used to explore scale, sight lines (due to the chaotic nature of elements), floor pattern, building color, and spatial relationships (Figure C-86).

C-77

C-78

FIGURES C-77–C-86
Architecture, interior design, models, renderings, drawings, and boards by Meyer, Scherer & Rockcastle LTD.

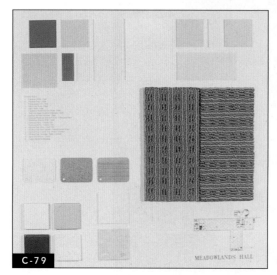

C-79

MEADOWLANDS HALL

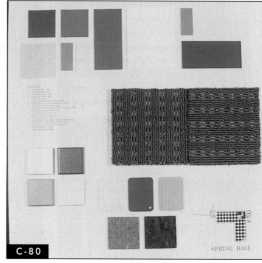

C-80

SPRING HALL

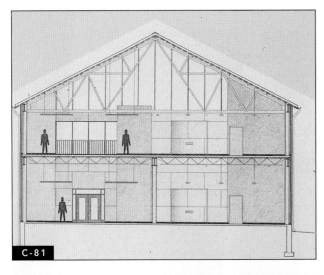

C-81

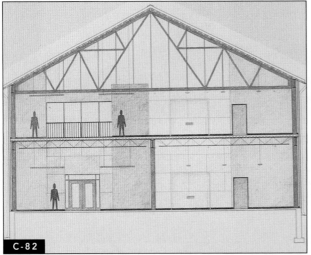

C-82

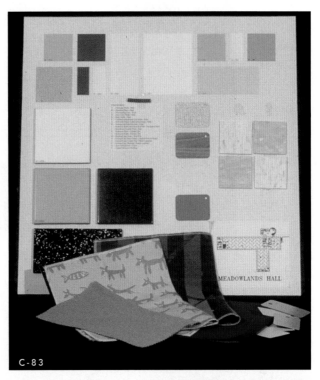

C-83

C-84

C-85

C-86

FIGURE C-87
Rendering by a professional design illustrator for a design-development presentation. Marker and colored pencil on bond paper. Notice the movement of color throughout the composition. Project: Ward House at Winchester Gardens, Maplewood, N.J. Design: Arthur Shuster Inc. Illustration: Janet Lawson Architectural Illustration.

FIGURE C-88
Screen shot of a simple Web-based portfolio created using Dreamweaver and a standard template, with a total time of less than two hours for completion.

FIGURE C-89A
Screen shot of the home page for Web-based portfolio created using Macromedia Dreamweaver. By Anne Harmer.

FIGURE C-89B
Screen shot of a single portfolio from the site shown in C-88a created using Adobe Photoshop. By Anne Harmer.

FIGURE C-90A
Screen shot of a CD-based portfolio gallery created using Portfolio by Extensis. By Randi Steinbrecher.

FIGURE C-90B
Screen shot of a portfolio page from the disk shown in Figure 90a. By Randi Steinbrecher. Sketch shown is after a Brunschwig & Fils advertisement.

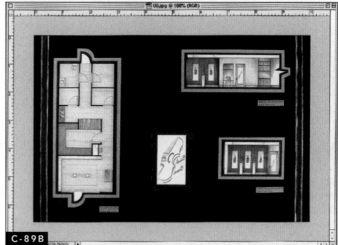

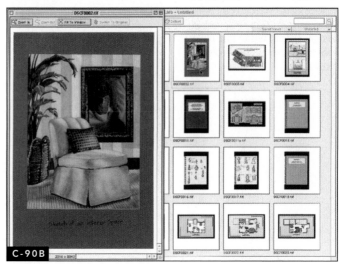

SCALE MODELS

INTRODUCTION TO SCALE MODELS

The use of three-dimensional scale models allows designers to study the volume of a given space. Unlike drawings and graphics, which exist on a two-dimensional surface, models reveal the three-dimensional qualities of form. Scale models provide designers with the opportunity to comprehensively study and review the elements of a design.

Scale models vary widely in terms of finish, refinement, and time spent in construction. Generally the level of refinement of a model reflects the stage of the design process in which it is constructed. This means that in the preliminary stages of design, models are often quickly constructed and reflect the preliminary nature of the design; these are referred to as STUDY MODELS or WORKING MODELS. As a project proceeds into design development, models often become more refined and detailed. Those models used as a means of presenting a fully developed finalized design are often very refined and painstakingly crafted and are commonly referred to as PRESENTATION MODELS or FINISHED MODELS.

Most study models present simplified or abstracted versions of finishes, materials, and colors, yet all elements must be presented in accurate scale. Presentation models also often depict design elements in a simplified manner, with all elements accurately scaled; however, they are considerably more refined than study models. On some occasions finished models are constructed for design presentations with all materials, colors, and finishes depicted accurately. These highly accurate models are most often constructed by professional model makers. Many architecture and design firms have full-time model makers on staff; other firms hire model-making consultants as required. These professionals employ a wide variety of materials, techniques, and equipment — ranging from band saws to laser cutters — in the construction of beautiful scale models.

The construction of any model must begin with deciding its purpose. If the purpose is study and eventual refinement of an in-progress design, a study model is constructed. If the model's purpose is to present a fully developed design to a client, a presentation model is constructed. Furthermore, in constructing a presentation model, thought should be given to the nature of the design presented as well as the audience. For example, if the model is meant to communicate the spatial relationships or functional aspects of a space, the model maker should simplify and abstract the finishes so that they are not the focus of the model.

Projects that are publicly funded often require presentation models to gain public approval, and projects funded by investors may also require presentation models. In these cases, the audience must be considered carefully and the model must clearly communicate the design. Models meant for a general audience may require very accurate, realistic depiction of finishes and are often made by professionals.

Models are highly useful as a means of study for students of design. Many design students are more comfortable designing spaces by drawing plans and elevations and avoid constructing scale models. The problem here is that most students have trouble visualizing the totality of a space when they limit their work to two-dimensional drawings. Without a doubt, the best way to come to know the totality of any space is to build a scale model; it is also a wonderful way for design students to improve design visualization skills.

Constructing quick study models of in-process designs allows students to "see" a space early in the design process. Study models are often constructed rapidly, using inexpensive, readily available materials. Given the way interior spaces are planned, interior study models are often constructed by attaching vertical elements directly to a drafted floor plan. A basic understanding of materials and construction techniques will allow design students to construct helpful study models.

MATERIALS AND TOOLS

PAPERBOARDS

Various types of paperboards available in art supply stores are used in scale model building. For the most part, paper products are inexpensive, lightweight, and easy to cut. Figure 6-1 illustrates a range of paperboards used in model building.

Foam board (also called foam core) is a type of paperboard consisting of polystyrene foam (or Styrofoam™) sandwiched between two sheets of paper. Foam core comes in a variety of thicknesses, often $3/16''$ or $1/8''$, and is readily available in bleached white paper with a white center. Also available are black foam core, consisting of black cover paper and a black foam center, and foam core that is primarily white with one colored top layer.

White foam board is commonly used for study models because its thickness relates well to standard scaled wall thicknesses. Most often foam board is left unpainted to serve as a neutral or abstract presentation of materials. Sometimes designers cap foam core edges with another paper such as bristol board or museum board to cover the exposed Styrofoam, which gives a more refined appearance.

Foam board is easily cut with snap-off cutters or X-acto™ knives. When cutting foam board, it is important to use very sharp blades and to cut in a minimum of three steps. The first cut is made through the top layer of paper, the second cut should go through the middle layer of Styrofoam, and the last cut must cut cleanly through the bottom paper layer (Figure 6-2).

Do not try to cut through foam board in less than these three steps; otherwise the effort will result in jagged edges. Only very sharp blades should be used, because dull ones produce poor results. When required, the paper can be peeled from away from the foam center and the foam can be cut, sanded, or scored. This allows for the creation of angles, curves, and other complex shapes (Figures 6-3, 6-4, and 6-5).

White glue works well in joining foam board. When required, straight pins are used to hold joints together while the glue dries. In complex models, angled weights and clamps may be used. Spray adhesive and double-sided tape also work with foam board. As stated, most often foam core is left unpainted, creating attractive, simple study models. If painting is desired, paint must be carefully tested on a scrap of foam core, as some paints dissolve the foam.

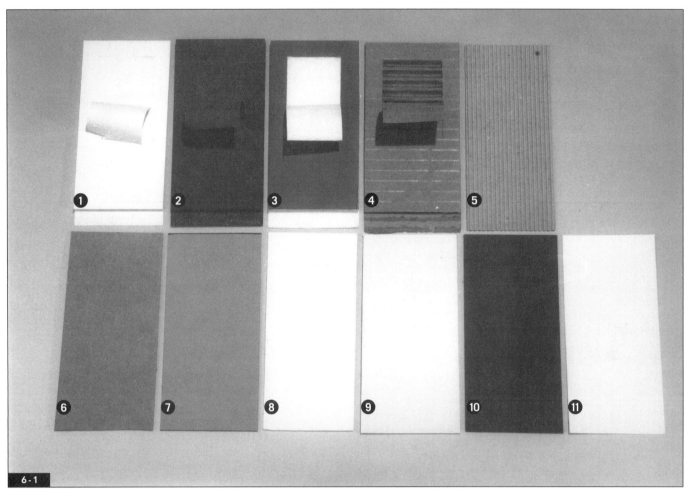

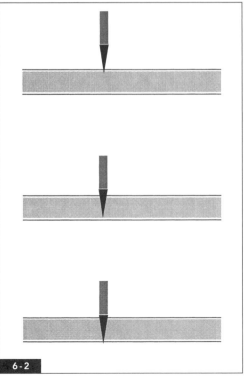

FIGURE 6-1
Various paperboards used in model making.

1. Foam board (white)
2. Foam board (black)
3. Foam board (colored)
4. Corrugated board (commonly called cardboard)
5. Ripple wrap
6. Chipboard
7. Mat board (with black core)
8. Museum board (white)
9. Illustration board
10. Mounting board (black)
11. Bristol board

Photograph by Bill Wikrent.

FIGURE 6-2
Cutting paperboard. When cutting paperboard, three separate cuts should be made. First the top paper surface is cut, then the middle surface, and finally, the bottom paper surface is cut.

Foam board is also used as a mounting surface for materials presentations, drawings, and renderings. Although it works well in this application, foam core can warp, depending on weather conditions, paper surfaces, and adhesives used.

GATOR BOARD™ (also called gator foam) is similar to foam core, in that it consists of foam sandwiched between layers of paper. This material is very sturdy and is difficult to cut. Gator Board is best cut on a band saw. If no saw is available, the material can be scored and

FIGURE 6-3
When using foam board, a 45-degree angle is cut by first peeling away a portion of the top surface that matches the thickness of the board. Then the inner material and bottom layer of paper are cut at 45 degrees. Two sheets cut this way can be joined together to form a 90-degree angle. Photograph by Bill Wikrent.

FIGURE 6-4
When using foam board, a 90-degree angle can be formed by removing a portion of the top paper surface that is twice the thickness of the foam board. Each side of the foam core is then cut away at a 45-degree angle with the backing paper left in place. The board is then folded to create a 90-degree angle with a continuous paper surface. Photograph by Bill Wikrent.

FIGURE 6-5
Create curves with paperboard by first scoring the material (leaving the backing paper intact) and then securing the board in place with glue. Photograph by Bill Wikrent.

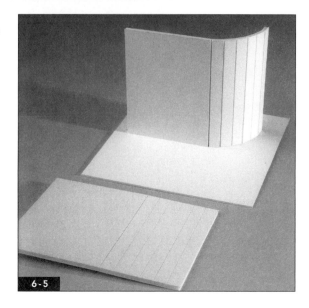

carefully snapped off along the scored edge. As with foam board, the outer layers of Gator Board can be peeled away, allowing the inner foam to be cut and sanded. White glue works well in Gator Board scale models, as do spray adhesives and double-sided tape.

Gator Board is available in bleached white as well as black; it also works well in presentation boards, especially for heavy items. Gator Board is used occasionally as a mounting surface for drawings and renderings because it does not warp as easily as foam board.

CORRUGATED BOARD (commonly called cardboard) is generally brown in color, inexpensive, and can be used in constructing study models. Corrugated board consists of heavy corrugated paper covered with outer layers of heavy brown paper. The outer layers of corrugated board may be peeled away to reveal the corrugated paper center. This corrugated center can then be used to indicate texture. Corrugated board works well in quick study models because it is widely available, inexpensive, and can be cut easily. Although it is easy to cut, this material requires the three-cut method discussed earlier in regard to foam core. White glue works well with corrugated board, as do spray adhesives and double-sided tape. FIGURE 6-6 shows a study model constructed of corrugated board and chipboard.

Another kind of paper that is currently available looks like the corrugated center portions of corrugated board; this is often referred to as RIPPLE WRAP. Ripple wrap is available in a wide range of colors and is used in the creation of presentation boards, notebook covers, and portfolio covers, as well as in model making.

CHIPBOARD looks like the outer layer of cardboard (corrugated board). It is extremely inexpensive and is used on quick study models. Chipboard cuts easily with a cutter or an X-acto blade and can be fastened with white glue, spray adhesive, or double-sided tape. Figure 6-6 shows a study model constructed of corru-

FIGURE 6-6
This study model for a workstation is constructed from corrugated board (for vertical partitions), chipboard (for the work suface), and tracing paper (for transparent sliding windows) and is held together with white glue.

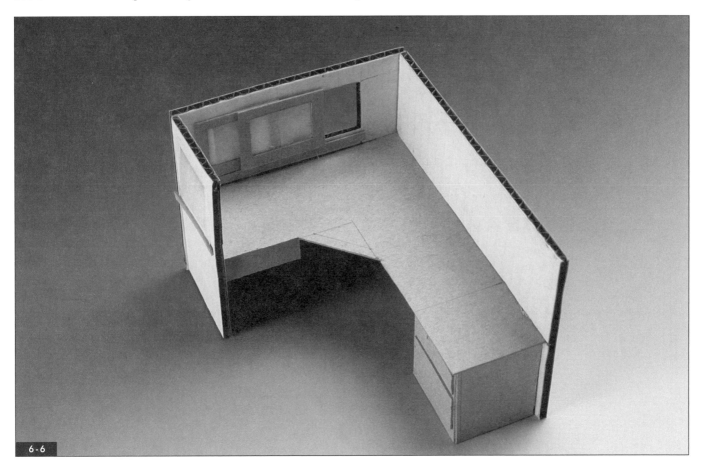

6-6

FIGURE 6-7
This conceptual study model, made of bristol board, is a vehicle for exploring various thematic issues for a particular project. Model by John Urban. Photograph by Bill Wikrent.

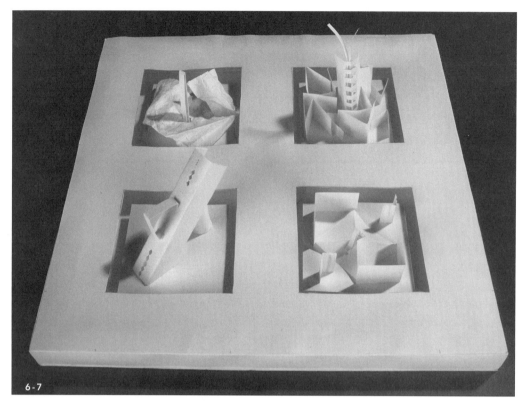

gated board and chipboard. MAT BOARD is paperboard with a colored top surface. It is available with a white or black paper center. Mat board is sometimes used to add color and details to models, and on some occasions models are constructed completely of mat board. MUSEUM BOARD generally has a high rag content and is white or off-white throughout. Museum board is used to create pristine study and presentation models because of its attractive appearance.

ILLUSTRATION BOARD most often has a white or buff-colored surface and a high rag content, and can be used for model making. Illustration board requires three cuts through the paper surfaces to produce a clean-looking cut area. Black MOUNTING BOARD is thin and easy to cut, as is BRISTOL BOARD (or bristol paper), which is often white. Figure 6-7 is a conceptual model made of bristol board.

Chipboard, mat board, museum board, black mounting board, and bristol board are easily cut, lightweight, easy to glue, and often used in model making. Because they are thinner than foam core, they work in smaller-scale models. In large-scale models these thinner paper boards are laminated (layered together using glue or double-sided tape) or used in conjunction with additional paperboard, wood, or plastic.

WOOD

Wood is used often in scale model building. Because it is more costly and time-consuming to work with, it is not used as often as paper products in quick study models. It is, however, used widely in models during the design development of a project and for final presentations. Because of its warmth and natural beauty, wood is often treated very simply and abstractly in models. It may be sanded, stained, or sealed but is rarely painted or heavily embellished. Wood is particularly useful in models where it is to be a major interior finish.

A variety of wood products useful in model building are available in hobby stores. Particular wood species offer certain advantages. Figure 6-8 illustrates wood products used in models.

FIGURE 6-8
Some examples of wood used in constructing presentation models.
1. Balsa wood (strips and blocks)
2. Cherry
3. Walnut
4. Basswood (strips, veneer, and scaled moldings)
Photograph by Bill Wikrent.

BALSA WOOD is a light and porous wood that can be cut with a blade or knife (or a saw on larger pieces) and requires no power tools for cutting. Because it is easy to carve, balsa wood is used for toy making, crafts, and scale model building. Balsa wood is readily available in blocks, strips, sheets, and veneers (very thin sheets) in a wide range of sizes. Because of its fibrous nature, this wood may appear rough even after sanding. Although balsa wood can be cut easily, it can be difficult to cut evenly because of the structure of the wood.

BASSWOOD is an attractive, smooth, light-colored hardwood that is very popular for model building. It has only slight graining patterns, giving it a neutral appearance useful in models. In addition, basswood is relatively easy to cut and work with. Unlike balsa wood, basswood can be sanded smooth if handled carefully. Basswood is sold at many hobby stores, especially those that specialize in railroad models or miniature houses. It is available in blocks, sheets, veneers, strips, dowels, cut with siding patterns, and in scaled ornamental moldings. Thin sheets and strips of basswood can be cut with a sharp X-acto blade or a utility knife, whereas thicker slabs and blocks require hand saws or power tools.

Other hardwood species such as walnut, mahogany, cherry, and teak — available in sheets, veneers, and blocks — are used in models. Because these woods have distinct patterns of graining and coloration, they are often used to accent basswood models. In constructing highly detailed models, it is helpful to use the actual wood species that is proposed for a particular design. Often hard-to-find wood veneers are available at local specialty woodworking shops.

White glue is often used in the construction of wood models. It is best applied sparingly, which provides better adhesion and a neat appearance. Because white glue requires time to dry, items should be weighted, clamped, or otherwise held in place as the glue dries. In some cases instant glue is used on wood models. Many expert model makers rely on slower versions of instant glue such as Slow Jet™ or Slo-Zap™, especially when gluing small or complex items.

PLASTICS AND FOAM

Plastics are used by professional model builders and by industrial designers for scale models, mock-ups, and working prototypes. Styrene, polystyrene, and Balsa-Foam™ are some of the most popular plastics for use in model and prototype construction. Figure 6-9 illustrates types of plastic used in model building.

STYRENE sheets, strips, rods, and I-beams are available at hobby shops in a range of sizes with a white finish. A variety of grooved and scored sheet styrene is available in patterns that resemble tiles, siding, and other finish materials. Sheet styrene is cut by scoring with a sharp blade and then snapping along the scored area. Sheet styrene is best glued with specialized plastic cement that creates a fast and strong bond that actually fuses the joint.

STYRENE FOAM insulation board is lightweight and readily available at lumberyards

FIGURE 6-9
Plastics are often used in study models and for portions of presentation models.

1. Styrene foam (cut into blocks)
2. Balsa-Foam™ (cut into cylinders)
3. Sintra™ (colored)
4. Sintra (white)
5. Styrene (strips, rods, grooved sheets, plain sheets)

Photograph by Bill Wikrent.

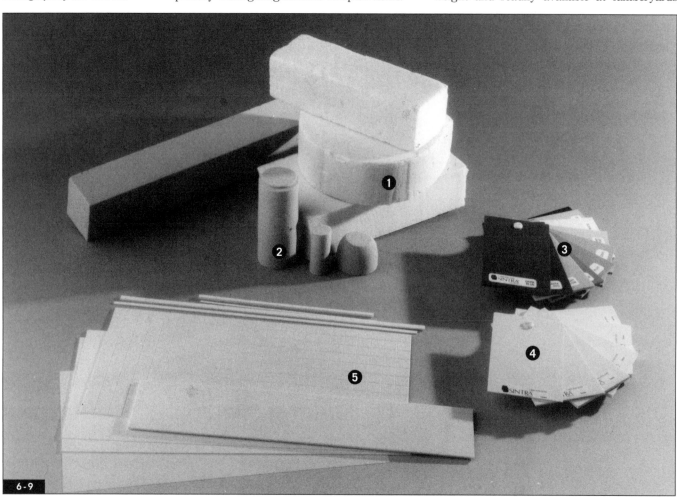

6-9

and home-improvement stores. This material is most often sold in blue, pink, and gray in a range of thicknesses. Sheets of styrene foam can be glued together (or laminated) to form the desired width and depth. The best means of cutting styrene foam is a hot wire cutter. Nonrepositionable spray adhesive works well as a glue in layering foam. Styrene foam presents a problem in terms of toxicity and does not accept paint well. It is best used unpainted in study models or as an abstraction of material form.

BALSA-FOAM is a tan-colored, nontoxic, phenolic polymer resin foam that is easier to work with than standard styrene foam. Balsa-Foam can be readily cut with simple hand tools (knife blades, cutters, and saws) and is easily glued with low-melt hot glue or spray adhesive. If required, Balsa-Foam can be painted with acrylic or enamel paints. It is available through model railroad shops and catalogs geared to industrial designers.

SINTRA™ is a polyvinyl chloride product used in point-of-purchase displays and signage construction. This material is used increasingly by model makers. Much like sheet styrene, thin sheets of Sintra are cut by scoring and breaking along the score. Sintra is available in varying thicknesses and colors and can sometimes be painted with acrylic paints over appropriate primers (this works only for models; displays require different paints). Paint may be applied by brush, airbrush, or spray can.

ADHESIVES AND TOOLS

Model making requires tremendous patience in measuring, cutting, gluing, and attaching. Certain tools and adhesive products can make the job of model construction easier. However, the most important tools of all are patience and allowing the proper amount of time. Figure 6-10 illustrates popular modeling tools and adhesives.

WHITE GLUE, such as Elmer's Glue-All™, is used a great deal in model construction. It works well on paper, foam core, Gator Board, and wood. White glue forms an excellent bond; however, it takes some time to dry. This means that the items being glued must be held in place by clamps, weights, or hands. Generally white glue should be applied in thin layers to create neat, tight joints. White glue applied in thick layers does not hold well and looks terrible.

RUBBER CEMENT is an excellent adhesive for bonding paper and light fabrics to paperboard in models or materials presentations. When using rubber cement, be sure to apply the cement lightly to both surfaces, let it dry a bit and become tacky, and then attach the two surfaces. This type of application allows for repositioning of the cement. Rubber cement is flammable and can produce toxic vapors.

INSTANT GLUES have the advantage of drying quickly and the disadvantage of drying so fast that mistakes are made. Many model builders use slow versions of instant glue, such as Slow Jet or Slo-Zap. These slower quick glues allow for objects to be set in place and repositioned. Once the items are in place, an accelerator such as Zip Kicker™ or Zap Kicker™ is sprayed on the joint, and the glue dries instantly.

The use of slow glues and accelerators is necessary in constructing detailed and refined models with complex elements. These instant glues work well on wood but not on styrene. They are highly toxic and flammable, and should be used only according to manufacturer's instructions in extremely well-ventilated work areas.

DOUBLE-SIDED TAPE (including transfer tape), masking tape, and painter's tape all work well in model construction. Double-sided tape is excellent for attaching and layering sheets of paper, foam core, and wood veneers. It works better than spray adhesive, which can cause warping of dissimilar surfaces.

TRANSFER TAPE is sold in rolls; it is sticky on both sides yet contains no sheet of plastic to hold the adhesive. It can be applied by hand or with a transfer tape gun (sold in some art supply stores). Transfer tape works well for layering paper and thin veneers and causes little telegraphing of the tape through the veneer.

FIGURE 6-10
Model-building tools and adhesives.

1. White glue
2. Slow instant glue
3. Glue accelerator
4. Glue stick
5. Rubber cement
6. Double-sided tape
7. Transfer tape
8. Masking tape
9. Painter's tape (removable)
10. Spray adhesive
11. Sandpaper
12. Small file
13. Tack cloth (for removing debris after sanding)
14. Small, heavy angle plate (used as a weight)
15. Large paper clips
16. Small clamps
17. Straight pins
18. Utility knife
19. Snap-off cutter
20. Excel™ (or X-acto) knife
21. Metal builder's square
22. Cork-backed metal ruler
23. Steel straightedge with knob
24. Cutting pad

Photograph by Bill Wikrent.

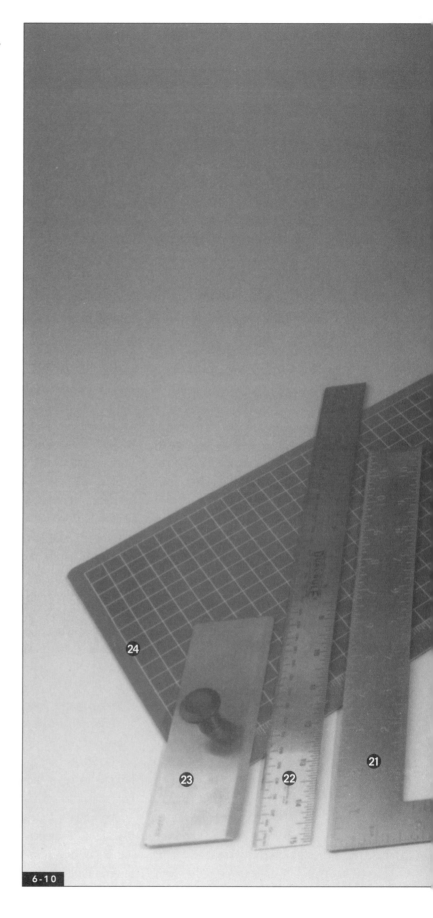

6-10

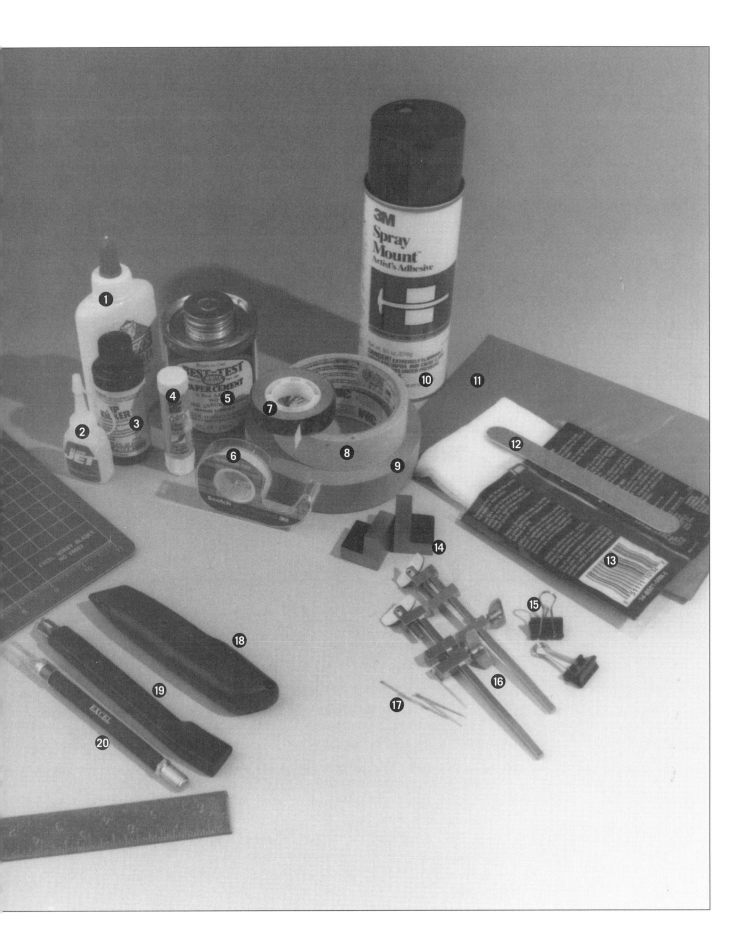

This tape is excellent for attaching paper to foam core or mat board and generally causes no warping.

MASKING and PAINTER'S TAPE work for masking off areas and bonding items together. Long-Mask™, or painter's tape, looks similar to masking tape but is blue in color. The advantage to painter's tape is that it is easily removable and leaves no residue even after several days. This allows the model maker to leave the tape in place while paints and glues dry, without having to remove the tape too soon.

SPRAY ADHESIVE is used like spray paint. The adhesive is sprayed from a can onto the appropriate surfaces. Some types of spray adhesive adhere permanently, and others allow for repositioning. Spray adhesives are very popular with design students. In model making, spray adhesive is most commonly used in attaching copies of plans and elevations onto foam core for use in study models. This is a fast and effective method of study model construction.

Although spray adhesive is quick, it is important to note that paper applied with spray mount to foam board will eventually wrinkle or bubble if applied to large surface areas. It is wise to use repositionable spray mount in model construction and materials presentations. However, almost all spray adhesives can cause wrinkling and warping of paper and foam board if left for any period of time. One trick to removing a spray adhesive is to use a hair dryer to warm it before attempting removal. The overspray from spray adhesives can be messy. These adhesives also generate fumes and are flammable.

STUDIO TAC™ is an alternative to spray adhesive. This is a double-sided adhesive sheet sold in a range of sizes. Studio Tac is peeled away from a backing paper and applied to the object for mounting; it is then peeled away from another backing surface and mounted. Studio Tac works best in adhering lightweight items such as paper and paperboard. It produces no overspray or fumes.

HOT GLUE guns are electric guns that heat and dispense hot (or very warm) glue. Glue guns hold sticks of glue that melt and are pushed through a nozzle; they are popular with many hobbyists and have some applications for models. However, hot glue is messy, hard to control, and in many cases does not produce a strong bond. Hot glue is used more often in the construction of quick study models than in refined presentation models. Hot glue can cause gaps to form in joints and can fail in completed models.

Generally hot glue is more useful in adhering materials to presentation boards than in assembling scale models. Glue guns range in size and in temperature. High-temperature glues work best for fabric, some plastics, glass, wood, and ceramic. Lower-temperature glues are often used for Styrofoam, paper, and more delicate materials.

X-acto knives and blades are commonly used in model building, as are snap-off cutters and utility knives. A wide range of blades are available for use with X-acto (or similar brand) knives. The range of blades provides for specialized cutting uses, although the classic fine-point blade (#11) is most useful in cutting paperboards. Cutters with snap-off blades also work well because they allow for easy changing of blades.

The key to using all types of knives and blades is to work with a sharp blade and make many cuts through the paperboard or wood. Foam board, mat board, museum board, bristol board, and cardboard all require at least three cuts through their surfaces. The three-cut method is the only way to achieve neat and tidy cuts, and it requires absolutely sharp blades.

A specially designed polyvinyl cutting pad is very useful for cutting all types of material. Most cutting pads have a grid pattern that allows for alignment. These pads protect table surfaces, provide a nice measured cutting surface, and seem to make blades last longer.

A cork-backed metal straightedge is an excellent cutting edge for model making. In addition, steel straightedges are available with knob holders that protect fingers from cutting accidents. Plastic rulers and triangles are not to be used for cutting edges because they are easily damaged and do not work well.

Professional model makers sometimes use heavy angled plates, as well as clamps, to hold pieces together while glue sets up. These are necessary for detailed and complex models and are not used as often by students for study models.

One busy professional model builder has stated that the six most important items for model making are a steel triangle with knob holder (to protect fingers), a polyvinyl cutting pad with a horizontal wood edge attached (for use in conjunction with the triangle), an X-acto knife, white glue, double-stick tape, and Long-Mask tape (Figure 6-11).

CONSTRUCTION AND USE OF MODELS

As stated, all types of model building require patience and time. The first step in model construction is careful consideration of the purpose of the model. If the purpose is for the designer(s) to study spatial relationships and proportions, a very quick study model can be constructed. Quick study models are most often constructed of chipboard, cardboard (corrugated board), mat board, museum board, or foam board.

As a project is refined, a more refined model may be used to study design details and finishes; in this case the study model must be more detailed and may be shown to a client for approval. Refined study models are often constructed of illustration board, mat board, museum board, foam core, or wood (or some combination of these materials). Refined study models may also include plastic or acrylic, for indication of glazed surfaces.

A common method of constructing a quick study model involves gluing orthographic drawings to chipboard, corrugated board, or foam core. This is done by first gluing the floor plan in place on the model-making material, such as foam board. The interior elevations are then glued onto foam core, chipboard, or cor-

FIGURE 6-11
Helpful tools for student paperboard models.
1. **Transfer tape**
2. **Painter's tape (blue)**
3. **Elmer's white glue**
4. **X-acto knife**
5. **Steel straightedge with knob (a metal triangle with knob also works well)**
6. **Cutting board fitted with wood to use with straightedge or triangle**
Photograph by Bill Wikrent.

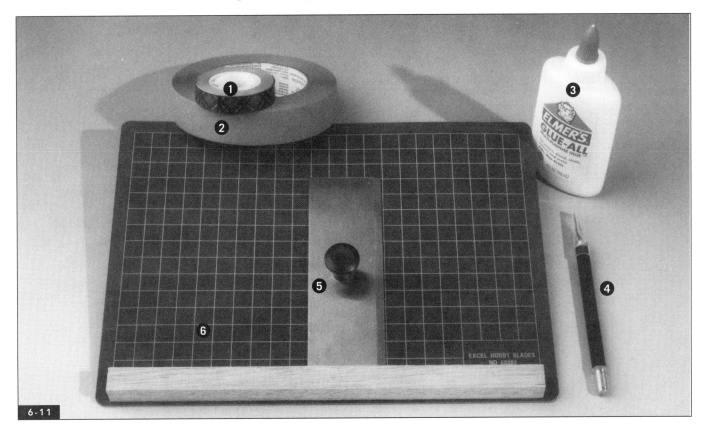

6-11

FIGURE 6-12A
Quick study models are often constructed by first attaching the floor plan to foam board, then attaching the elevations. It is best to plan ahead and leave extra room at either side of the appropriate elevations in order to attach the adjacent walls. Photograph by Bill Wikrent.

FIGURE 6-12B
The walls are glued into place on the plan. Notice that the extra room at each side of the first wall elevation allows for gluing and joining the adjacent wall. Photograph by Bill Wikrent.

FIGURE 6-12C
An overview of the steps of construction. Photograph by Bill Wikrent.

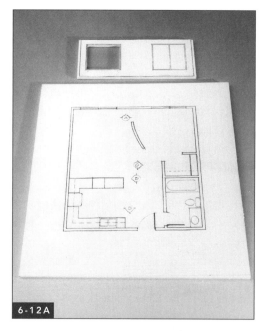

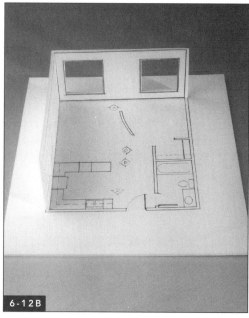

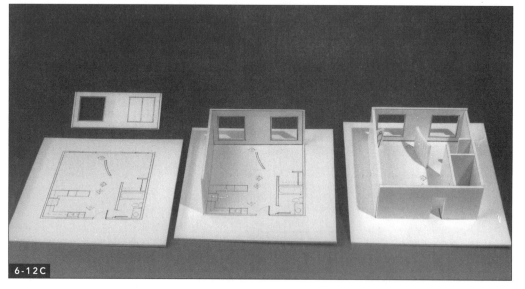

rugated board, attached to the plan, and glued in place. It is advantageous to use scaled human figures in study models. These can be drawn by hand and glued to foam core.

When gluing orthographic drawings, it is important to consider the eventual thickness of the walls and to plan accordingly. Figures 6-12a, b, c illustrate the steps in constructing this type of study model. Figure 6-13 depicts a model constructed similarly, with the exception that the orthographic drawings are attached to a building section, creating a sectional model. Figures 6-14a, 6-14b, and 6-15 show student study models constucted to examine spatial relationships. A more complex model constructed by attaching foam core to orthographic projection drawings can be found in Figures 6-16a–6-16d.

The materials selected for a model must relate to its scale. For example, a model constructed in ¼" scale requires exterior walls that scale to roughly ¹⁄₁₆"; in this case thin museum board or mat board would be an appropriate choice (Figure 6-17). In some cases, the paper used in constructing the study model can be rendered.

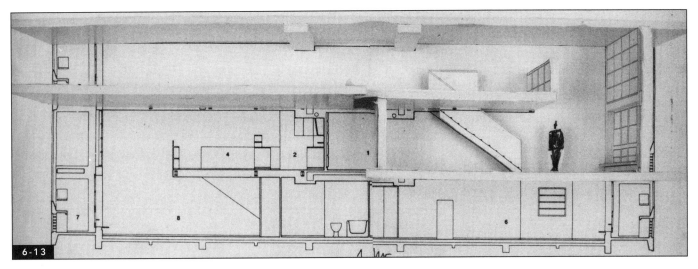

FIGURE 6-13
A sectional model (a section fragment model) of the Unité d'Habitation, designed by Le Corbusier. This model was part of a demonstration of quick and efficient model building for students. Model by Thomas Oliphant. Photograph by Bill Wikrent.

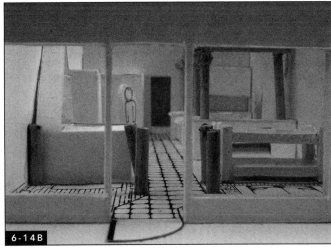

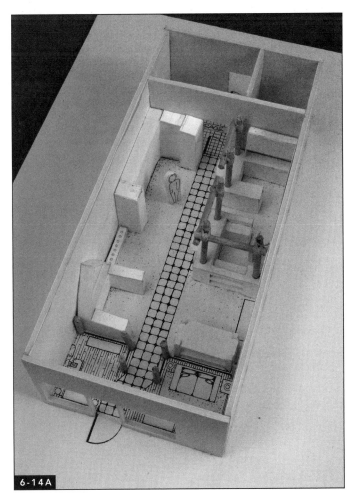

FIGURES 6-14A, 6-14B
This study model, constucted early in the design process, was used to study spatial relationships and scale issues on a retail project. The model is constructed in the manner described in Figures 6-12a, b, c. Design and model by Denise Haertl. Photograph by Bill Wikrent.

6-15

FIGURE 6-15
This study model was used to present the design for a class critique. The model is constructed in the manner described in Figures 6-12a, b, c. Design and model by Anne Cleary. Photograph by Bill Wikrent.

6-16B

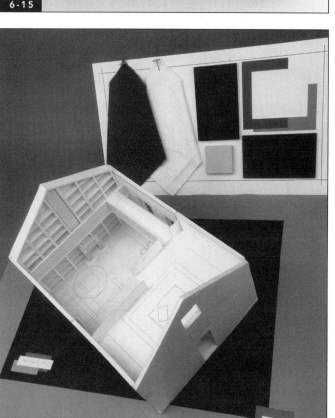

6-16A

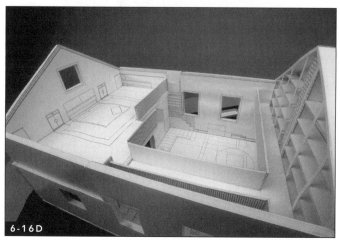

6-16C

FIGURES 6-16A, B, C, AND D
This foam board and paper model was built to depict the design of a small two-story building. Due to the nature of the design and the scale of the project, the model was designed in two parts, the top of which can be removed for better viewing of the first story. Special care was given to accurately portray specially designed cabinetry and millwork details. Design and model by Siv Jane Refsnes. Photograph by Bill Wikrent.

6-16D

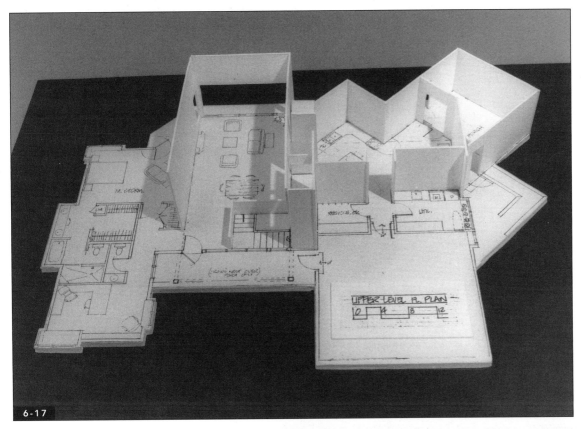

6-17

Some designers prefer pristine monochromatic models. In such cases simply gluing an elevation onto paperboard is not appropriate. A model like this requires that measurements be taken from orthographic drawings and transferred to paperboard. The paperboard is cut to the correct dimensions, and the model is then glued in place. Figure 6-18 illustrates a study model constructed by transferring dimensions instead of attaching elevations.

For the most part, it is best to avoid using manufactured dollhouse products in study models. Such items tend to be too busy and distracting. Instead, abstracting materials to simple forms is useful and less distracting. However, some milled wood items such as paneling and interior moldings can be used to good effect in study models. Figures 6-19a and 6-19b are simple models with abstracted finishes. Figures C-50a and C-50b depict a colored presentation model with abstracted versions of finish materials applied in a visually successful manner.

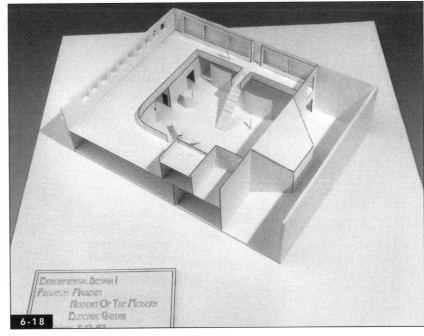

6-18

FIGURE 6-17
A model built to study wall heights, constructed of museum board mounted on black foam board. Design by Courtney Nystuen. Model by Leanne Larson and the author. Photograph by Bill Wikrent.

FIGURE 6-18
Study model constructed of illustration board. Model by Eric Zeimet. Photograph by Bill Wikrent.

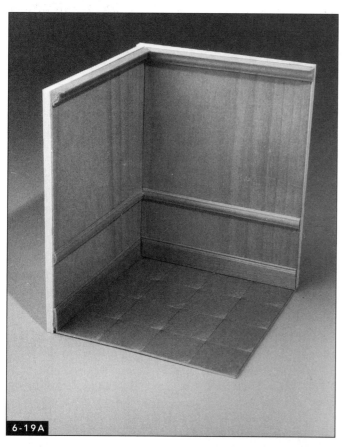

6-19A

6-19B

FIGURE 6-19A
A vignette model built to study wall finishes, constructed of foam board, rendered mat board, basswood veneer, and basswood dollhouse moldings. Photograph by Bill Wikrent.

FIGURE 6-19B
A vignette model built to study wall finishes and design, constructed of mat board, rendered mat board, ripple wrap (metallic finish), and basswood veneer. Photograph by Bill Wikrent.

FIGURE 6-20
A rendered flip-up model. Constructed of rendered bond paper on black foam board. Model by Ardella Pieper. Photograph by Bill Wikrent.

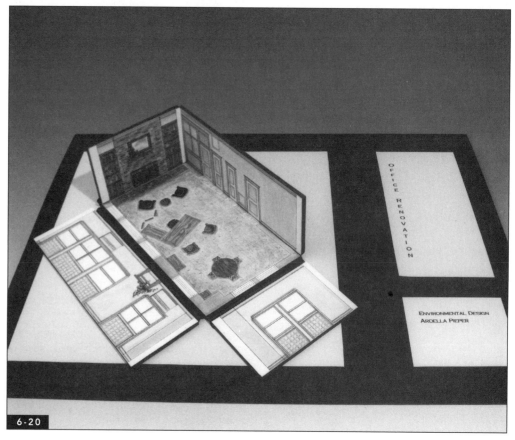

6-20

FLIP-UP MODELS

Simple square or rectilinear spaces can be illustrated with flip-up models. These models use floor plans and interior elevations that are rendered and glued onto a paperboard surface. The elevations are then attached to the plan with a single strip of tape placed on both back surfaces. The tape serves as a hinge and allows the elevations to flip up into place. The elevations can be taped into place as needed for study and review (Figure 6-20).

Creating flip-up models is a way to use drawing skills as an aid in model making, and these models can be stored flat for inclusion in a portfolio. The limitation of flip-up models is that they work only for very simple floor plans and are less realistic spatially than standard models.

SCALE MODELS IN PROFESSIONAL PRACTICE

Some design firms use scale models a great deal; others use them rarely. Highly refined presentation models take hours to build and are very costly. For this reason some designers do not use them. However, many designers have a commitment to study projects fully during the design process, and this requires the use of scale models. It also requires that design contracts include the costs of model building.

Larger firms often have a fully equipped model shop where a range of models are constructed for study and presentation. In many firms, designers build only study models, and professional model builders are hired to build presentation models.

Firms that use models as a fundamental part of the design process often construct many in the course of a project. This means that a series of models are constructed that reflect the levels of refinement of the design. Figures 6-21– 6-25 illustrate a series of models built for one design project. Figures C-51 and C-52 are color images from this project.

On very large design projects, such as hotels and entertainment facilities, full-scale mock-ups may be constructed. It is not unusual for large hotel projects to employ full-size room mock-ups for viewing by investors or owners. Unusual design details may also require full-scale mock-ups as a means of study prior to construction.

6-21

FIGURE 6-21
An overhead view of a large study model built for a professional project, constructed of bond paper, foam board, plastic, teak veneer, metal screen, and fabric. Design and model by Meyer, Scherer, & Rockcastle, Ltd. Photograph by Bill Wikrent.

FIGURE 6-22
An overhead view of a smaller study model built for a professional project (also shown in Figure 6-21), constructed of bond paper, foam board, plastic, basswood, teak veneer, and fabric. Design and model by Meyer, Scherer & Rockcastle Ltd. Photograph by Bill Wikrent.

FIGURE 6-23
Side view of the model shown in Figure 6-22, constructed of bond paper, foamboard, plastic, basswood, teak veneer, and fabric. Design and model by Meyer, Scherer & Rockcastle Ltd. Photograph by Bill Wikrent.

Industrial designers create a number of study models throughout the design process. These models are made of a variety of materials, ranging from foam board to styrene and Balsa-Foam (Figures 6-26 and 6-27). In an ongoing process of refinement, industrial designers often create many models for each project, ending with absolutely accurate presentation models that can be mistaken for the real thing.

In the specialized process of designing furniture, it is necessary to construct many models and mock-ups. Furniture study models are often constructed of corrugated board, chipboard, foam board, or styrene. As a design becomes refined, it is often necessary to move to large-scale mock-ups or prototypes as a means of studying form as well as working out construction issues. Prototypes are required to perform as the actual products will, so they are often constructed of materials very similar to the actual final product (Figures 6-28 and 6-29).

FIGURE 6-24
Furniture models for the project featured in Figures 6-21, 6-22, and 6-23, constructed of assorted wood. Design and model by Meyer, Scherer & Rockcastle Ltd. Photograph by Bill Wikrent.

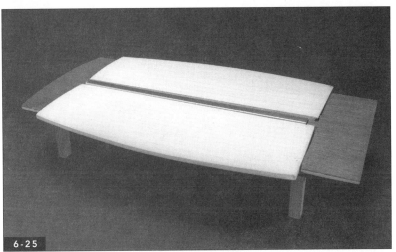

FIGURE 6-25
Furniture model for the project featured in Figures 6-21, 6-22, and 6-23, constructed of assorted wood and metal. Design and model by Meyer, Scherer & Rockcastle Ltd. Photograph by Bill Wikrent.

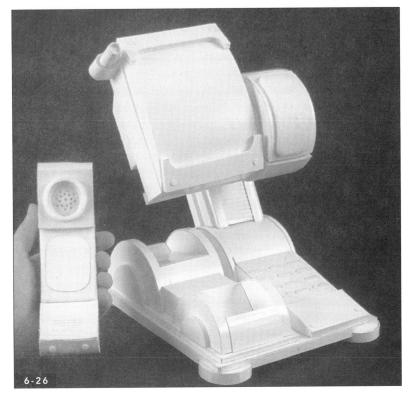

FIGURE 6-26
Study model of a videophone, constructed of foam board. Design and model by Evan Sparks. Photograph by Bill Wikrent.

FIGURE 6-27
Study model of a portable stereo, constructed of Balsa Foam. Design and model by Jill Holterhaus. Photograph by Bill Wikrent.

FIGURE 6-28
Chair prototype constructed of wood and steel. Designed and made by Thomas Oliphant. Photograph by Kathy Fogerty.

FIGURE 6-29
Chair prototype (on right) shown with actual finished chair (on left). Designed and made by Thomas Oliphant. Photograph by Kathy Fogerty.

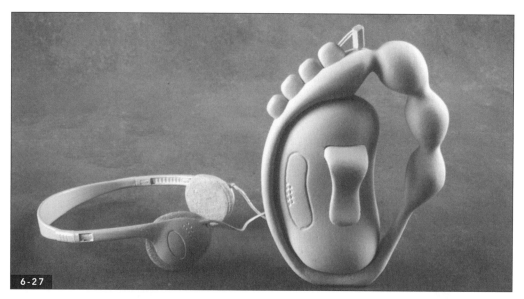

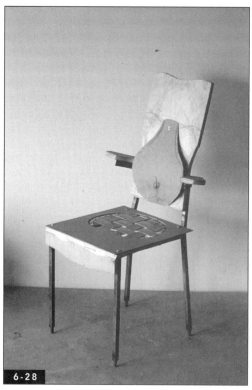

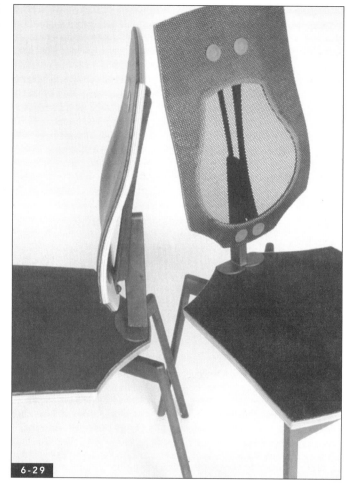

REFERENCES

Mills, Criss. *Designing with Models.* New York: John Wiley and Sons, 2000.

Shimizu, Yoshiharu. *Models and Prototypes: Clay, Plaster, Styrofoam, Paper.* Tokyo: Graphic-sha Publishing Company, 1991.

PRESENTING MATERIALS AND FINISHES

INTRODUCTION TO MATERIALS PRESENTATIONS

Most professional interior design projects involve study, review, and refinement of interior architectural finishes and materials, as well as furnishings, fixtures, and equipment. Finish materials, furnishings, and fixtures must be studied individually and also be viewed as parts of a whole. All of these items must be evaluated in terms of life-safety issues and performance as well as from an aesthetic standpoint. This chapter focuses only on the presentation of these items and does not cover the important issues of life safety, performance, and specification.

A formal materials presentation is not of particular importance to the individual designer as an aid in the design process. It is most common for designers to gather a variety of samples and make preliminary decisions without pinning anything down. Most designers can work from large samples kept loose (unmounted) while in the preliminary stages of a design (Figure 7-1). It is necessary to create formal presentations for clients, end users, or investors only when selections have been determined or narrowed down. Large projects, or those with many team members, may in rare cases require a materials presentation as a communication and design aid. These cases are the exceptions, not the rule.

Early in the space-planning process many designers begin to consider architectural finishes and materials. After careful study, preliminary selection of finishes, materials, and furnishings can be made. These preliminary selections are presented to the client or end user in a way that reflects the preliminary nature of the selections.

Often preliminary selections of materials are presented at the same time as preliminary plans, elevations, perspective or axonometric drawings, and perhaps study models. All of the elements used in a particular presentation must be consistent graphically, and they work best if they contain unifying elements. For example, if it is used in a preliminary presentation, a materials board may incorporate the graphics found in the title block of drawings. Or perhaps the format of a materials board can be consistent with the format used to present renderings. In many cases, materials boards are keyed graphically to floor plans and serve as an aid in understanding elements of the design presented.

Some designers prefer to keep the preliminary materials presentation casual, with all

7-1

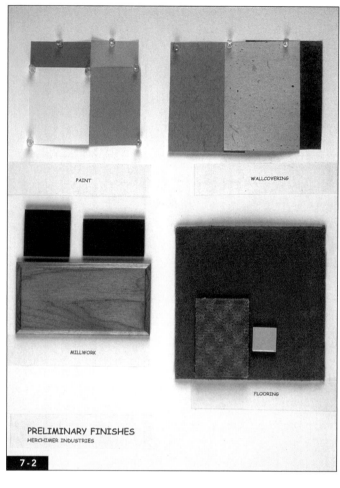

PAINT
WALLCOVERING
MILLWORK
FLOORING

PRELIMINARY FINISHES
HERCHIMER INDUSTRIES

7-2

FIGURE 7-1
Many designers prefer to keep materials loose and unmounted, especially in preliminary presentations. Photograph by Bill Wikrent.

FIGURE 7-2
This preliminary presentation of finishes makes use of foam board, pushpins, and simple titles. This type of presentation allows for easy removal of the samples for inspection or replacement. Photograph by Bill Wikrent.

elements remaining loose and unmounted. Providing loose items allows the presentation audience to touch and easily examine the samples. Keeping things loose also allows the client to understand clearly the preliminary nature of the selection and imparts a sense that there is plenty of room for decision making.

Many designers mount preliminary selections on presentation boards so that the client or end user gets a sense that decisions have been made and are being communicated. Another method of preliminary presentation calls for pinning samples down on a board with pushpins so that they can easily be removed for examination by the client (Figure 7-2).

As a project moves forward, it is important that materials presentations clearly reflect the given stages of the design. Many designers create a materials presentation as part of the final visual presentation, which takes place at the end

of design development phase of a project. Large and complex projects often require several materials presentations, which occur at key points in the design development process. Some projects, however, may require no formal materials presentation during the entire design process.

One extremely successful residential designer never mounts materials onto boards for any project. He keeps all samples loose and arranges them on a worktable for his clients' review. Several designers interviewed prefer to drape fabrics on full-size furniture samples and keep all finishes unmounted for client approval.

Clearly there is variation in the manner in which finalized selections of materials, furnishings, and finishes are presented to clients. Many designers pride themselves on consistent, well-crafted materials presentations, whereas others prefer to keep samples loose and informal. Many firms have standards for the way presentation boards are prepared. These standards include preferred board size, color, graphics, and methods for attaching samples, as well as the level of formality conveyed in the presentations.

The standards employed by an individual firm allow presentations to distinctly reflect the concerns and focus of the firm and at the same time clearly convey the selections for a particular project. Final presentations often include drawings, renderings, models, and materials boards, all of which must appear visually cohesive and logical.

On some projects, all of the elements for a final presentation, including materials boards, must be packed for travel. This means that all necessary items are included, and everything of importance must be packed and organized for the designer's arrival in a strange city. Organizing a final presentation for travel can take weeks of preparation. There are large projects that include more than 50 materials boards that must be packed for travel and presentation to large audiences. Presentations of this sort must be organized in a clear and logical fashion that leaves no margin for error.

The variation in practice and presentation of interior design projects requires that design students develop a range of skills in preparing materials presentations. Fortunately, internships often provide an excellent opportunity for students to become involved in creating many types of design presentations, including materials presentations, thus allowing the students to see particular office standards as they relate to these presentations.

Although there is great diversity as to formality of presentation and office graphic standards, there are numerous factors common to all materials presentations. These have to do with legibility, organization, graphic cohesion, quality of craftsmanship, techniques, and tools, and appropriateness. All design students can benefit from a clear understanding of these factors in developing visual skills and creating meaningful presentations.

MATERIALS AND MEDIA

Many of the materials used in presentation boards are discussed in previous chapters. Information on types of paper and drawing tools can be found in Chapter 1; additional information on paper and rendering media is found in Chapter 5. For descriptions of paperboards, adhesives, and cutting tools, refer to Chapter 6.

Most materials presentations require sturdy backing materials, most often a type of paperboard. Foam board is often used in such presentations because it is sturdy yet lightweight and easy to work with. Samples, titles, and notes can be applied directly to the top paper surface of the foam core. In some cases white foam board is used as the surface to which all samples are applied; a mat board border is also added to the surface of the foam board (Figures 7-3a and b). This type of presentation has the added feature of resisting warping, making it useful for student portfolios, which otherwise fall prey to warping and wrinkling. While many prefer white foam board, black foam board is favored by others for more dramatic presentations. Figures C-54 and C-55 depict attractive, well-organized professional presentations mounted directly on white foam-core board.

In some presentations foam board is covered with mat board, illustration board, bond paper, or Canson™ paper. Samples and titles are then mounted to the top paper surface. When thinner papers such as bond paper or Canson paper are used, the entire surface can be laid out with titles and notes and printed on a large-format copy machine; samples are then added to the appropriate locations (Figures 7-4, 7-5a, and 7-5b). Some words of warning about the use of lightweight paper applied to boards: warping and wrinkling are huge problems if spray adhesive is used; two-sided tape is far superior. For color illustrations of presentations employing paper board, see C-60a, C-60b, C-61, C-63a, C-63b, and C-64.

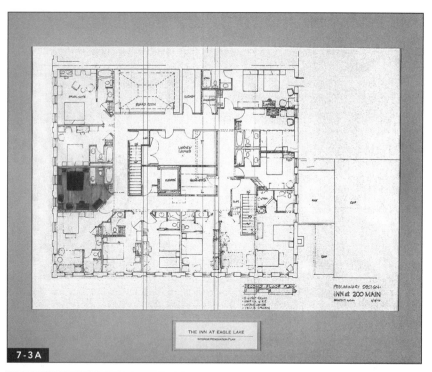

7-3A

7-3B

Smaller or lightweight materials may be mounted on lighter-weight boards such as mat board, illustration board, or museum board. However, lighter boards can appear flimsy and will not support heavy materials such as tile or stone samples. Mat board and museum board are sometimes cut with windows; samples are mounted behind the windows just as artwork is matted (for further information, see the discussion later in this chapter under "Window Matting").

Materials presented in professional practice are often large and quite heavy. Full-size ceramic tile, glass, and stone samples are particularly heavy. For this reason Gator Board or wood panels are used as a mounting surface in some professional presentations. Large pieces of Gator Board can be used with minimal warping, as can wood panels. Gator Board and wood also allow for the mounting of very heavy samples (see Figures C-73, C-74, C-75, and C-76).

Professional practice also requires very large-scale sample mock-ups to be provided on some jobs. For example, it is not uncommon to create 3' by 3' ceramic tile sample mock-ups for large projects such as retail malls and airports. These large-scale samples are often provided by the appropriate subcontractors on a project. However, in some cases they are created by design firms.

Nontraditional projects often require nontraditional materials presentations. One designer uses galvanized sheet metal, with magnets holding samples in place, for nontraditional

FIGURES 7-3A, 7-3B
Samples, titles, and notes can be applied directly to the top paper surface of white foam board, as shown in this sample board. Here colored mat board has been used to create a frame around the entire composition. The project floor plan is presented similarly with the drawing taped to the foam core to prevent warping and wrinkling. The similar treatment of these elements creates a cohesive presentation that

is less likely to warp than many other techniques. Photograph by Bill Wikrent.

FIGURE 7-4
This simple traditional board was made by photocopying the titles and borders onto bond paper, mounting the bond paper onto foam board, and attaching samples directly to the bond paper or board. Photograph by Bill Wikrent.

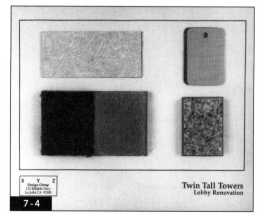

7-4

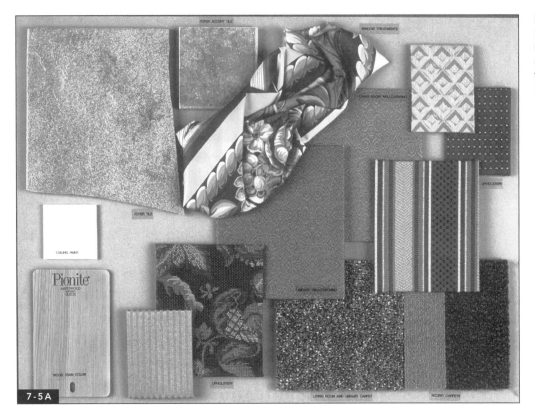

FIGURES 7-5A, 7-5B
Materials sample boards with samples surface-mounted on colored paper, mounted on black foam board. By Daniel Effenheim. Photograph by Andrew Bottolfson.

SEATING AREA, FLORIDA ROOM, AND CORRIDOR FINISHES

STONECREEK MANOR

FIGURE 7-6
This board employs bond paper mounted to foam board, with the materials arranged in a nontraditional manner. The bond paper contains a scanned image of the design parti. Photograph by Bill Wikrent.

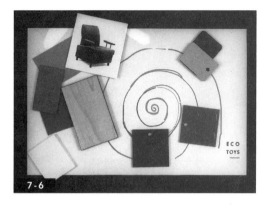

presentations. A recent presentation made use of chain-link fencing panels as a mounting surface. Clearly appropriateness is important in selecting nontraditional presentation modes (Figures 7-6, 7-7, 7-8, and C-56).

A variety of adhesives is used to mount samples, and a variety of mounting techniques is employed in materials presentations (see "Techniques and Methods of Presentation" later in this chapter).

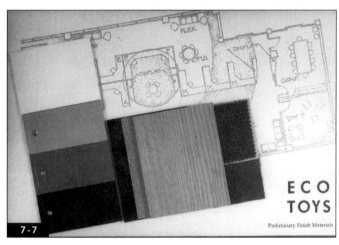

FIGURE 7-7
This board employs bond paper mounted to foam board, with the materials arranged in a nontraditional manner. The bond paper contains a scanned and manipulated image of the floor plan. Photograph by Bill Wikrent.

FIGURE 7-8
This nontraditional board consists of rendered illustration board and draped samples. Photograph by Bill Wikrent.

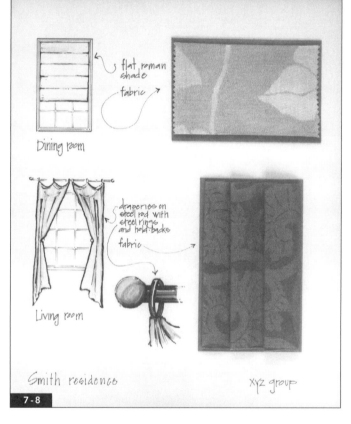

ORGANIZATION AND COMPOSITION

In materials presentations there is great variety in the placement of samples and materials, yet designers generally agree on the importance of planning the arrangement of presentation graphics.

Stylistically boards may vary greatly. However, regardless of style or method of sample organization, some basic principles of graphic design should be employed in laying out presentation boards. For example, the use of a grid

can do wonders for any presentation (see Chapter 6). Traditionally presentations with multiple boards should have a consistent compositional orientation: all boards should be formatted vertically, all horizontally, all square, and so forth.

Regardless of the presentation style, materials boards should have actual or implied borders. A border may be drawn, printed, or created with graphic tape (plastic or vinyl tape is available in a range of thicknesses and colors), or the border area may be left blank, with no samples or titles placed within a given area. Figure 7-9 shows thumbnail sketches of border arrangements.

There are distinct, diverse opinions regarding the organization of samples for presentations (Figure 7-10). One school of thought calls for materials to be laid out in relation to their actual physical location. This means that all flooring is placed at the bottom of the arrangement, furnishings are placed above flooring, wall finishes are placed above flooring, win-

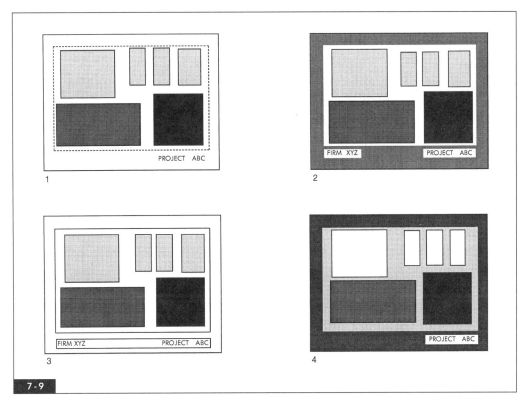

FIGURE 7-9
Boards look best with some type of border.

1. Borders may be implied (dashed lines), with no items displayed beyond the implied borders.

2. Borders may be defined with a window mat.

3. Borders can be drawn onto the board surface or applied with graphic tape.

4. Borders may be defined with a sheet of colored paper mounted on foam board.

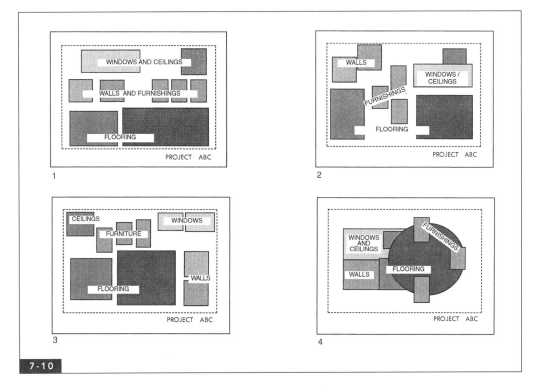

FIGURE 7-10
Board organization.

1. Materials applied in relation to their location in the environment: flooring at the bottom, walls above flooring, ceiling materials at top of board.

2. Materials applied in relation to proximity or physical contact; for example, flooring adjacent to related furnishings and finishes.

3. Materials placed according to their visual impact on the composition; for example, large areas of flooring represented by large samples.

4. Materials placed in relation to a graphic element or design parti; in this example, the materials form a collage relating to the floor plan.

dow treatments and ceiling materials are placed at the top of the arrangement.

It is also common for designers to place items that relate to one another in close proximity on the presentation board. For example, a picture of a chair will be mounted adjacent to the wood finish and upholstery samples for that chair. This method is useful for clients who are not accustomed to viewing presentation boards, such as corporate officers or homeowners.

Another school of thought calls for materials to be placed according to their visual impact within the composition. For example, on a project with hundreds of yards of rubber floor tile and very little carpeting, the presentation may show large samples of rubber flooring and smaller samples of carpeting.

Some designers place samples of exactly the same size on the board and lay them out in equally spaced horizontal bands. Others place important items in the center of the presentation and spin additional samples out from the center. A few designers use the floor plan of a given space as an abstract diagram for laying out the materials on a presentation board.

There is a bit of controversy in regard to whether samples should physically touch one another on presentation boards. For years designers were trained to lay out samples with blank spaces (negative space) between samples. In current practice this is no longer considered important by some designers, who think that items that will touch in reality should touch on boards.

Many designers place black or white cloth tape on the edges of materials boards. The tape can hide the several layers of material that would otherwise be exposed at the edge and creates a neat, clean look. A black taped edge creates a distinct border, whereas a white taped edge is less visually dominant. Certain designers find a taped edge unnecessary if the boards have been cut cleanly.

On occasion clients require that materials boards be framed and placed behind glass. This is most common when presentations will be viewed by investors or hung in the sales or leasing office of a developer of commercial real estate. In these cases the particular needs of the audience must be considered in the titling and layout of the boards.

TITLES, KEYS, AND LEGENDS

It is imperative that all materials presentations clearly communicate the items selected. This means that samples must be titled, referenced, or keyed. There are two basic systems of referencing samples and images on presentation boards. One method requires that all items be titled or labeled directly on the front of the board, adjacent or very close to the appropriate sample. Another method allows for samples to be keyed and referenced with a legend on the front or back of the board or on an accompanying document. Designers and firms most often have office standards that call for some form of one of these methods. Figure 7-11 shows thumbnails of some methods of titling and keying boards.

There are many board-titling methods. Some designers prefer labels to be kept simple; for example, a carpet sample may simply be labeled "Carpet — Master Bedroom" or "Carpet." Other designers prefer that actual specifications be included in the title; for example, the carpet would be labeled "Carpet — Master Bedroom, Wool Berber, 42 oz., Helios Carpet Mills." Some designers prefer simple titles on the front of the board with full specifications keyed to the back of the board or keyed to a floor plan. Figure 7-12 shows a board with samples keyed to a floor plan.

Systems for keying or referencing samples vary as well. Some designers prefer a letter or number code that relates to the type of sample used. For example, carpet may be listed as "C-1," wallcovering as "WC-1," and both are then fully referenced on the back of the board. Other designers prefer a simple numbering or lettering system starting with "1" or "A," running through all of the samples and referenced on the back.

Some designers prefer a system that employs no titles or codes on the front of the presentations. Instead a duplicate image of the

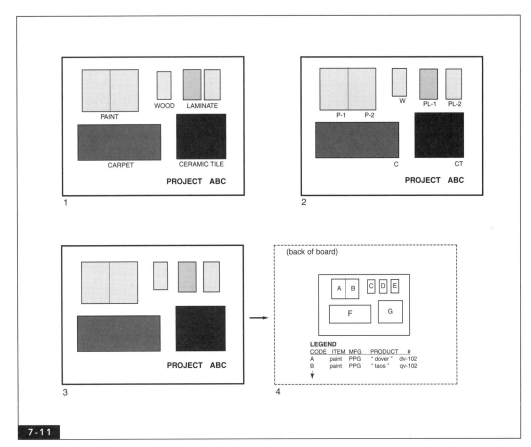

FIGURE 7-11
Board titles.

1. Materials may be titled directly on the board.

2. Materials may be titled using a code system, with a legend or key placed on the back of the board.

3. This example employs no titles on the face of the board; instead a coding system and legend are used on the back of the board.

4. Legend on the back of board shown in 3.

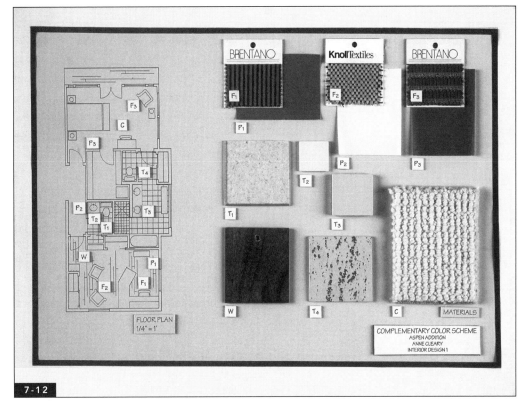

FIGURE 7-12
Materials sample board making use of titles keyed to a floor plan. By Anne Cleary. Photograph by Andrew Bottolfson.

board appears on the back with samples specified or referenced. It is also common to key materials to related floor plans or elevations and use the orthographic drawings as part of the reference system. For example, a materials board may have the code "C-1" for a particular carpet; the locations for the carpet are then shown on an accompanying floor plan.

There are many ways to create the actual titles used on boards. The simplest titles are created by hand lettering. In some cases lettering is drawn directly on the top surface of the presentation board. A more professional look is created by using machines that print type onto plastic tape, such as Kroy™ or Merlin™ machines. After the machine expels the printed tape, a plastic backing is peeled away and the tape is mounted to the board surface or raised mat board title plates, much as in hand lettering. It is imperative that the tape lettering is neatly cut and applied to boards with the use of guidelines. Figure C-64 shows tape titles used in a presentation.

Appliqué film (sticky back) is commonly used in titling boards and drawings for presentation. Almost any graphics may be photocopied onto sticky back. The film is then cut to size and the backing surface removed, allowing the graphic to be applied to any paper surface. Sticky back works well in creating neat titles and unusual graphics, such as logos for boards and drawings. Sticky back can be found at most commercial photocopier supply stores and is available in a range of finishes from matte to glossy. Designers often select a matte finish for titling materials boards. It is imperative that appliqué film is measured and cut neatly (an X-acto works well). In applying film to any surface, vertical and horizontal guidelines are required. For more information on appliqué films, see Chapter 1.

Most computer word-processing software will allow for printing a range of type styles. This means that students and designers with computers can create beautiful titles by simple computer generation of the appropriate words. The titles may then be mounted directly, or first applied to paperboard and then mounted (with the use of guidelines).

Titles, borders, and notes and additional information can be laid out on a large sheet of paper and photocopied using a large-format copier (or a standard copier for boards 11" by 17" and smaller). The large copy is then mounted on paperboard and samples are attached. This method allows titles and logos to be printed on colored papers that accept photocopy toner. The colored paper is then mounted on paperboard, and samples are applied to the colored paper. Figure 7-13 is a presentation board with drawings, titles, and borders copied directly onto colored paper, with surface-mounted samples.

FIGURE 7-13
Board with drawings, titles, and samples surface mounted on kraft paper, mounted on black foam board. By Daniel Effenheim. Photograph by Andrew Bottolfson.

FLOORPLAN
SCALE: 1/4"= 1'-O"

PERSPECTIVE
CASH DESK AREA

ENVIRONMENTAL DESIGN   RETAIL SPACE   DANIEL L. EFFENHEIM

7-13

TECHNIQUES AND METHODS OF PRESENTATION

Currently, given the time constraints of professional practice, most designers mount or attach samples to the front surface of a presentation board. This method requires samples to be neatly mounted with all edges trimmed or wrapped.

Fabrics are often wrapped around cardboard (or mat board) and taped or glued in place. This treatment produces neat, uniform samples with no unraveled edges. Figure 7-14 illustrates the construction of these samples. The same wrapping method can be used on formal boards for paint samples (Figure 7-15). When it is necessary to save time, fabric samples can be neatly trimmed and placed on mat board, which is then glued to the presentation board. In appropriate circumstances, fabric samples may be draped and glued in place.

Pictures or photocopies of furnishings and equipment look best if they are mounted (with double-sided tape, Studio Tac, or spray mount) on mat board, which is then trimmed and mounted directly on the presentation board. Placing these items on mat board allows them to sit on the surface of the presentation board, creating a shadow line and adding a professional finish to the board; it also can prevent warping. The fastest method of trimming photos that are mounted on mat board is to use a large paper cutter with a sharp blade (Figure 7-16). This is quicker than cutting with a utility knife or X-acto. Replacement blades are available for paper cutters and should be replaced as necessary.

When mounting heavy objects such as tile, stone, or metal panels it is sometimes necessary to score the mounting board surface prior to applying glue. Scoring the surface

FIGURE 7-14
In wrapping fabric samples, first allow an appropriate amount of material for wrapping. Then pull the ends firmly in place and secure with glue or tape. Adding a piece of paperboard to the back of the wrapped sample allows for easy mounting and gluing. Photograph by Bill Wikrent.

7-14

FIGURE 7-15
Paint samples can be wrapped around a cardboard form and held in place with tape. Photograph by Bill Wikrent.

7-15

FIGURE 7-16
Photographs look best mounted on mat paperboard and then trimmed and glued onto a board. A paper cutter makes quick work of trimming. Photograph by Bill Wikrent.

7-16

adds texture to the board and increases the bonding capacity of most glues. This is especially necessary if Canson or another art paper is applied on top of a mounting board. Often the paper must be cut away to reveal the mounting surface, so objects are glued directly to the backing board. This prevents the sample from pulling the Canson paper from the backing board. A consistent, thin application of white glue can often bond heavy samples to boards. In rare cases, contact cement is used, but because it is toxic and rather unpleasant to work with, it should be used as a last resort.

Especially large or heavy samples may require two layers of foam board to be used as backing. This allows one layer of the foam board to be cut away so that the sample may be recessed into the opening.

Plastic laminates and other samples may have product numbers printed on them. These printed numbers can often be removed with an electric eraser. Bestine™ or another solvent can also be used to remove stubborn printed information.

Designers use a variety of adhesive products in mounting samples and materials. A relatively thin application of white glue works beautifully in adhering lighter- and medium-weight samples. However, white glue will cause light papers (tracing paper, vellum, bond) to wrinkle. In mounting these papers, double-sided tape, rubber cement, or spray-on adhesive (for small areas) can work well. Studio Tac works well in adhering paper and light samples to board surfaces.

Hot glue can work wonders in creating materials presentations if it is used on light- to medium-weight items with large flat surface areas. Heavier samples will not bond well with hot glue. A fairly thin, consistent application works best. Big globs of glue are not only messy, but do not create enough surface area of glue for a good bond. It is imperative that care is taken to prevent the hot glue from spilling onto the presentation board surface.

Sometimes it is necessary to remove an item that has been glued permanently in place. Hand-held hair dryers may work to warm and loosen a variety of adhesives, such as spray-on adhesive, StudioTac, hot glue, rubber cement, and sticky back. A warm setting is usually best because a hot setting may cause melting or warping.

There are some technical issues to consider in mounting a presentation. It is generally a mistake to use spray adhesive to mount large bond or print paper drawings to foam board or mat board. Boards mounted in this fashion will wrinkle or warp — or both. It is far superior to use Studio Tac or rubber cement to mount these lightweight drawings. In some cases drawings may be mounted on Canson or other art papers, which creates a thinner presentation format that can be inserted into a portfolio.

Some designers prefer to use large black clips (available at office supply stores) to attach drawings to foam board or precut plywood sheets (the exact size of the drawing's surface). This allows drawings to be easily removed and replaced with revised drawings.

WINDOW MATTING

Some designers and educators prefer formal boards with samples placed behind neatly cut window mats. Clearly, window mats create tidy and clean presentation boards. However, cutting a window for each sample is time-consuming. Because time and budgets are constant factors in design practice, some designers have forsaken this presentation method, and others use individual window mats only for very formal presentations or those that will eventually hang in sales rooms or developers' offices. Some design firms continue to employ window-matted presentation boards.

Window matting requires that the board be designed and laid out with all of the samples and items in place. Window locations are drawn on the surface of the mat board and then cut in the marked locations. If a beveled edge is required, I recommend using a commercially available mat cutter. Mat cutters range in price from about $30 to more than $1,000. Mat cutters generally provide a housing for a cutting blade that slides along a metal straightedge, providing a beautiful beveled or straight cut. Most mat cutters create a beveled edge by making cuts from the back of the mat board surface; this can become quite confusing when many windows are to be cut.

When cutting windows by hand, it is imperative to use a very sharp blade. It is also important that the cutting blade is used to make a minimum of three cuts: one through the top, one through the middle, and one through the bottom paper surface. Making three cuts will create clean, sharp edges. It is also a good idea to use a fresh blade for each window. To avoid overshooting the corners of windows with the blade, try to precut corners (Figure 7-17). A nail file can be used to smooth ragged cuts when necessary.

In window matting, samples are attached to the backing board, then the front board with windows is placed on top (Figure 7-18). In some cases, the mat board lies on top of the samples to create a presentation where the samples are recessed behind the windows (Figure 7-19). It is common for boards with window mats to have taped edges that conceal the many layers of material involved. In presentations employing window mats it is also common to include window-matted drawings. In these cases, a window is cut in a board and that board is hinged (using tape) to a backing board. The flat drawing is then taped over the back of the window (Figure 7-20) or attached to the backing board. Archival mat board, backing board, and hinge tape are used for matting drawings that should be preserved. Figures C-53a and C-53b show a materials presentation in which some elements are window matted and others are surface mounted.

DIGITAL TECHNOLOGY

Increasingly designers are relying on digital technology when preparing materials presentations as well as documenting various selections and options. Currently digital cameras and scanners are used to capture materials, samples, and product imagery. For example, several firms that I have interviewed scan all samples for use in specification books. Many of these firms also scan all components of visual presentations to preserve images and retain accurate records, this was previously done at many firms using traditional photography. Firms working on long-distance projects use scanned versions of presentations as a means of communicating. In many cases, digital files containing visual presentations are sent via e-mail for client review. In other cases, the actual presentation boards are sent or left with the client and the designer retains digital files and then is able to discuss elements of the presentation over the phone or via e-mail.

Current methods of documenting finish selections include scanning actual materials and importing them directly onto design drawings such as orthographic drawings and three-dimensional views generated on CADD or drawn by hand. This is done easily with a range of products, but I favor Photoshop Elements®, a reasonably priced image-editing, photo-retouching, and Web graphics software product. Using this software, drawings can be imported via scanning, as can all of the desired finish materials. The various finish materials can then be imported directly onto the appropriate places on plans, elevations, and three-dimensional views (Figure C-18).

Complete virtual boards can be created by scanning materials and adding text (Figure C-57). In a few hours most students can develop the basic skills required for creating digital renderings and materials boards using this product. It is worth noting that there is a range of software designed for this purpose. Photoshop Elements is useful due to its reasonable price and wide range of applications; however, there are many useful products on the market. It is also worth noting that these virtual sample presentations lack the textural quality available with true finish materials; they are nonetheless worthwhile, especially in terms of setting a conceptual direction or being used in conjuction with the actual samples.

The Internet has become a powerful tool for obtaining design and building product information and related visual imagery. When items are not available in firm or school product libraries, many people seek them via the Internet. Specification information, visual information, product guides, and sometimes pricing are available on the Internet. There is a range in terms of the accuracy of the visual imagery found on the

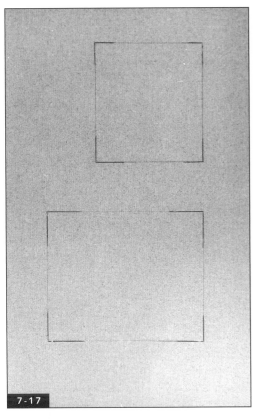

7-17

7-18

FIGURE 7-17
When cutting window mats by hand, it helps to precut the corners. Photograph by Bill Wikrent.

FIGURE 7-18
Window mats can allow items to project from the windows. Photographs by Bill Wikrent.

7-19

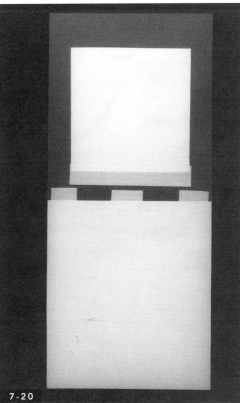

7-20

FIGURE 7-19
The nature of some materials requires items to be recessed beneath window mats. Photograph by Bill Wikrent.

FIGURE 7-20
Interior view of matted flat artwork. The drawing is taped to the back of the window, and the backing board is hinged at the top with tape. To preserve artwork, only archival materials should come in contact with the artwork. Photograph by Bill Wikrent.

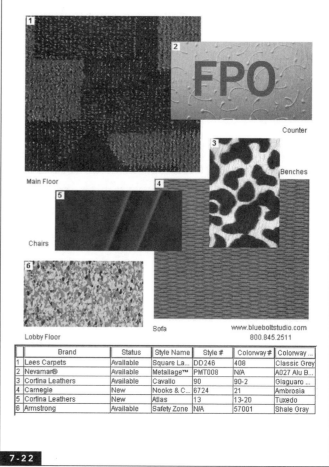

FIGURE 7-21
This enlarged view of a virtual carpet sample obtained from BlueBolt's online service contains visual information as well as product specification information. Courtesy of BlueBolt.

FIGURE 7-22
This virtual sample presentation obtained from BlueBolt's online service incorporates the item shown in Figure 7-21 as well as additional samples. A legend, corresponding titles, and product information are readily included. Courtesy of BlueBolt. Figures C-58 and C-59 show color boards from BlueBolt.

Internet, therefore, many designers continue to use real samples when digital images are not useful or appropriate.

One solution to the problems related to the visual accuracy of Web-obtained samples is available through the services of BlueBolt. This company provides an online resource with a library of more than 50,000 interior finish products. Design students as well as practicing professionals can use BlueBolt's search and selection tools. Color- and pattern-accurate images are consistent for lighting and scale. Up-to-date specifications and the ability to create digital sample boards with an automatically integrated legend and titles are features that are available at no cost.

For educational content specifically tailored to design students as well as the ability to order material samples online, individual students and educational institutions may pur-

chase a subscription to the service. Interestingly, because it's an online resource, work can be easily archived and stored on BlueBolt Network. The service also allows for e-mail transmission of digital sample boards. Figures 7-21 and 7-22 are images of products and specifications from BlueBolt. Figures C-58 and C-59 are color images of a sample board created through the use of this service.

DESIGNING THE TOTAL PRESENTATION

Many of the materials and methods discussed in this chapter are used not only for materials sample boards but in mounting drawings, renderings, models, and other elements used in visual presentations. When multiple elements are combined for a visual presentation, all of them must be consistent graphically and must contain unifying elements. This sounds easy but is typically rather complex. For example, a presentation may include sheets of orthographic drawings or construction documents, renderings, models, and materials boards. Creating unity among such varied formats can be problematic.

The key is to seek a unifying element(s) that will hold the presentation together visually and conceptually. Project graphics, including title blocks, logos, and/or conceptual diagrams, may be employed as unifying elements. For instance, the graphics found in the title block on a sheet of orthographic drawings may be used on materials boards and mounted renderings to unify the presentation. In some cases, the actual format of the boards is used as a unifying element (Figures C-60a and C-60b). For example, all of the two-dimensional elements of a presentation can be mounted on boards with consistent horizontal bands at the bottom, in a consistent color.

Formal materials presentations employing window-matted materials may require that renderings are window matted and titled similarly to create unity and consistency. Certainly there are no hard-and-fast rules in bringing together the many visual aids used in design presentations. However, consistency, clarity, legibility, and craftsmanship are worthy goals. In all cases it is important to carefully consider the presentation audience. An audience familiar with design drawings will require far fewer visual aids than one unfamiliar with viewing floor plans and elevations. Moreover, an unfamiliar audience requires far clearer titling and greater graphic consistency than a group of design professionals.

The foregoing considerations point to the need for design presentations to be designed. Students must see unity of presentation as a design problem rather than an afterthought. In designing and developing a presentation, it is worthwhile to follow the steps of the design process. The presentation should be analyzed, a list of criteria created, and research regarding the audience and available materials undertaken. Synthesis is achieved by the creation of thumbnail drawings and design sketches. The design of the presentation must be evaluated, and only then should the presentation be created.

In analyzing design presentations, it is important first to consider the stage of the design process that is to be communicated. Preliminary presentations are quite different from final design development presentations. Analysis must include the relative sizes of elements, the number of components presented, and the various formats to be employed. The size of the audience and the layout of the room used for the presentation influence its relative size and format. Time as well as budgetary constraints must be considered.

Once the important issues are analyzed, several sketches can be made of possible presentation formats, and these should be reviewed and evaluated. Possible presentation formats include renderings and materials formally mounted on boards. As stated previously, some situations call for nontraditional board presentations (Figures 7-23 and 7-24). On some occa-

FIGURE 7-23
Inspiration board created as a starting point for a project. Constructed of a game board, fabric, and paper mounted on foam board. Photograph by Bill Wikrent.

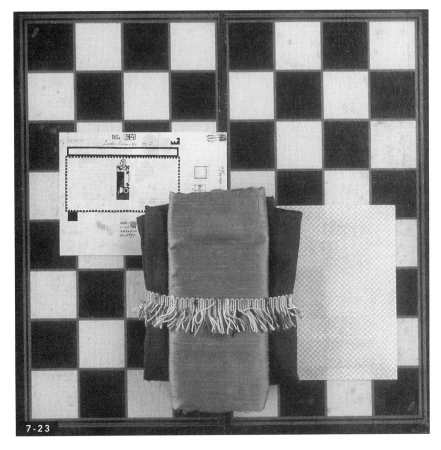

7-23

sions drawings, renderings, sketches, and materials are left unmounted and are simply pinned up in the design firm's conference room (or in some appropriate viewing area), and the client is invited to view the work. In these instances full-size samples of furnishings and equipment may be placed in the viewing area as well. Figures C-60a–C-65c are examples of student presentations. Case studies highlighting methods of visual presentation used in two professional design projects are illustrated in Figures C-66a–C-88.

FIGURE 7-24
A presentation board used to communicate a marketing message. Specialized presentations created to communicate a firm's strengths for a given project are commonly used by practicing designers. This nontraditional board is constructed of Masonite, paper, a clear plastic panel, images copied onto clear transparencies, nuts, and bolts. Clear plastic panels can also be used for reflected ceiling plans mounted on top of floor plans. Photograph by Bill Wikrent.

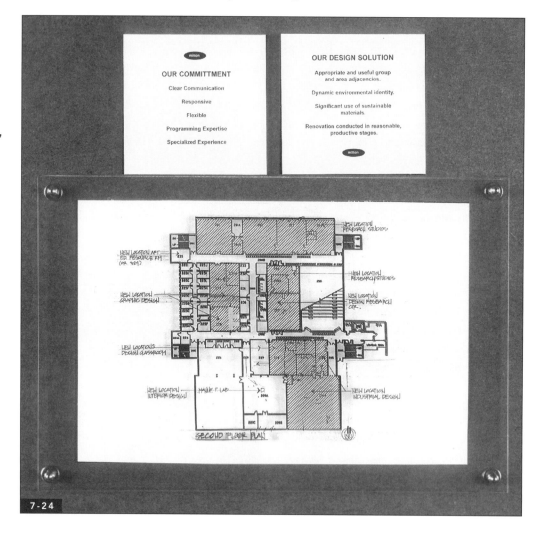

REFERENCES

Leach, Sid Delmar. *Techniques of Interior Design Rendering and Presentation*. New York: Architectural Record Books, 1978.

Tate, Allen. *The Making of Interiors*. New York: Harper & Row, 1987.

PORTFOLIOS AND RESUMES

The mere word *portfolio* can strike fear in the heart of a soon-to-be design graduate. This is because in representing a student's body of work, the portfolio is often the key to getting an excellent entry-level job or internship. And often the portfolio becomes symbolic of a student's fears about graduation and employment.

Yes, portfolios can be scary business. They require planning and organization, an expenditure of money, excellent design skills, and a huge amount of effort. Working on your portfolio also signifies that the next step is interviewing, followed by working. This is the goal of many individuals pursuing an education in design. Therefore, working on a portfolio is a commitment to working in design. And, of course, anyone who will hire you without looking at your work is probably not really hiring you to do design.

Creating a portfolio along with a resume, cover letter, and other related items is a necessary step in moving forward as a designer. This is true whether one is searching for an internship, an entry-level job, or a new job within the design community after years of experience. The graphic design of one's portfolio, resume, and cover letter must be appropriate to the intended audience, most often a design director, managing designer, or human resources

director of a firm or corporation. These professionals are busy people who will be reviewing a great deal of information. As a result, economy and organization are key factors in the design of one's employment-generating tools. A basic understanding of the principles of graphic design and general hiring practices can help in creating employment-seeking materials. Some of those principles and concepts are covered in this chapter.

Although some basics are covered here, it is most useful for interior designers and design students to enroll in an introductory graphic design course (more advanced courses are also highly beneficial). Graphic design is a fascinating discipline with a rich history and vast application in the practice of interior design.

GRAPHIC DESIGN COMPONENTS

GRIDS

Good graphic design allows for good communication. Organization and composition lead to clear communication and are important principles of graphic design. For years graphic designers have employed grids as a means of composing and organizing information. Grids

FIGURE 8-1A
Grids provide the framework for page design. These are examples of simple multicolumn grids and columns divided into blocks.

FIGURE 8-1B
Text and images can be structured using grids.

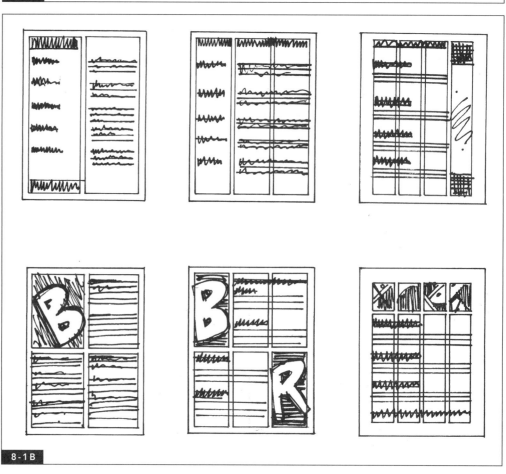

provide the framework for the design of any page or two-dimensional surface. Writing in *Grids* (1996), André Jute states, "The primary purpose of the grid is to create order out of chaos." He goes on to say, "Of all the tools available to help the designer to present a concept in a thoroughly professional manner, none is more powerful than the grid."

Grids offer structure and aid in the organization of data, allowing the reader to easily locate and comprehend information. In addition, grids are very helpful for individuals with little experience in graphic design and page layout. Components of a grid include the actual page size, the margins at the four edges of the page, and the printed area. The printed area is often divided into columns, further dividing the grid structure.

In many areas of graphic design, such as book and magazine design, margins are set according to printing and publication constraints. In resume and portfolio design, however, margins are set rather arbitrarily, based on individual preference. Margins may be equal and uniform or asymmetrical, focusing attention on a particular portion of the page. With the margins established, the total print area is defined and columns can be created within the print area. Columns are useful because most people prefer to read short lines of text rather than long lines. Simple grids employ a limited number of columns to carry data. Some occasions call for many columns and further division within columns (usually into blocks). Regardless of the number or width of columns, it is essential that spaces between columns are left blank for ease of reading and clarity of communication. Figures 8-1a and 8-1b depict some simple grids.

Thumbnail sketches are required in laying out the elements of a grid. Thumbnails may be drawn by hand or quickly generated by computer. When drawing thumbnails by hand, it is best to work in scale. This means that the thumbnail sketches of an 8½-by-11-inch resume should be drawn in a workable scale.

Grid thumbnails are constructed easily with the use of appropriate computer software, such as PageMaker™ and QuarkXPress™. Margins and columns are quickly indicated, allowing the designer to evaluate the layout immediately. In creating hand-drawn or computer-generated grids, it is important to experiment with a range of options. It is also essential to estimate the amount of text required for the document, with important headings or areas of text identified, as one creates thumbnails.

TYPE

According to Jute (1996), the main purpose of the grid is to organize various typefaces and integrate type and illustrations of varying format and origin. This means that type and illustrations become part of the grid and are significant elements of composition. Understanding basic information about typography is essential for successful graphic design.

Typefaces can be divided into two main categories for purposes of classification: serif and sans serif (Figure 8-2). Serif typefaces have main strokes that end in cross strokes or accents. Sans serif typefaces do not have these cross strokes or accents. Serif typefaces are thought to work best for long passages of text, in that the serif leads the eye across the page. Sans serif typefaces are considered highly legible for a word or group of words that stands alone, such as a headline. Within the two classifications there are many varying typefaces. For example, Avant Garde, Gill Sans, and Helvetica are sans serif typefaces. Garamond, Bodoni, and Palatino are serif typefaces.

Most word-processing or page-design programs allow for the creation of a number of style choices within a typeface. Underline, *Italics,* **Bold,** ALL CAPS, SMALL CAPS, Shadow, Outline, and Strike Through are generally available. Very often these styles are overused by those without graphic design experience. Overusing underline, bold, outline, or shadow style can destroy consistency and legibility. To

SERIF
Serif

SANS SERIF
Sans Serif

8-2

FIGURE 8-2
Examples of serif and sans serif type.

This is
aligned flush
left, ragged
right.

This is
aligned flush
right, ragged
left.

This is justi-
fied and is
aligned both
left and right.

This is
centered

8-3

FIGURE 8-3
Examples of alignment.

add emphasis within lines of text, it is often best to use the italic style in place of bold or underline. Writing in *The Non-Designer's Type Book* (1998), Robin Williams states, "Rarely should you use all caps and never should you underline. Never. That's a law." Williams continues to describe only headings, headlines, and subtitles as benefiting from the use of bold style.

Williams goes on to discuss other options for emphasizing type, such as using a bold italic version of the same typeface or a completely different bold typeface. There is much agreement with Williams' admonishments against using all bolded type in the world of professional graphic design; however, many resume writing guides call for their use. This points to the fact that professional graphic designers are trained to create emphasis through the use of various design elements rather than simply relying on bold type, caps, or other styles.

Word-processing and page-design programs allow for the size of type to be altered instantly. Text is easiest to read when set at 9, 10, 11, or 12 points. Most text used in resumes and business correspondence is set at 10, 11, or 12 points. Many graphic designers insist that smaller type, such as 10 or 11 points, is actually easier to read than is 12-point type for text. Titles for portfolio elements are generally larger. The size of type selected affects column width. In general practice, column width is limited to fewer than 65 characters. Therefore, when small-size type is used, columns are generally narrow, which is often easy to read at a glance.

Jute (1996) sets forth a useful rule of thumb regarding type selection: a designer should remain limited to "sixteen fonts as follows: two typefaces, in two sizes, in two weights, in two styles." It is important to note that Jute is referring to an entire unit of design, such as a book or magazine; clearly a resume or brochure should employ fewer fonts. In graphic design, restraint will consistently produce the best results for those with limited experience.

The alignment of type in a column has an influence on the composition of the page and the legibility of the document. *Alignment* refers to the way type is aligned in columns. Word-processing and page-design software allow for a range of alignment. Left-aligned (flush left) type is aligned to the left column margin. Right-aligned type is aligned to the right column margin. Center alignment centers text in the column. Justified alignment creates type that is aligned to both the right and left margins (see Figure 8-3).

Left-aligned text is considered very readable and is the standard setting (default) for most word-processing programs. Center-aligned text can appear quite formal; however, centering large blocks of text can diminish legibility. Right-aligned text is somewhat unusual, but in some cases it is useful. Although justified text creates blocks of type with crisp margins, it can become heavy compositionally.

Proper spacing between letters, words, and paragraphs is important. Most word-processing and page-design programs automatically establish spacing between characters. However, in certain cases there appears to be too much space between characters, and the spacing requires adjustment. Adjusting the space between pairs of letters is called *kerning.* The amount of space between lines of type is called *leading.* Leading can be adjusted in most word-processing or page-design programs. For purposes of legibility, it is common to increase leading as line length increases.

The preceding discussions of grids and typography are related to the design of resumes, personal identity systems, and business correspondence. Although grids are very useful in the design and layout of portfolios, most portfolios do not require extensive text. Therefore, portfolios will be discussed separately in this chapter.

Most individuals seeking design-related jobs should create the following: a resume, cover letters or letters of application, a thank-you letter, an acceptance letter, and a refusal letter. In addition, most recent graduates find that a promotional mailer sample portfolio can help in getting one's foot in the door for interviews. Most firms receive cover letters and resumes constantly, and it is often the graphic strength of resumes or promotional mailers that gives potential employers a glimpse of what sets special applicants apart from the crowd.

THE RESUME

In *Your First Resume* (1992), Ron Fry defines a resume as "a written document that attempts to communicate what you can do for an employer — by informing him what you have already done — and motivate him to meet you. However, content alone cannot do that job; presentation is almost equally important."

The resume is an essential tool in finding work in design; it is a means of illustrating one's strengths and opening doors to interviews. With the cover letter and the appropriate samples of work, it is an introduction to potential employers. This means your resume must be well considered and professional.

Most individuals responsible for hiring new employees are very busy and must wade through large numbers of resumes and cover letters. For this reason, a resume must clearly illustrate one's attributes in an eye-catching manner. It must be brief and legible, and at the same time elevate one above other applicants.

Designers' resumes are different on the whole from those of many other business professionals. Because we do creative work, our resumes may be presented in a creative manner. In fact, many of those hiring design professionals look for creative (yet concise and legible) resumes. Burdette Bostwick states in *Resume Writing* (1990) that creative resumes do not follow a formal pattern or standard format. Burdette goes on to describe the necessity of including only relevant, condensed information in creative resumes. In designing and writing a creative resume one must meet all of the requirements of a traditional resume, yet do so in a creative manner.

Where I teach, we often have successful professional designers discuss resumes with our senior students. I must say that the students are always amazed that the visiting professionals never agree about resume and portfolio styles and formats. Typically professionals involved in facilities management or office planning and furniture dealerships are looking for more restrained traditional resume design. Yet designers engaged in retail, hospitality, or exhibition design are looking for extremely creative, nontraditional resume designs.

The disagreement among design professionals points to a key in resume writing. It is necessary to analyze carefully your own personality, strengths, weaknesses, and employment objectives prior to writing and designing your resume. It is only after you figure out who you are, what you are comfortable with, and what your objectives are that you can create a resume that reflects these issues. The creative resume must reflect you and illustrate who you are.

If you are comfortable with a simple, straightforward resume, that is what you must use. If, on the other hand, you are most comfortable with a dynamic or nontraditional resume, you must undertake to create one. These differing resume styles will clearly appeal to different employers and will set you on your way to making the appropriate employment connection.

One caveat about the creative resume: Do not go overboard with poorly refined designs or an unstructured, ill-conceived resume and use the excuse of "creativity" to get away with it. Resumes must necessarily be professional-looking and legible, and work within standard business practices.

There are some basic guidelines for designing creative resumes. The use of a grid is highly beneficial for all resumes; designers should employ some form of grid to provide graphic structure. Generally employers will find it easiest to deal with a standard letter-size paper format. Most business correspondence is formatted this way. I have found that resumes printed with a horizontal orientation may become lost in files; using nonstandard paper sizes can present problems because odd sheets of paper also tend to get lost.

In designing your resume it is important to show restraint in type selection (most often, no more than two different typefaces). It is also important to use restraint in kerning and leading. The paper selected should allow for legibility. Very dark or highly decorative papers may present problems; they can be distracting and can thwart photocopying. It is also best to avoid folds and staples, both of which can be problematic in filing.

Additional guidelines for resumes include careful consideration of the location of your name. Although there are a number of appropriate locations, it is never a good idea to make the name hard to locate. Some employers prefer the name to be placed close to the top margin for filing purposes. Generally speaking, your name, address, and phone number should be presented in a straightforward manner. Do not confuse creativity with unduly clever complications that can frustrate potential employers. Remember, the goals are to attract attention, sell yourself, and allow employers to find you (see Figures 8-4– 8-10c).

Creative resumes can be organized in a chronological or functional format. A chronological resume describes work experience in a reverse chronological (last first) order. This type of resume often lists employers' names, position titles, and the dates the positions were held as a means of organizing information. Short statements relating to activities, duties, and accomplishment are clustered with each position. Chronological organization makes it easy for an employer to quickly determine work history and education. Chronological resumes are most commonly used by designers with several years of experience in design and by those remaining in a given field.

Functional organization groups work experience by function and job duties. Functional resumes highlight related work experience and focus attention on the type of job held rather than chronology. The organization of a functional resume allows for emphasis on particular experiences by organizing relevant skills into skill group paragraphs. This type of resume organization is useful for designers who may have held non-design-related jobs but wish to focus attention on design experience. This may be particularly true for recent design graduates who have held a nondesign job but wish to focus attention on a previously held successful internship. The functional resume also provides an opportunity to describe skills that may transfer to a design position from another profession, such as project management.

Burdette Bostwick (1990) has identified a basic resume, appropriate for those entering the job market with little experience. A basic resume focuses attention on career objectives and education and may include extracurricular activities, useful skills such as languages other than English, summer jobs, volunteer work, and interesting hobbies. For those seeking a design-related position, computer skills and specialized class work should be emphasized in the resume and highlighted in the portfolio. In writing all types of resume it is best to use action words to describe experience. Words such as *accomplished, achieved,* and *created* work well to insert energy into the described activities.

Many employers look for an employment objective as part of an entry-level resume. If included, this should be a briefly stated objective for the immediate future — the next two to three years. A well-stated objective can tell an employer a great deal about you and your communication skills. A vague, poorly stated objective can land your resume in the trash. Some employers find objectives trite and tedious. Therefore, if you do not have a genuine objective, it may be best to omit this feature. It is also worthwile to review and edit the objective for a particular job application so that it is in keeping with the position.

Recent graduates should assess the strengths of their educational programs and highlight them in their resumes. Course work in construction and construction documents,

RACHEL EIDET

312 12TH STREET

MENOMONIE, WI 54751

715-235-3841

eidetr@post.uwstout.edu

OBJECTIVE

To obtain a job position or internship in which I will be able to use both technical and creative skills to enhance all aspects of design in relation to the graphic design field

ACADEMIC BACKGROUND

UNIVERSITY OF WISCONSIN - STOUT
Menomonie, Wisconsin
Malcolm Baldrige Recipient 2001
Bachelor of Fine Arts in Art
Graphic Design Concentration
Graduation Date: May 11, 2002
Cum Laude

WORK EXPERIENCE

FREELANCE GRAPHIC DESIGNER The High Sierra Group Chippewa Falls, Wisconsin	JULY 2002 - PRESENT
FREELANCE GRAPHIC DESIGNER Northtown Ford-Mercury Menomonie, Wisconsin	AUGUST - SEPTEMBER 2002
COMPUTER LAB SUPERVISOR University of Wisconsin - Stout Menomonie, Wisconsin	APRIL - MAY 2002
VOLLEYBALL REFEREE Community Services & Recreation Dept. Menomonie, Wisconsin	NOVEMBER 1998 - MARCH 2002
FLORAL DESIGNER Becky's Floral & Gift Shoppe Mankato, Minnesota	MAY - AUGUST 2000
SALES ASSOCIATE Herberger's Department Store Shoe Department Mankato, Minnesota	MAY 1997 - JANUARY 2000

COLLEGE ACTIVITIES HONORS & AWARDS

VARSITY VOLLEYBALL	FALL 1998 - FALL 2001
Tri-Captain	2001
All-Conference Honorable Mention	2001 & 2000
All-Conference All-Defensive Team	2001
Best Defensive Player	2001 & 1999
All-Tournament Teams	2001 & 2000
(UW-River Falls (2), Ohio Northern, St. Norbert)	2001
(Bethel, Hamline, Eau Claire)	2000
Most Hustle Award	2000
LEAD DESIGNER UW-Stout and Varsity Volleyball T-shirts and Sweatshirts	1999 - 2001
CHANCELLOR ACADEMIC AWARD	FALL 1999 & 2001
AIGA MINNESOTA CHAPTER	2002

8-4

FIGURE 8-4
Graphic design student resume.
Design by Rachel Eidet.

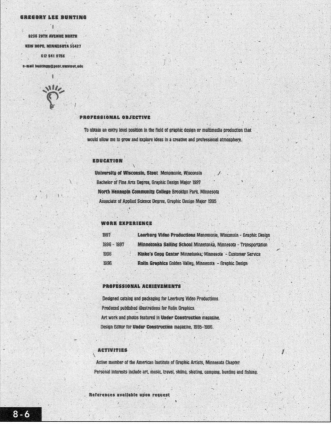

FIGURE 8.5
Graphic design student resume.
Design by David Winkler.

FIGURE 8-6
Graphic design student resume.
Design by Greg Bunting.

FIGURE 8-7
Interior design student resume.
Design by Ardella Pieper.

anneCLEARY

301 E. McArthur Street
Appleton, WI 54911
414.734.5663

Education

University of Wisconsin-Stout
Menomonie, WI 54751
I am currently a junior in the Bachelor of Fine Arts program, with a concentration in Graphic Design.
August 1996 to present

Fashion Institute of Technology
Seventh Avenue at 27th Street
New York, New York 10001
I graduated with an Associate Degree, with honors, in Fashion Design.
January 1995 to December 1995

University of Wisconsin-Stout
Menomonie, WI 54751
Double major in Fashion Design and Studio Art.
August 1993 to December 1994

Design Experience

I worked with Patrick Robinson of Anne Klein, as a class critic at F.I.T.

Work experience

Dayton's Department Store
Fox River Mall
Appleton, WI
Sales Associate, Junior Sportswear Department
I assisted guests with selection and purchase of merchandise, and was also responsible for maintenance of the selling floor, as well as opening and closing procedures.
February 1996 to August 1996

Pechman's Professional Color Lab
Kaukauna, WI
I worked in the art department touching up negatives and spotting photographs.
June 1996 to August 1996

Pine Lake United Methodist Church Camp
Westfield, WI
Waterfront Director
I was in charge of the supervision and coordination of a safe waterfront area and activities.
Summer 1994 and 1993

Activities

I am currently a member of the Graphic Design Association at UW-Stout.

Awards and Recognition

A painting of mine was chosen for the Student Art Show at UW-Stout.
Spring 1997

A pastel and charcoal drawing was also chosen to be in one of the Student Art Shows.
Spring 1994

Deans List, 3.8 cumulative gpa.
Fall 1993 to present

As a freshmen, I received an Academic Honors Scholarship for the 1993-1994 academic year at UW-Stout. It was awarded to those in top 10% of their High School class.
September 1993

Technical experience

I am familiar with Quark XPress, Freehand, Photoshop, CAD, and IBM Wordperfect.

Other Experience

I spent a summer living with a French family in Marseille France and traveling throughout the country.
Summer 1992

Portfolio and references available upon request.

8-8

JASON GILMOUR
GRAPHIC DESIGN
PHOTOGRAPHY

618½ 3RD ST. #6 MENOMONIE WI 54751
715.235.2573 GILMOURJ@POST.UWSTOUT.EDU

OBJECTIVE	To utilize my design skills and talent in a creative fashion for a business seeking to aesthetically improve the design quality of its clientele.
EDUCATION	1997 University of Wisconsin-Stout Bachelor of Fine Arts degree Graphic Design major 3.4 cumulative GPA
WORK EXPERIENCE	SKYLINE DISPLAYS, INC. *Design Intern* [July 1996 to Sept. 1997] Worked in marketing and commercial graphics/production department scanning chromes, producing comps, and various in-house and client-based design projects THE STOUTONIA (weekly campus newspaper) *Staff Photographer* [Sept. 1995 to April 1996] Photographed 2-3 events per week around campus and rolled and developed film *Photography Editor* [April 1996 to Dec. 1997] Hired photographers, trained them in photojournalism and darkroom techniques, dispersed photo assignments, critiqued photos, managed darkroom, chose photos to publish, scanned film, color corrected, assisted in layout and design of newspaper, assisted in maintaining of several computers, and wrote music reviews and several editorials SPORTS STAR PHOTOGRAPHY *Photographer* [July 1997 to present] Assisted photographers and photographed at youth sports team photo shoots
EXTRA-CURRICULAR	AIGA Minnesota Chapter Member [Sept. 1997 to present] Graphic Design Association (UW-Stout) Member [Sept. 1995 to Dec. 1997] Art & Design computer lab Volunteer Monitor [Sept. 1994 to May 1996] Chi Alpha/Christians in Action Member [Sept. 1993 to Sept. 1997] President [Oct. 1994 to May 1996] Power 100 (campus radio station) Disc Jockey [Sept. 1993 to May 1995] Co-ed & league softball Utility [May 1993 to present]
PORTFOLIO & REFERENCES	Available upon request

8-9

FIGURE 8-8
Graphic design student resume.
Design by Anne Cleary.

FIGURE 8-9
Graphic design student resume.
Design by Jason Gilmour.

TIMOTHY O'KEEFFE

NORTON

SCHOOL

E6511

STATE RD.

COLFAX,

WISCONSIN,

54730

715.

962.

3850

EDUCATION
MFA 1992   Cranbrook Academy of Art
Bloomfield Hills, Michigan
BFA 1986   School of Visual Arts
New York, New York
1980   Colorado Institute of Art
Denver, Colorado

EXPERIENCE
1996 - Present
University of Wisconsin Stout, Menomonie, WI
Assistant Professor, full time, tenure track. Presently teaching
all levels of Graphic design course work, including interactive
design using Macintosh computers and related design software.
chair of the department computer committee, overseeing the
budget, maintenance, and development of labs.

1993 -1996
University of Wisconsin Oshkosh, Oshkosh, WI
Assistant Professor, full time, tenure track. Teaching duties
included intro to advanced level classes using Macintosh
computers and Design related software. Curriculum includes;
learning/mastering software (Quark, Illustrator, Photoshop,
Fontographer, Streamline, and Painter), Graphic design history,
theory, and compositional skills, with an emphasis on strong
typography. Director of the Art Dept. Computer Lab,
overseeing the budget, maintenance, and development of lab.
In addition to classroom and lab responsibilities, currently
serving on the department Advising Committee, Faculty
Advisor of student co-operative learning program for Design
Area, and Redevelopment of the Graphic Communication Area
Curriculum to meet the challenges of present and future.

1992
Eastern Michigan University, Ypsilanti, MI
Adjunct faculty. Sophomore (205) level typography class.
Curriculum included; history, theory, mechanical and
compositional skills .

1989-1990
The Museum of Modern Art, New York, N.Y.
Senior designer. Position requirements included, design of all
phases of exhibition materials (exhibition identity, signage,
exhibition text design, publications, invitations, advertisements,
and associated ephemera) and in-house materials (signage,
stationary systems, etc.) for the museum and museum stores.

1989
The Atlantic Monthly Press, New York, N.Y.
Assistant to the art director. Designed book dust jackets and
interiors. Responsible for production and trafficking of seasonal
lists.

8-10A

8-10B

8-10C

FIGURES 8-10A,8-10B, 8-10C
Professional resumes require
careful consideration in organization and design. This resume
belongs to a professional graphic
designer. Design by Timothy O'Ke-
effe.

business, specialized computer software, human factors, universal design, and related fine-arts activities should be noted. This does not mean that you should list every course taken. Instead, focus on what made your education extraordinary. Student membership in design organizations and service projects should be included as well. Remember, your resume must set you apart from the competition.

Recent graduates with prior nonrelated education and work experience often employ a combination of the functional and chronological resume formats. This can be done by clustering related activities chronologically and emphasizing skills and experiences. It is exceedingly important that individuals with multiple life experiences seek interesting and appropriate ways to communicate them in resumes. It is also important for those with a few years of design experience to alter the basic resume to clearly communicate experience.

Currently potential employers may request that a resume be sent via e-mail. This is worth doing because it lands the resume in the correct hands, often immediately. To preserve the graphic integrity of the resume it is best to send it as an attachment rather than as lines of text to the e-mail message. Prior to sending a resume in this fashion it is worthwhile to send a test message to be sure that the resume document can be opened. If the document was created in a program not available on the recieving end, the document may not open. Therefore it may be advisable to save the resume in a format that can be opened by Web browsers or in a standard software program such as Microsoft Word®.

Some large corporations use computer tracking systems to search through hundreds of applicant resumes. Although these systems are not generally used by design firms, they are used by companies that may hire interior designers. It can prove worthwhile to inquire whether or not a particular large corporation or governmental agency makes use of such a tracking system because a creative resume may prove less than ideal in these situations. Because tracking systems rely on scanning resumes and creating a database through the use of key words, certain graphic nuances may be lost, to say the least. If documents are to be scanned, it is useful to simplify the resume and perhaps use less italicized type and more bold type.

Spelling and grammatical errors will land a beautifully designed and produced resume and cover letter in the garbage can or shredder. Check, check, and check again prior to mailing anything to potential employers.

ADDITIONAL CORRESPONDENCE

It is customary to send a cover letter with a resume as means of stating your interest in a job. In addition, a thank-you letter, letter of acknowledgment, and letter accepting or declining an offer are useful. One of the best reasons to design an original, creative resume is that you can use the grid (or format), type, font, and any logo on all correspondence used for your job search. A cover letter using design components found in the resume is an attractive and enticing promotional item. Following up an interview with a similarly designed thank-you card is an excellent idea that says volumes about a designer's skills and professionalism.

There are varying circumstances encountered in applying for a job. For example, a position may be advertised or communicated by word of mouth. In other cases a resume and cover letter may be sent to a huge number of firms and companies (this is known as broadcasting or generalized mailing). Because there is a range of circumstances, a cover letter must be sent with the resume as a means of introducing yourself, describing your interest in a position, and briefly listing your qualifications.

A successful cover letter generates enough interest for the reader to turn the page and review your resume. In most cases a brief cover letter is best — everyone's time is valuable. Although there are significant variations, most cover letters include an introductory paragraph. This is where you describe your interest in the company and state that you are answering an ad or that a mutual acquaintance links you to the employer. In a generalized mailing it is common to simply introduce yourself, whereas in a letter targeted for a particular position you may lead with why you are interested in working for the particular firm or company.

The cover letter then continues with a partial list of your qualifications (including information about your recent degree or job). The final paragraph should recap, with interest and enthusiasm, the points stated. Be clear and brief; do not waste the reader's time by going over in detail what is covered in your resume. Some applicants find it useful to include a stamped postcard with the resume and cover letter. The postcard can be preprinted with responses such as "We are not hiring at this time," to be mailed back to the applicant.

All forms of business correspondence discussed require accuracy and correct spelling and grammar (do not rely on spell-check alone). By being brief and to the point, you demonstrate business acumen and professionalism. Although a resume can be quite nontraditional and creative, other forms of correspondence should follow standard business conventions. A good book on resume writing and job seeking can be worth the cost.

Employers are often deluged with resumes and cover letters from recent graduates. An excellent resume and cover letter go a long way in getting the door open. However, in some cases more is required. It may be necessary to actually include samples of work with a resume and cover letter. Most often this entails creating a mailer or sample portfolio. (See Figures 8-11a–8-16c).

A sample portfolio is an interesting means of offering a quick look at your work. I have found that recent graduates with well-designed sample portfolios, also known as "mailers," cause quite a stir with employers and are often called for interviews. In designing sample portfolios, careful consideration must be given to items for inclusion and the overall cost of mail-

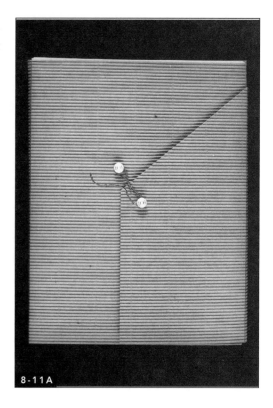

8-11A

ing. Sample portfolios are expensive, time-consuming, and should be used only for targeted firms or known job openings.

The most inexpensive sample portfolios contain reduced black-and-white copies of design projects and student work. These may be photocopies or images scanned into a computer and used in conjunction with page-design software. Reduced color photocopies are also an option for sample portfolios. Graphic designers and product designers use slides extensively in sample portfolios; interior designers use them less often.

Sending samples of work along with a resume and cover letter creates the need for a well-designed package to house the items. When designing a sample package it is important to consider mailing regulations and ease of opening and review. In some cases the package can be designed for return, with postage and return instructions enclosed. However, the party who receives the documents has absolutely no responsibility to return them. Digital portfolios work in a manner similar to sample portfolios, and those are covered in detail at the end of this chapter.

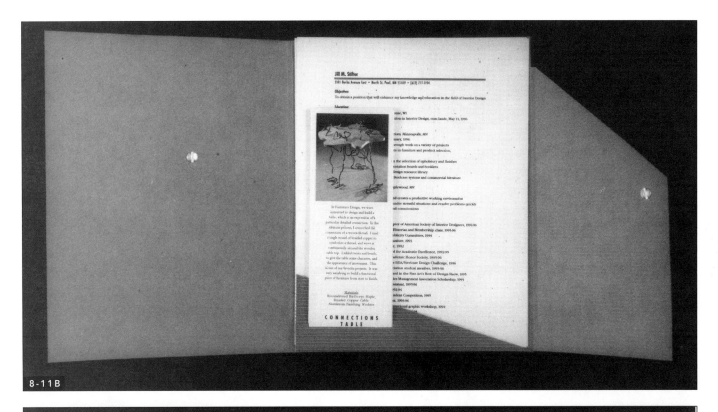

8-11B

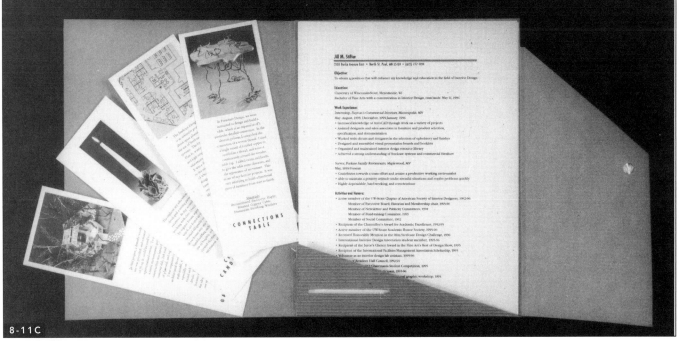

8-11C

FIGURE 8-11A
Sample portfolio ready for mailing. By Jill Stifter. Photograph by Bill Wikrent.

FIGURE 8-11B
Sample portfolio as seen when opened. By Jill Stifter. Photograph by Bill Wikrent.

FIGURE 8-11C
Sample portfolio as seen with contents fully displayed. Photographs of special projects were reduced and mounted on well-designed project cards; a resume and a reply card are included. By Jill Stifter. Photograph by Bill Wikrent.

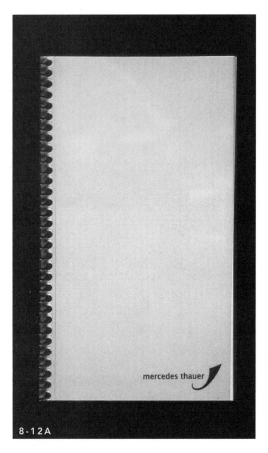

8-12A

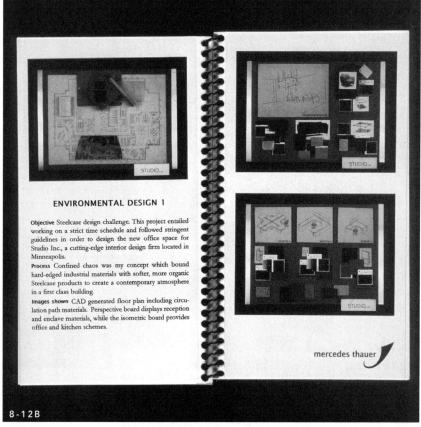

ENVIRONMENTAL DESIGN 1

Objective Steelcase design challenge. This project entailed working on a strict time schedule and followed stringent guidelines in order to design the new office space for Studio Inc., a cutting-edge interior design firm located in Minneapolis.

Process Confined chaos was my concept which bound hard-edged industrial materials with softer, more organic Steelcase products to create a contemporary atmosphere in a first class building.

Images shown CAD generated floor plan including circulation path materials. Perspective board displays reception and enclave materials, while the isometric board provides office and kitchen schemes.

mercedes thauer

8-12B

FIGURE 8-12A
Sample portfolio, closed, with view of cover. By Mercedes Thauer. Photograph by Bill Wikrent.

FIGURE 8-12B
Sample portfolio, opened. By Mercedes Thauer. Photograph by Bill Wikrent.

FIGURE 8-12C
Sample portfolio, opened. By Mercedes Thauer. Photograph by Bill Wikrent.

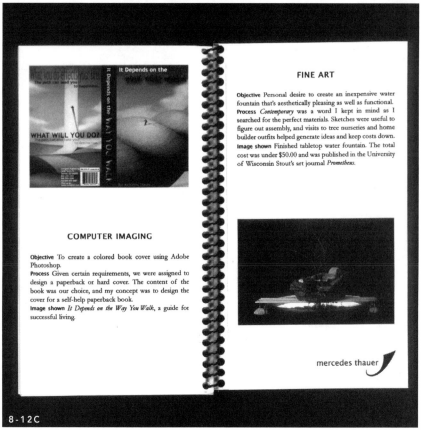

COMPUTER IMAGING

Objective To create a colored book cover using Adobe Photoshop.

Process Given certain requirements, we were assigned to design a paperback or hard cover. The content of the book was our choice, and my concept was to design the cover for a self-help paperback book.

Image shown *It Depends on the Way You Walk*, a guide for successful living.

FINE ART

Objective Personal desire to create an inexpensive water fountain that's aesthetically pleasing as well as functional.

Process *Contemporary* was a word I kept in mind as I searched for the perfect materials. Sketches were useful to figure out assembly, and visits to tree nurseries and home builder outfits helped generate ideas and keep costs down.

Image shown Finished tabletop water fountain. The total cost was under $50.00 and was published in the University of Wisconsin Stout's art journal *Prometheus*.

mercedes thauer

8-12C

8-13A

FIGURE 8-13A
Sample portfolio, closed, with view of cover. This was created several years ago as a tool for entry-level design employment by the owner of the firm featured in Figures 8-14a and 8-14b. By Kathryn Pertzsch. Photograph by Bill Wikrent.

FIGURE 8-13B
Sample portfolio opened to reveal "chain set." By Kathryn Pertzsch. Photograph by Bill Wikrent.

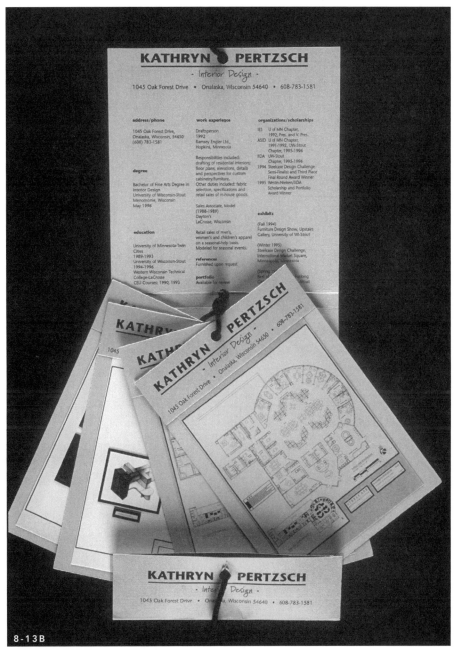

8-13B

FIGURE 8-14A
Professional brochure for firm owned by the creator of Figures 8-13a and 8-13b. Firm: Pertzsch Design Inc. Design by Susan C. Schuyler of the Creative Edge. Photograph by Bill Wikrent.

FIGURE 8-14B
Brochure opened to reveal interior contents. Firm: Pertzsch Design Inc. Design by Susan C. Schuyler of the Creative Edge. Photograph by Bill Wikrent.

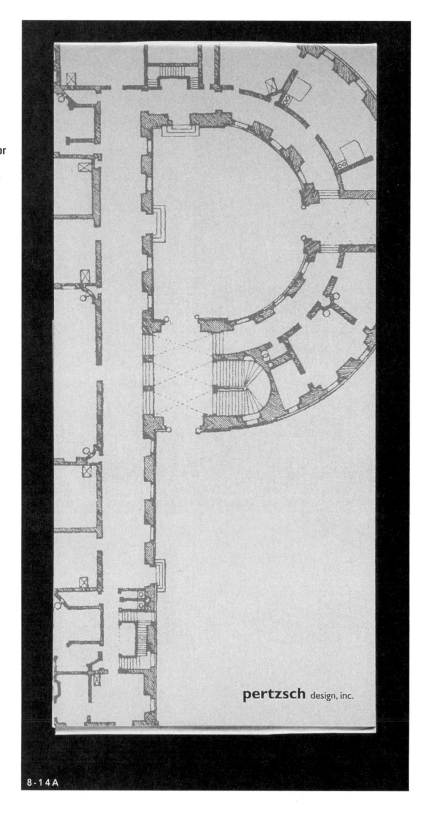

8-14A

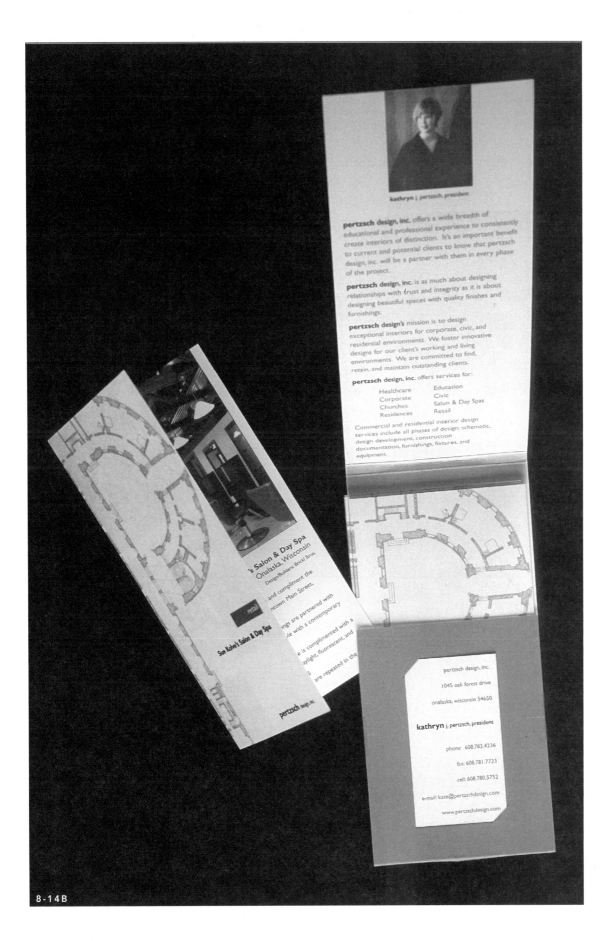

kathryn j. pertzsch, president

pertzsch design, inc. offers a wide breadth of educational and professional experience to consistently create interiors of distinction. It's an important benefit to current and potential clients to know that pertzsch design, inc. will be a partner with them in every phase of the project.

pertzsch design, inc. is as much about designing relationships with trust and integrity as it is about designing beautiful spaces with quality finishes and furnishings.

pertzsch design's mission is to design exceptional interiors for corporate, civic, and residential environments. We foster innovative designs for our client's working and living environments. We are committed to find, retain, and maintain outstanding clients.

pertzsch design, inc. offers services for:

Healthcare	Education
Corporate	Civic
Churches	Salon & Day Spas
Residences	Retail

Commercial and residential interior design services include all phases of design: schematic, design development, construction documentation, furnishings, fixtures, and equipment.

's Salon & Day Spa
Onalaska, Wisconsin
Design/Builders Brickl Bros

and compliment the
ntown Main Street.

ings are partnered with
le with a contemporary

e is complimented with a
ylight, fluorescent, and
are repeated in the

pertzsch design, inc.

Sue Kolve's Salon & Day Spa

pertzsch design, inc.

1045 oak forest drive

onalaska, wisconsin 54650

kathryn j. pertzsch, president

phone: 608.783.4236

fax: 608.781.7723

cell: 608.780.5752

e-mail: kate@pertzschdesign.com

www.pertzschdesign.com

8-14B

8-15

FIGURE 8-15
Sample portfolio on a chain. By
Ardella Pieper. Photograph by Bill
Wikrent.

FIGURE 8-16A
Resume and related business card
created by a graphic design student. By Rachel Eidet. Photograph
by Bill Wikrent.

FIGURE 8-16B
Cover of sample portfolio created
by a graphic design student. By
Rachel Eidet. Photograph by Bill
Wikrent.

FIGURE 8-16C
Interior of sample portfolio cre-
ated by a graphic design student.
By Rachel Eidet. Photograph by
Bill Wikrent.

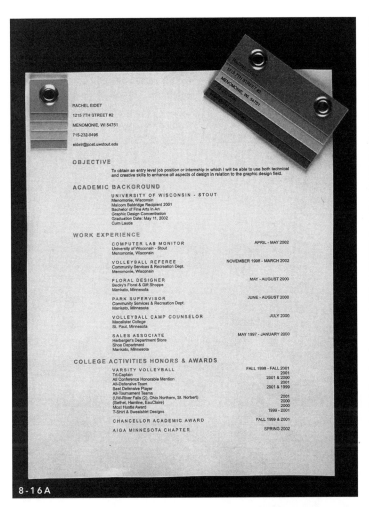

8-16A

8-16B

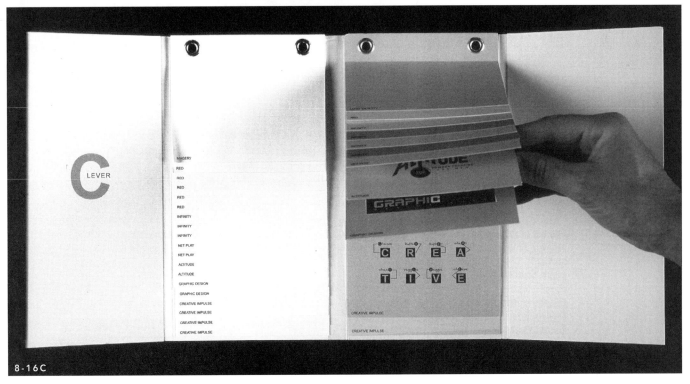

8-16C

FIGURE 8-17
Portfolios and presentation cases.

1. **Zippered presentation case with binder, sheets, and sheet protectors**
2. **Zippered portfolio for use with individual boards (no binder)**
3. **Hard-sided portfolio (no binder)**
4. **Attaché case (individual boards, no binder)**
5. **Handmade box (individual boards, no binder)**
6. **Small presentation case with binder, sheets, and sheet protectors (excellent for photographic and smaller images)**
7. **Inexpensive coated paper or fiber portfolio (no binder)**
8. **Easel binder with sheets and sheet protectors (usually no larger than 18" x 24")**

FIGURE 8-18A
Student project booklet (exterior) created for a furniture design class. By Sarah Amundsen. Photograph by Bill Wikrent.

FIGURE 8-18B
Student project booklet opened to display sketches and finished product. By Sarah Amundsen. Photograph by Bill Wikrent.

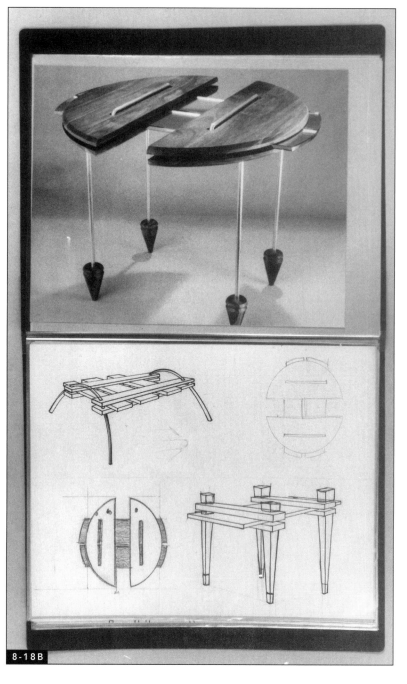

8-19A

FIGURE 8-19A
Student project booklet (exterior cover) created for an interior design studio project. By Ardella Pieper. Photograph by Bill Wikrent.

FIGURE 8-19B
Student project booklet (in use) created for an interior design studio project. By Ardella Pieper. Photograph by Bill Wikrent.

8-19B

THE PORTFOLIO

Putting together a design portfolio requires the selection of appropriate items for inclusion, the selection of a format (or grid) for the items included, the selection of an actual portfolio case to house the contents, and some practice in presenting a portfolio.

The selection of items is a primary step in creating a portfolio. This requires taking an inventory of all student projects and assignments, as well as items completed during an internship or specialized study. It is important to assess the items honestly and decide which projects are excellent and ready for inclusion, which items require reworking, and which should be tossed out.

In selecting items, it is essential to include a range of project types. Residential, commercial, small and simple, large, concrete, realizable and highly conceptual projects all have a place in a portfolio. It is also useful to include a range of types of presentation. Currently it is important to include computer-aided drafting and design (CADD) pieces and additional computer-generated imagery, as well as construction documents, if possible.

Many soon-to-be graduates wonder whether all projects should be presented completely consistently, or whether projects should be treated individually in terms of graphics and format. Unfortunately, there is no hard-and-fast answer to this question. Like resumes, portfolios reflect the tastes and personality of the individual. This means that for some a portfolio that is completely consistent graphically is the only possibility; for others a diverse portfolio with a range of project formats, sizes, and styles is best.

Creating a portfolio that is completely consistent means that all items must be exactly the same size, similar in color, and consistent graphically. This often requires that all projects be redone for inclusion in the portfolio, an expensive and time-consuming proposition. Another drawback is that this type of portfolio presentation does not show projects as they were done for class assignments and therefore may not indicate growth or improvement (see Figures C-60a and C-60b for an example of a consistent portfolio format).

Portfolios that present projects with a range of graphic styles require some element of unity to tie the projects together. In these portfolios the quality must be consistent, so often a few projects are redone for greater legibility or graphic unity. It is also useful to limit, to some degree, variation in the size of boards and sheets presented because too much variety in size can be confusing and messy.

Regardless of the consistency of format, all portfolio presentations benefit from elements that add unity and cohesion. The best way to create graphic unity is to use a consistent or similar grid for all projects presented. When this is not possible, a consistent typeface, title block, or logo may be employed. In some cases, perhaps the only possible unifying element is the size of items presented.

Students often ask how many projects to include, and that is difficult to answer. The best way to decide on quantity is to take an inventory of the projects you wish to present, then do a mock-up presentation or run-through and check for time. It is best to limit the presentation to a half hour (for entry-level jobs). Although many interviews go on for longer than an hour, some are cut short, and you must make sure all the best work is presented in the time allotted. First interviews often take between a half hour and a full hour. When setting up an interview, it is reasonable to ask how much time will be allowed. Knowledge about the interview time combined with knowledge about the potential employer can allow you to edit items in the portfolio.

Questions often arise as to sequence or organization of projects. Much like resumes, portfolios may be organized chronologically or functionally. Generally one's best projects are completed in the last two years of school, with the finest completed in the last studio courses. There is merit in presenting the most recent projects first and working backward.

Grouping projects in terms of scope and function also has merit because it allows one to target certain areas for certain interviews. For example, if hospitality projects are clustered together, one can focus on them in an interview with a hospitality-oriented firm. When clustering projects functionally, it is common to lead with the strongest projects and work backward.

Organizing projects purely in terms of quality also has merit. Presenting the strongest projects first can generate excitement. This allows for weaker projects to be seen as building blocks. I think it is a mistake to lead with weak projects in the hope that you will build excitement as quality increases. Weak projects seen too early will generally put off a potential employer. Moreover, there is always the possibility that the potential employer will be called away in the middle of the interview, not having seen the best work.

One of the biggest problems for interior designers in creating entry-level portfolios is the size and weight of many presentation boards. It is difficult to include many thick boards of mounted materials in a standard zipper portfolio case with plastic sleeves. One way around this problem is to include all drawings, renderings, and graphics simply mounted or copied onto paper, held inside sleeves. Only materials presentations are then mounted on paperboard. The materials boards can be removed from the portfolio and presented as the employer reviews the project drawings in the sleeves.

Some recent graduates opt for a thin box-like portfolio and present all projects mounted on boards or plates. The boards are carried to the interview in the portfolio or presentation case, then removed and handed in stacks to the interviewer. Some students decide that they wish to have a more compact portfolio and choose to reduce all project documents to fit a smaller case. This creates a manageable portfolio; however, reducing all student work is time-consuming and expensive.

Practicing designers usually have photographs taken of built projects and combine these with sketches and reduced working drawings. Photographs, sketches, and reduced drawings can be included in small, very manageable portfolios or binders. Figure 8-17 illustrates some popular portfolios and presentation cases.

Some design graduates manage the size problem by presenting multiple portfolio cases. This is most often done with special projects, such as a thesis or long-term project. Putting special projects into separate portfolios can add interest to the presentation. However, it may be a mistake to use more than two individual portfolios because they can become difficult to handle if the applicant is nervous. Figures 8-18a, 8-18b, 8-19a, and 8-19b are samples of project notebooks.

In the case of technical drawings, it is perfectly appropriate to hand them to an interviewer as flat stapled sheets, rolled drawings, or a small booklet. These drawings, such as construction documents and CADD drawings, are important to bring to interviews and are often presented outside the traditional portfolio case. It is worth practicing arriving in the room for the interview with a portfolio case and rolls of drawings. Remember, you will need to shake someone's hand at the same time you are setting down your portfolio, drawings, and perhaps a coat or bag.

It is important to include design-process documents with finished presentation drawings in the portfolio. Employers often wish to see how a potential employee thinks and the nature of his or her design process. The best way to document the design process in student projects is to save everything — all research, notes, doodles, schedules, bubble diagrams, sketches, and so forth. At the end of the project these process documents and sketches can be photocopied and bound into a project booklet. The project booklet is then available for discussion during the interview. Retaining sketches, notes, and drawings is also important for practicing designers, who should keep these items for reference (and for interviews).

THE DIGITAL PORTFOLIO

Increasingly interior designers are using digital portfolios as components of a complete package, which often includes a physical portfolio, resume, and perhaps a mailer or sample protflio. Digital portfolios provide an excellent vehicle for relaying the types of visual imagery and project information found in standard interior-design portfolios. There are significant issues involved in creating digital portfolios, and these relate to the use and selection of software, organizing and obtaining digital images, and the decision about whether to create a Web-based portfolio or a compact disk (CD). These issues present something of a roadblock to many students and designers, which is unfortunate, because despite having to deal with these issues, digital portfolios can be easier than one might think to create.

Initial digital-portfolio development involves many of the same steps as a developing a "real" or physical portfolio. Decisions about what to include and the manner in which to include it must be made well in advance of stiting down to the computer with Web-authoring software or a CD to burn. Consistency between the digital portfolio and the actual physical portfolio is a worthy goal and can be accomplished with some thought and planning. Very often digital images of the actual pages of the physical portfolio are used to create the "pages" of the digital portfolio. Therefore, selecting background colors or type styles consistent with the elements of the physical portfolio is worthwhile when possible.

Interior designers and design students often produce large presentation boards containing items and elements created by hand. This means that in order to include this non-technology-based material it must be scanned, or photographed with a digital camera to prepare it for inclusion in a digital portfolio.

Many colleges and universities provide digital-photography services. In cases where this type of service is not available students can photograph their own work using standard or digital cameras. High-quality cameras must be used to avoid distortion, poor color rendition, and generally poor quality results. Standard photographs can be made into digital image files at most places that process standard film. In place of photography, many copy and reprographics shops provide scanning and digital file-creation services for all but the largest presentation boards. With the desired digital images on hand, the actual digital portfolio can be authored.

Digital portfolio-authoring programs are those that allow text, links, digital images, and often audio and video to be imported and viewed. Adobe Photoshop®, Macromedia Dreamweaver®, and Microsoft FrontPage® are commonly used among students with whom I come in contact. Adobe Photoshop Elements® is less expensive than the standard version of Photoshop, and it allows for easy creation of a Web gallery, Although it does have some design limitations, given the price it is quite useful. Netscape Communicator comes with a free authoring program called Composer®; Front-Page Express comes with Windows 98®. These free options allow for the creation of gallery pages that can be used to create a simple digital portfolio.

Most digital portfolios start with a main page, which provides some sort of introduction as well as links to the various pages of the portfolio. Each page or slide should then link back to the main page or provide some form of navigation. Photoshop, Dreamweaver, and FrontPage all provide standardized templates that allow for quick and easy generation of digital portfolios. Working with standardized templates is useful for those with little experience using Web-authoring software, but it can be limiting in terms of font selection, layout, and backgound colors and styles (Figures 8-20a, 8-20b, C-88, C-89a, and C-89b).

I agree with Robin Williams, writing in *The Non-Designer's Web Book* (2000), "It's easy to make a web page; to make a well-designed web page, however, is not so easy." Web-authoring software allows those of us who do not know HTML (HyperText Markup Language) or *anything* about the design of Web sites to create Web pages and digital portfolios easily using templates. This means that one must consider the amount of time available and use standardized templates if time is short due to the learning curve involved in going beyond the template. However, it's worthwhile to spend time developing a more well-designed digital portfolio as time allows. For those interested in spending the time necessary to move away from standardized templates, I recom-

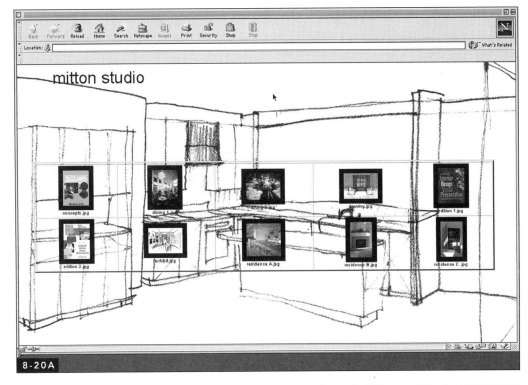

FIGURE 8-20A
Simple Web page from a site made in less than two hours, containing a gallery of thumbnail images. Made with a Photoshop Elements standard template. Architectural photographs by Ed Gohlich.

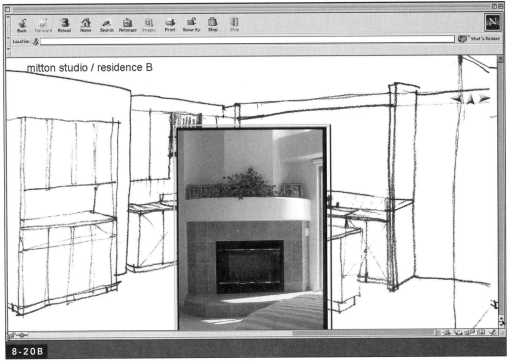

FIGURE 8-20B
A larger image located on a separate page on the same Web site as Figure 8-10a. Made with a Photoshop Elements standard template. Architectural photograph by Ed Gohlich.

mend reading Williams' book, which is easy to understand and covers all aspects of Web-site creation. Additionally *The Web Style Guide: Basic Principles for Creating Web Sites,* by Horton and Lynch (2002), is useful.

Once all of the elements of the portfolio are complete — with desired text, links, and visual imagery in place — the portfolio can be burned to a CD or uploaded to a server for use as a Web site. The decision about which format to use for the digital portfolio requires thought and careful consideration of related advantages and disadvantages. Advantages of creating a Web-based portfolio include the fact that when produced properly they open easily using standard Web browsers, avoiding issues of computer-platform compatibility. In addition, Web-based portfolios are viewed easily by potential employers as directed in a cover letter or resume, and there is no CD to misplace.

The primary disadvantage of Web-based portfolios relates to their need to be posted to a server or host so that the site is accessible via the Internet. Most colleges and universities currently offer students space on the institution's server; however, this service is often stopped shortly after graduation — when the site is most necessary. There are a variety of commercial server options available. Fee-based servers are run on a for-profit basis, generally requiring a monthly fee for server space. There are also a number of free servers available. Many Internet service providers, online services (such as AOL), and computer software and hardware manufacturers provice free space on servers. However, these services often come with a fair amount of online advertising, which can be less than ideal.

The digital portfolio can also be burned to a CD and sent to potential employers. Advantages of CD-based portfolios include the fact that they are relatively inexpensive, do not rely on a server, and are easily included with resumes or mailers. They can also be labeled easily using readily available software to create an identity consistent with the resume and portfolio (see Figure 8-21). Disadvantages of CD-based portfolios relate to issues of computer-platform compatiblility, meaning that a disk created on a Mac is not readily opened on a PC. To ensure that the disk can be opened on either platform, a hybrid disk must be created. Software used to create hybrid disks includes Toast and Easy CD Creator by Roxio, both of which have additional capacities related to the viewing and organizing of images, videos, and sound.

Because CDs are read by browsers using the "file system protocol" and Web sites are read using "hypertext transfer protocol"(http), one cannot simply put the HTML pages created by Web-authoring software onto a CD — it won't automatically "run" and open to the main page. Creating a self-starting CD on a Windows-based computer inolves adding one or two small files to the root directory of the CD during creation. One file is called "autorun.inf," which is required to auto-launch a program with an ".exe" extension. If the file that is to be auto-started is not a program (Web pages, for example), then a second intermediary .exe file should also be added to the root level. One such file is "ShelExec.exe," which associates the Web-page file with a default browser and launches the page in that program. ShelExec.exe can be downloaded as freeware.

Creating a self-starting CD for use on a Mac involves using Toast software during the creation of the CD and specifying a file to open automatically. It is important to note that this and the previous paragraph describe creating a CD that operates like a Web site. Some designers and students are perfectly content with simply creating a CD containing a gallery of images with minimal text in which images can be selected and enlarged. This is done easily with the software that is shipped with most CD burners.

In situations when there are many graphic images to view, store, and edit, specialized software can be used. For example, Extensis Portfolio® creates a catalog of a large database of images. The images can be viewed as a list, thumbnails, or a slide show; can have significant text added; and can be found via a keyword search. This product also readily installs the software necessary for viewing files directly onto the CD. Design firms, educators, and museums use this powerful software, which is also rather expensive. Increasingly my students are using this product as a means of storing digital images of projects for future use and as long-term digital file storage (see Figures C-90a and C-90b). It is not likely that

8-21

FIGURE 8-21
CD labels are created easily and are best handled in a manner graphically consistent with the resume or mailer. By Anne Cleary. Photograph by Bill Wikrent.

all computers will have the programs needed to open and view customized slide shows and specialized CAD images. In cases where these items are used, it is necessary to include viewer software on the CD as well as instructions for use.

My interviews with those hiring designers consistently point to a willingness to review digital portfolios. All of those interviewed to date have stated that they would be willing to access a Web site *if* the resume and cover letter indicated a high-caliber applicant. One firm expressed concern about inserting an unkown CD into the company's computer system due to a fear of viruses. However, the digital portfolio is consistently seen by employers as a way to get one's foot in the door, paving the way for the "real" portfolio. Therefore, the digital portfolio is a worthwhile tool for recording and sharing one's work, but it should be used as part of a total package that relies on the resume, cover letter, and physical portfolio to convey strengths, skills, and knowledge.

Clearly, developing a successful resume and portfolio takes work, talent, and time. The graphic design and organization of these elements deserve careful consideration and a serious look inward. By taking an honest inventory of your objectives, work, interests, talents, and skills, you can design a system that communicates your identity to potential employers. Developing a schedule and budget for your portfolio system in your final semester at school is extremely helpful. Researching potential employers and firms early in your last year of school is highly advisable. Practicing professionals are well advised to save everything (make copies!) for inclusion in a future portfolio — because in a designer's life learning never ends.

REFERENCES

Benun, Ilise. *Self Promotion Online.* Cincinnati, Ohio: North Light Books, 2001.

Berry, Wayne. *15 Seconds: Creating a CD-ROM from a Web Site* [online]. Available at www.15seconds.com/issue/990708.htm, 1999.

Berryman, Gregg. *Designing Creative Portfolios.* Menlo Park, Calif.: Crisp Publications, 1994.

———. *Designing Creative Resumes.* Menlo Park, Calif.: Crisp Publications, 1990.

Bostwick, Burdette. *Resume Writing.* New York: John Wiley & Sons, 1990.

Horton, S., and P. Lynch. *Web Style Guide: Basic Design Principles for Creating Web Sites.* New Haven, Conn.: Yale University Press, 2002.

Kirby, J. Douglas. *Educational Technology: Digital Portfolios* [online]. Available at www.dkirby.com/edtech/digitalportfolio.htm, 2002.

Linton, Harold. *Portfolio Design.* New York: W. W. Norton, 2000.

Marquand, Ed. *Graphic Design Presentations.* New York: Van Nostrand Reinhold, 1986.

Oldach, Mark. *Creativity for Graphic Designers.* New York: McGraw-Hill, 1998.

Rich, Jason. *Job Hunting for the Utterly Confused.* Cincinnati, Ohio: North Light Books, 1995.

Swan, Alan. *The New Graphic Design School.* New York: John Wiley & Sons, 1997.

Williams, Robin. *The Non-Designer's Web Book.* Berkeley, Calif.: Peachpit Press, 2000.

———. *The Little Mac Book.* Berkeley, Calif.: Peachpit Press, 1999.

———. *The Non-Designer's Type Book.* Berkeley, Calif.: Peachpit Press, 1998.

DIRECTORY OF FEATURED PROFESSIONALS

Craig Beddow, AIA
Beddow Design • Digital Architecture
4036 Colfax Avenue South
Minneapolis, MN 55409

CNH Architects Inc.
7300 West 147th Street, Suite 504
Saint Paul, MN 55124

Ellerbe Becket
800 LaSalle Avenue
Minneapolis, MN 55402-2014

BlueBolt Network
www.blueboltstudio.com
1-800-845-2511

Aj Dumas
Mind's Eye Design
2681 118th Street
Chippewa Falls, WI 54729

Kathy Fogerty
1070 Ashland
Saint Paul, MN 55104

Ed Gohlich
P.O. Box 180919
Coronado, CA 92178

Janet Lawson
Architectural Illustration
112 North Third Street, Suite 206
Minneapolis, MN 55401

Peter Lee
1331 North East Tyler, Studio 232
Minneapolis, MN 55413

Robert Lownes
Design Visualizations
www.designvisualizations.com

Meyer, Scherer & Rockcastle Ltd.
119 North Second Street
Minneapolis, MN 55401-1420

Courtney Nystuen
P.O. Box 111
Menomonie, WI 54751

Thomas Oliphant Studio
1500 Jackson Street N.E.
Minneapolis, MN 55413

Arthur Shuster, Inc.
1995 Oakcrest Avenue West
Saint Paul, MN 55113

Smart Associates
119 North Fourth Street, Suite 506
Minneapolis, MN 55401

TKDA
Engineers, Architects, Planners
1500 Piper Jaffray Plaza, Suite 506
444 Cedar Street
Saint Paul, MN 55101

Bill Wikrent
University of Wisconsin–Stout
Menomonie, WI 54751

DRAWING ELEVATIONS: A RESIDENTIAL CASE STUDY

Many students find drawing interior elevations confusing at first. This is due to the fact that interior elevations convey spatial information using specific drawing conventions. These conventions often cause elevations to look very different from a perspective drawing of the same space.

Reviewing the interior photographs of an actual house and the related interior elevations provides a clearer understanding of the standard drawing conventions employed. In reviewing the drawings and photographs it will be helpful to make special note of the lack of perspective lines found in elevations. Additionally, the location of each elevation reference symbol on the floor plan and its influence on the manner in which the elevation is constructed is of significant importance.

FIGURE A-1
An AutoCAD-generated floor plan for a multilevel residence with standard interior elevation symbols shown in locations viewed in the photographs and elevations. Residence designed by Kristine Recker-Simpson. Drawing by Randi Steinbrecher.

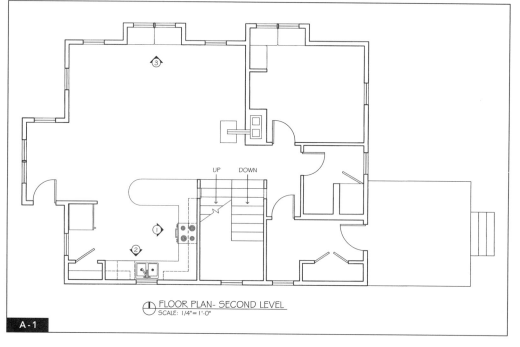

FIGURE A-2
Photograph of the view referenced in elevation symbol 1.

FIGURE A-3
AutoCAD-generated interior elevation drawing of the view referenced in symbol 1. Note that given the location (in plan) of the reference symbol, the base cabinets on the left and the base and upper cabinets on the right have been cut through and shown with a bold line weight.

FIGURE A-4
Photograph of the view of the kitchen similar to that referenced in elevation symbol 2.

FIGURE A-5
AutoCAD-generated interior elevation drawing of the view referenced in symbol 2. Note that given the location (in plan) of the reference symbol, the base and upper cabinets on the left have been cut through and shown with a bold line weight.

FIGURE A-6
Photograph of the view of the sitting area referenced in elevation symbol 3.

FIGURE A-7
AutoCAD-generated interior elevation drawing of the view referenced in symbol 3.

A-2

① ELEVATION- SECOND LEVEL
SCALE: 3/4"= 1'-0"

A-3

A-4

A-5

A-6

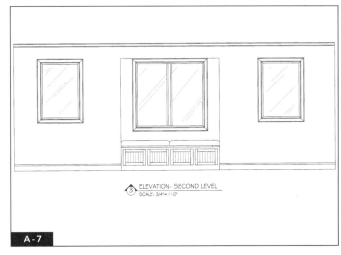

③ ELEVATION- SECOND LEVEL
SCALE: 3/4"= 1'-0"

A-7

COLOR THEORY FOR RENDERING

Color rendering requires a basic understanding of color theory, especially the properties of color and how to approximate these with various media or pigments.

Hue. What we often call a color should actually be referred to as a hue. Green and orange are both hues. Hue is changed only when mixed with another hue. Green mixed with blue changes the hue to greenish blue.

Value. This term refers to lightness or darkness. Adding white lightens a color without changing the hue; this is also true of adding black to darken a color. *Value* also refers to the manner in which light falls on an object illuminating its surfaces.

Chroma. Also referred to as intensity or saturation, *chroma* describes the purity or level of brightness of a color. Describing something as being dull or bright is a way of referring to chroma.

Hue, value, and chroma are all properties of color and are part of color rendering. Consider the following example. When rendering a faded red chair, we must select the correct hue — red. The red must be not bright, but faded; this means the chroma is not highly saturated. The chair must have light, medium, and dark values applied to various locations based on the light source — these values are necessary in rendering.

When using markers, the following can be done to achieve properties of color:

Hue. Sometimes a desired marker hue does not exist. Layering two marker hues can sometimes produce the appropriate hue. For example, red-orange is often created by layering orange and red. In some cases the hue can be altered with the application of colored pencil over the marker color. Hue is also altered by making a pool of color on tracing paper and "picking it up" with a colorless blender; the blender is then dabbed on in the desired locations.

Value. The best way to create value with markers is to lay gray marker in the appropriate locations prior to the colored marker application. This is done by locating the light, medium, and dark areas of the form, then light, medium, and gray markers can be underlaid. Colored marker is then applied on top of the gray, and the values are complete. Sometimes the complementary color may be underlaid in place of gray. A wash of gray or complementary colored pencil may also be applied on top of marker in the appropriate locations.

To create highlights or light areas, it is sometimes necessary to wash over marker with light-colored pencil, especially white or beige. Washes of dry pastel may also be used to lighten or darken areas and to achieve value gradation. Small amounts of white gouache or white-out pen (pen only — not liquid from a bottle) also work for highlights.

Chroma. Marker chroma is often dulled by the application of a layer of complementary-hued marker, colored pencil, or dry pastel. Chroma may be brightened with the application of a similar hue of marker, pencil, or pastel. For example, to brighten dull green marker color, apply a brighter green colored pencil layer on top of the marker.

It is worthwhile to experiment with multiple layers of markers, washes of pencil, and pastel to vary hue, chroma, and value to enrich a rendering.

SCALE FIGURES AND ENTOURAGE

Adding scale figures to orthographic projections, perspectives, and paraline drawings provides a touch of realism and clarifies relative proportions. Adding plants, animals, and other elements of everyday life can also enliven drawings. It is also helpful to trace figures or cut and paste photographs onto CADD-generated drawings.

A number of books are available with scaled figures and entourage elements such as plants, cars, boats, and sports equipment. These books contain hundreds of images, free of copyright restrictions, that are easily traced onto transparent paper. Images from magazines can also be traced into drawings. Many designers prefer to draw their own scale figures, reflective of personal style. Figure A-8 shows a step-by-step creation of stylized human figures.

Human figures must be placed at the appropriate height and locations in a drawing. In orthographic projections and paraline drawings, most adult figures should be drawn with eye levels at about five to six feet. In perspective drawings, most adult figures should be placed with eye level at about five to six feet, which is the standard horizon-line location. In perspectives drawn with nonstandard horizon lines (those above or below eye level), scale figures are placed at five to six feet, which may be far above or below the horizon line. Figure A-9 shows placement of human figures in two-point perspective.

I recommend keeping a file filled with entourage elements such as plants, window coverings, and decorative objects. Mail-order catalogs, plant catalogs, equipment catalogs, and magazines provide excellent images for entourage elements. Items from a clip file can be drawn or traced using a quick stylized approach that allows for elimination of details. These traced items should be simplified to speed the drawing process and to avoid overwhelming the composition. Figures A-10, A-11, and A-12 are simplified drawings of human figures and plants that may be traced.

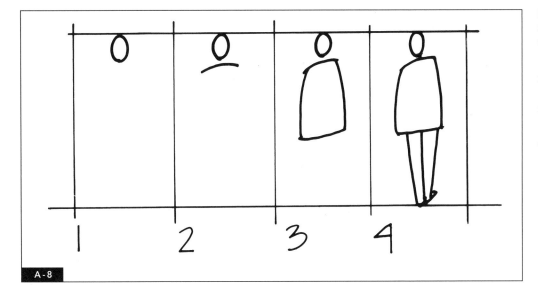

FIGURE A-8
Step-by-step drawing of human figures.

1. Draw a small oval head.
2. Draw curved shoulders slightly below head.
3. Draw torso extending downward from shoulders.
4. Draw legs below torso; legs can be slightly uneven.

FIGURE A-9
Figures and other scale elements
diminish in size as they recede
from the viewer. A standard adult
figure will diminish in size in
accordance with the location of
the horizon line.

FIGURE A-10
These simplified scale figures can
be copied, reduced, or enlarged
as necessary and traced for
inclusion in drawings, as shown
in Figure A-9. The horizon line is
shown at a standard five to six
feet above floor level.

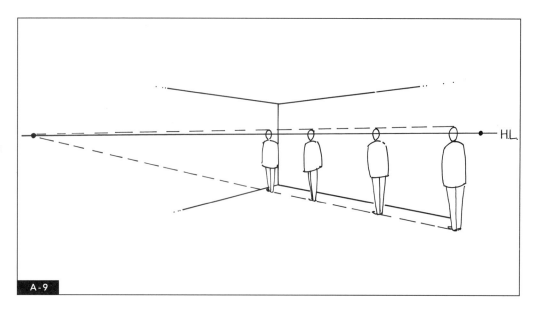

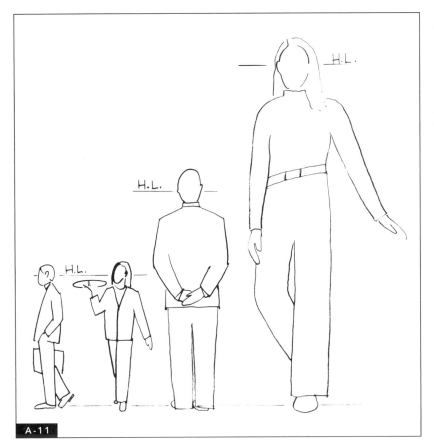

A-11

FIGURE A-11
These simplified scale figures can be copied, reduced, or enlarged as necessary and traced for inclusion in drawings, as shown in Figure A-9. The horizon line is shown at a standard five to six feet above floor level.

FIGURE A-12
These simplified plants can be copied and traced for inclusion in drawings.

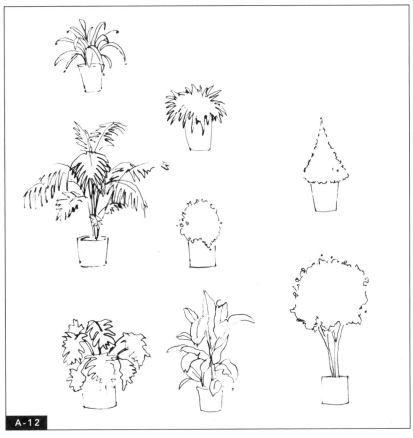

A-12

TWO-POINT PERSPECTIVE GRID

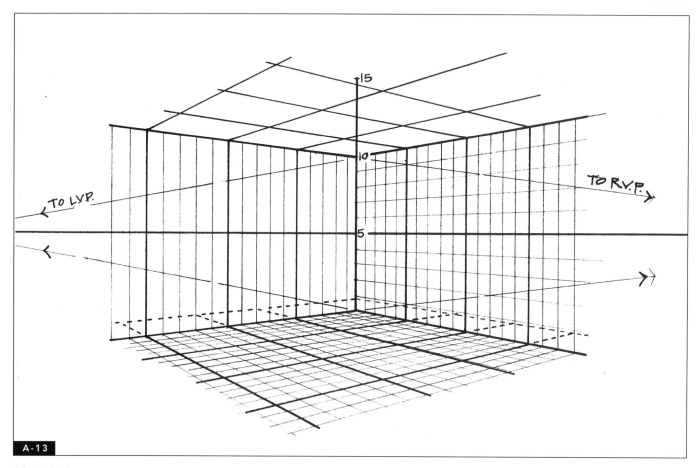

A-13

FIGURE A-13
This basic two-point perspective
grid can be copied and used as
an aid in constructing drawings,
as shown in Figures 4-13a–h.
Note that the horizon line or
viewer's eye level is at five feet
above the floor.

FLOOR PLANS OF PROFESSIONAL CASE STUDY: SCIENCE MUSEUM OF MINNESOTA

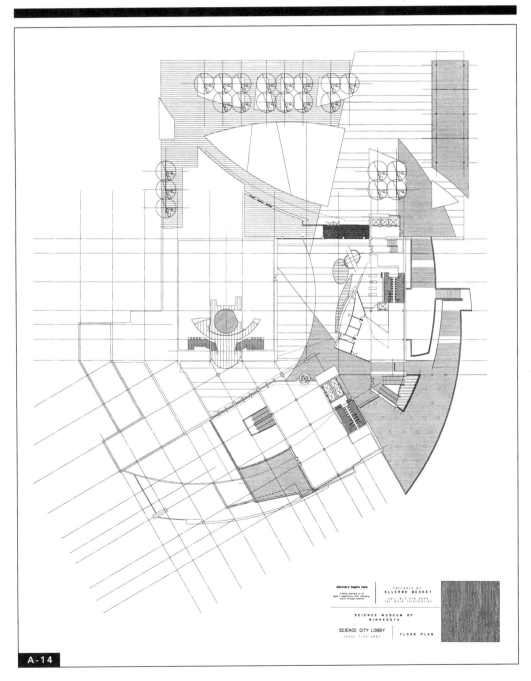

FIGURE A-14
Floor plan, level six, Science Museum of Minnesota, featured in Figures C-66–C-76. By Ellerbe Becket. Courtesy of Ellerbe Becket and the Science Museum of Minnesota.

INDEX

Page numbers in italic refer to illustrations.